30' 68° 30' 67° 30' 66°

Maine

43°

350 0 10
340
330
320
310
300

ANNUAL INCREASE 4'

AGONIC 00' W. (1976)

270 90

180

30°

42°

100

50

30

NORTHEAST PEAK

20

10

20

4¾

30'

4

1½

10

50

20

10

10

10

50

20

40

100

40

3¾

30

20

30

41°

4½

3

G E O R G E S   B A N K

40

30

30'

50

Oceanographer Canyon
Lydonia Canyon
Gilbert Canyon

500

100

NUMERALS INDICATE
DEPTH IN FATHOMS

ONE FATHOM = SIX FEET

30'

Georges Bank

- Five fathoms or less
- Ten fathoms with lesser depths
- Twenty fathoms

0 10 20 30
NAUTICAL MILES

30' 68° 30' 67° 30' 66°

Also by Geoffrey Moorhouse

THE OTHER ENGLAND

AGAINST ALL REASON

CALCUTTA

THE MISSIONARIES

THE FEARFUL VOID

THE DIPLOMATS

THE BEST LOVED GAME

The Boat and the Town

The Boat and the Town

by Geoffrey Moorhouse

LITTLE BROWN AND COMPANY · BOSTON · TORONTO

FIRST AMERICAN EDITION

LIBRARY OF CONGRESS CATALOGING IN PUBLICATION DATA
Moorhouse, Geoffrey, 1931–
    The boat and the town.

    1. Fishermen—New England. 2. Lobster
fisheries—New England. 3. Herring fisheries—
New England. I. Title.
SH221.5.N4M66 1979   974.4'5   79-13898
ISBN 0-316-58060-0

BP

Designed by D. Christine Benders

PRINTED IN THE UNITED STATES OF AMERICA

To
the men I sailed with
and their people

AUTHOR'S NOTE

IT WOULD BE misleading to call this piece of writing a novel, when it so conspicuously fails to pass the test set by H. L. Mencken, for one. "The novel, properly conceived," he wrote, "is a means of uplifting the spirit; its aim is to inspire, not merely to satisfy the low curiosity of man in man." I'm afraid the highest claim I can make for this book is that it may satisfy some curiosity, though I wouldn't, myself, think such satisfaction either "merely" or "low." At the same time as not being a novel, however, this is also not a work of nonfiction in the accepted sense. To pass that test, I understand, a book must describe events and people as faithfully as a good newspaper should, so that anything and anyone in it can be identified by the reader who wants to check up. I cannot claim such fidelity, either for my fishing boat or its crew, or for any of the other figures in the foreground of my text. They do not exist outside these pages, in the way that I have set them down.

And yet this piece of writing is an attempt to tell a truth about a particular way of life, and it is set in a reality of time and place. It is the product of my own experience, working as a fisherman on the North American Atlantic coast between the summers of 1976 and 1977. I sailed in a number of vessels and labored through the seasons alongside more men than ever the Boat could contain. When at last I began to write, I found that I could not do justice to my subject by following my original intention, which was to produce a straightforward documentary account of that year. Too many images would have been blurred that way, too many figures would have appeared in outline and not in the round, too many feelings would have gone unremarked. It was clear that I must enlist imagination to describe adequately what was felt, and sometimes to fuse characteristics from half a dozen different people into one so that a reader might more fully understand a way of life. Therefore my book is balanced between the reality that a historian would require, and the imaginative reconstruction that he would quite rightly not allow. Thus, the sinking of the *Argo Merchant* is a matter of fact, and the refrigerated trucks of Gangloff and Downham do run from Indiana to the Atlantic coast; but Jonathan and Ellen and Big Boy and the rest of those whose lives surround the Boat were fashioned by me to tell this tale. No one who knows New England will have any difficulty in recognizing the Town, but he should not look for my characters there, for they are not to be found. If he is frustrated because I have not properly named the place, I hope he will at least accept my intention. I have seen the Town as a paradigm of all the fishing communities in the world, and I have wished to express this by the device of anonymity. I salute them all.

The Boat and the Town

SUMMER

THE BOAT MOVED down the inner harbor as though she were going to do battle. Some vessels slip out to sea as easily as an otter takes to the water, while others butt along with a carnival roll which suggests that no serious business can be at hand. The Boat's movement was different from all of these and it came most of all from her lines, which were generally upright or horizontal and without much dash. The southern yard that built her had mounted a spacious wheelhouse upon a high fo'c'sle, which rose abruptly from the working deck; and, as the deck ran cleanly, without superstructure, to the stern, the Boat in silhouette had something characteristic of a tug. Her stem, however, was as sharp as a warship's, though it flared out massively to accommodate the full extent of her beam, on which much of her tonnage was spent. She ran to seventy-seven feet from stem to stern, scarcely more than three times longer than she was wide, yet there was nothing ungainly about this. The working deck was empty, except for the hatch on which the banding table was perched, and the steel bench by the starboard rail, where the traps would come aboard. It was without bulwarks at the stern, so that the traps could be shot straight into the wake when a trawl was being set, and it was very low upon the water. It looked cleared for action as the Boat moved away from the dock with a small bone in her teeth. She had been a gleaming white overall when the southerners painted her, but four years of the Atlantic had turned her piebald, with rusty stains pouring down from the scuppers and dribbling out of the portholes. There was yet, however, something naval and neat about her appearance, something belligerent about her stance, something disciplined about that deck space. She might have been a fleet auxiliary. She did not much look like the fisherman she was.

It was a long run down the harbor, which was effectively a wide bay at its seaward end, with a breakwater swinging out from the rocky edge of the Point, like a door left half open. The dock was two and a half miles above this, where the Town was snugged down protectively around the fish quays, the processing plants, the yacht marinas, and the wastelands of the inner harbor. The weather at sea had to be brutal to make much more than ripples up there, for the land flowed hilly on either side, set so angular that all manner of projecting knolls broke the force of the onshore winds unless these came directly up from the south through the half-open doorway. There was just one place at the very top of the harbor, a ravaged plateau of dusty ruts and trampled beer cans and parked refrigerator trucks, where you could stand at the water's edge upon stinking mud and look straight out to the distant sea. If there was any sort of southerly breeze then, the grit would fly like small sandstorms and men would blink as they shouldered their way out of the green liquor store just across the road, and hang more firmly onto their six-packs, which were uniformly swathed in brown paper bags. Women traversing the Stop & Shop parking lot, a long way up the road, would clutch at hats if they wore them, and strain necks to one side as though jamming a telephone there to leave arms free, whether they wore hats or not; and grimace to each other in exasperation.

In high summer, though, the Town was more often glad for any breeze that penetrated its screens. The lucky ones were those in the clapboard homes that rose in terraces and dabs of white and olive, blue and brown, yellow and pink, on the landward slope of the inner harbor. They got anything that was going to relieve the sticky heat, which pressed upon them like a poultice. The people facing them across the harbor, along the undulating arm of land that shielded the Town from the open Atlantic, sweltered until the fall, but gave some thanks when winter came and blistered them with cold marginally less than that suffered by their townsfolk opposite.

At the top of the harbor, the two were divided not only by water but by the state fish pier, which ran neatly down the middle for a few hundred yards, a tongue of concrete bearing sheds and plant for gutting herrings, and devices that would suck fish from holds and pour flashing cascades of them into trucks with high sides but no tops—a process that excited clouds of gulls which otherwise lined the adjacent roofs, quietly digesting and beadily awaiting the next call. Along one side of the pier, in the shade of the sheds, men were mending nets and the crew of the coast guard cutter, dapper in blue drills and baseball caps, were fiddling methodically with cotton waste and brasswork. Along the other side, two wooden wharves stood out at right angles. A battered old mackerel seiner was tied up at one: the other was empty except for a small clutter of fish boxes and stove-in traps. This was the dock which the Boat had just left.

As she backed off from her wharf in an arc, then paused before moving forward down the harbor, the turbulence created by her screws rocked the pontoons of the Pier 7 yacht basin and made the pleasure craft there sway tipsily in response. A couple of girls in frayed and legless jeans and halter tops paused from their dreamy game of painting a cabin roof and wondered whether they could safely wheedle a lobster from the crew when the Boat came back. That man in the stern was reckoned to be a hard case and would probably demand his own price, especially after a week or more at sea. And Big Boy, still a little bleary from last night's long succession of Russian Velvets, which had been undiluted by love or anything else, stood challenging their gaze while he wistfully imagined his palms round the buttocks of the blonde one with the cocky little breasts. She might go, with a bit of persuasion. Nothin's easy, he thought; and bent down again by the starboard cleat to unhitch the mooring rope and stow it away.

There were many pleasure craft along this reach of the inner harbor, though on the other side of the state fish pier nothing but fishermen and coastguardsmen was ever to be found. The Boat began to make way toward the first of the channel marker buoys, angling to its left side where the water was a good twenty feet deeper than to starboard. In this deeper water, beyond the bobbing ketches and sloops and the tethered motorboats, a large freighter from Iceland was berthed alongside the biggest processing plant of all, her frozen cargo already half emptied into the factory's maw, whence it would eventually issue in the form of fish sticks which, with french fries and maybe cole slaw, would relieve an otherwise unmitigated working diet of hamburger, pizza, pastrami, and steak, across the length and breadth of a fiercely meat-eating continent. As the Boat swept past the Icelander, the crew of the fisherman glanced up at her towering sides and at the palleted blocks swinging up from her holds. They regarded her with the curiosity of seamen and without the brooding suspicion of threatened tradesmen, though almost every other boat in port was nagged with the worry of this frozen commerce. Their own catch, however, would be sold fresh and expensively, bound for consumption by people in New York to whom pizza and hamburger represented little more than snacks to fill in the gaps between helpings of more delicate and more exclusive food.

Round the Icelander's stern a cove opened into the arm of land, lined with more fishing wharves and pleasure craft moorings. To the dazzle of brilliant sunlight upon water was added the white flash and glaring splutter of oxyacetylene torches, for a deep-sea dragger was hauled up on the railway lines of the repair yard in the cove, and men were welding some new piece of metal to her curving green hull. "That's all right," Big Boy shouted up to Yank, who was leaning over the fo'c'sle rail. "Brancaleone's made enough this month to stick ashore awhiles." Brancaleone was the captain of the dragger, probably the most successful skipper in port, a high-liner who kept his boat at sea in weather that caused fainter hearts to run for home, and who had a most remarkable instinct for finding cod and haddock, hake and halibut, redfish and yellowtail (it mattered not much which) in great quantity on every trip he made. Yank was Big Boy's buddy, no more New Englander than he, but, having served as a Marine in Vietnam and having consequently enjoyed R and R in Sydney, he had acquired his label from Australians and had been pleased to perpetuate it when he came home because it reminded folks of where he'd been and made him feel distinctive.

The repair yard lay inside the promontory of the Neck, on whose outer point stood a building beloved of the artists who thronged the Neck, especially in summer, and serviceable to the mariners who came and went through all seasons of the year. Its steep-pitched roofs were gray and punctured by dormer windows, but its walls and its totem chimney glowed with the warmth of that same boxcar red which coated many a house and barn (not to mention railroad depots) from the Rhode Island state line right up to the borders of Maine and Canada; and westward, too. In large white lettering along the side of the biggest shed were the words MANUFACTORY. ESTABLISHED 1863, while a smaller wall alongside said SEA JACKET MARINE PAINTS. On the seaward side of the building came the legend COPPER PAINT, which had told mariners for a hundred years and more that here they could obtain the materials to protect their hulls from the insidious penetrations of worms and mollusks. This building was one of the first landmarks they spotted when they came out of the Atlantic and rounded the breakwater. It told them they were almost home and dry.

It marked the beginning and the end of the inner harbor. Facing it across the water was the very heart of the Town, rising to a low ridge from the coves and inlets of its habitat. Once, the buildings of the Town had run right down from that ridge and huddled together around Harbor Cove and the adjacent refuges; streets had come downhill and continued upon the planking of the wharves so that a drunken pedestrian, missing his own doorway, might easily have walked straight on until he tripped over a bollard and took a header into the water. But in some postwar flush of dollars and enthusiasm, civic iconoclasts had, in the name of urban renewal, torn down much of the waterfront, at which point the dollars had run out, leaving a strip of no-man's-land between the wharves and the Town, which a variety of entrepreneurs had sought to fill with the spasmodic and almost always unlovely insertion of trading posts of one kind or another, generally fashioned in brick, concrete, or asbestos; where, before, everything down there had been wooden and boxcar red. In just one instance, the transformation had run to charm rather than to ugliness. The Town House Restaurant was now established in something like a Swiss chalet, with the piles of a wharf on two of its sides, so that diners could masticate their chowder and their sole meunière within spitting distance of genuine fishing boats. But Main Street was some distance up toward the ridge: and there, on a bench thoughtfully stationed outside the premises of the Harry Stathopoulos Insurance Agency, old men who had been to sea all their lives would sit and think and gossip for hours, with their backs to it now; and occasionally spit into the gutter before creaking home to hamburger or pizza. A few blocks above Main Street rose City Hall, which seemed unable to make up its mind whether it was derived from Versailles or Huddersfield. It was largely red brick, but it had an ambitious stone portico upheld by Corinthian columns, slated pinnacles at the corners of its roof, and a distinctly municipal tower of stone capped by greened copper. If you were sailing home from the sea, this reared above the Town as another landmark, one of four that stood out on this side of the harbor. The other three were churches and of them the grandest by far was the Portuguese church. This had two towers, campaniles set either side of the west door and, in between, a statue of the Virgin, who was blessing the Town with her right hand held high while her left cradled not a Child, but a fishing schooner.

The Boat had to turn toward the Town and away from the Neck, round another buoy, as she bore down toward the Manufactory. And then, after moving across the harbor for some distance, she straightened up again at the entrance to the main channel, which was marked by buoys all the way to the sea. This was where the harbor became a bay, a mile across in parts, and in summer it was a trial to the fishermen, for it was then a playground of amateurs who hoisted sail and gunned engines with sometimes scant attention to the rule of the road at sea. Of these the most negligent by far were the rollicking playboys in their dandy launches, top heavy with superstructure, saddled with upholstery, whippy with aerials on which they could receive radio and television signals from National Weather Service, Citizen's Band, Station WVCA, or the whole mind-blowing range of Channels 2 through 56 from Boston, Providence, Concord, Manchester and points all (you name it, they'd got it). They were at their most alarming when they were dashing headlong across the channel so as to get to the Cut before the road bridge was let down again — the Cut being a narrow channel, turbulent when the tide was at the turn, which led into a river replete with marinas on the Town's western outskirts, the river itself winding through mud flats and sandbanks and headlands beyond the Cut until it found its way to the sea again, away to the north of the Town. For the Town was tucked into the underside of the Cape, which was itself all but an island, a great rocky knob sticking out into the ocean, hanging to the mainland by the threads of two bridges. Many of the playboys heading for the river were simply taking a shortcut up the coast. And all under the glaring eye of the man at the wheel who stood, cast in bronze, oilskinned, sou'westered and seabooted, his arms firmly braced against the spokes of his Stoddart, gazing forever beyond these frivolities to some point on the ocean's rim.

The working Town was left behind now, as the Boat

stood away to starboard of the small island which had once been grazing for sheep but had long since been abandoned to rats and a navigation light. To her right, the bay became thickly wooded above its shoreline strip of rock and sand. To her left, beyond the island, along the harbor's seaward arm, the meandering community of East Main Street and the variegated culture of the Neck had given way, after a short but proper interval of untenanted road, to the distant habitations of the Point. That this was a colony of some exclusive kind was instantly proclaimed by gateposts set on either side of the road, which forbade trespassing, and by a man in a white pith helmet who patrolled the entrance (his services paid for by subscription of those within) to advise all comers — or nearly all — that the notice on the gateposts meant what it said. A huge boulder behind the entrance concealed "Sunset Rock," on whose veranda this Monday morning could be seen a young couple who, if they did not belong there, had apparently arrived by any of the four cars drawn up on the terrace below them. He was clad in rugby shirt and shorts, she in tennis whites; and while he alone had his back to the water, she, with her arms round his neck, was most certainly not taking in a view which at that moment included the Boat plodding picturesquely off to work. The Point was a bit like that, though its inhabitants mostly relished their seaside views and rather gloried in their connections with the Town, to which they imputed a proximity that in no sense it really enjoyed. Beyond "Sunset Rock" came a succession of lawns and hedges and brick walls and thickets of trees and, at distances that were not always within hailing, dwellings which ranged from Yankee Baronial in stone, through clapboard Palladian (complete with plastic urns along the roofline) to wide-verandaed, jutting-eaved haciendas-by-the-sea. The grandest of all these homes, built by someone heavily

under the influence of Jefferson and Monticello, had six
columns to its pedimented frontage. This was flanked by
great magnolias which, though now past their best, had
been gorgeously creamy in spring. Along that very private
road just below the lawns, an occasional antique motor car
trundled along, a genuine old crock with gleaming brasswork and canvas roof thrown back to leave its occupants
free as the air.

As the Boat lined up for the channel, her five men
lounged in the wheelhouse, chaffing each other about
their weekend ashore. The Skipper was catching up on the
gossip, for his wife had steadfastly refused to shift house
from Rhode Island to the Town when the company had
engaged him to run the Boat, so he drove back and forth
between his times at sea. He was a young man with a
deceptively benign face, who had graduated college in
commercial fishing (just as, in Milwaukee, someone might
major in brewing) and had headed for deep-sea lobstering
as the quickest way of making enough dollars to buy his
own vessel and be his own boss. With a grin on his face and
an occasional question, he steered his crew through
reminiscence as deftly as his fingers stroked the wheel into
fractional movements that would position the Boat perfectly for passage through the oncoming traffic of inshore
fishermen, hurrying to market with whatever they had
been able to catch within sight of the Cape. Big Boy,
garrulous by nature, needed little steering and was enjoying himself vastly with the tale of how he'd breezed over to
a neighboring town and had hammered on the door of a
girlfriend there, threatening to kick it down if she didn't
open up, which she obediently did. "So I says to her,
'C'mon,' I says, 'I'm as horny as a bull and I want it now.
Let's go.' She wasn't havin' any. So I threw her over my
shoulder and I nailed her on the bed. Right there. And she
loved it." His pale eyes shone bright with the thought of

this prowess, his gut wobbled with his laughter (for Big
Boy rarely failed to see the funny side of things) and even
the blue lobster tattooed upon his left calf stirred a little in
response. Yank had his eyes focused on the approaching
breakwater, but his nostrils twitched slightly and his lips
didn't quite curl at the punch line. For he alone knew that
Big Boy had been smashed by midnight and it was more
than unlikely that he had been able to leave his unstable
mooring in the Schooner Bar. But when Carlo, sitting on
the chart table at the back of the wheelhouse, laughed
knowingly and said, "Christ, Big Boy, you must've sobered
up fast after 'leven o'clock," Yank half-turned his head
with menace. "How the hell would you know? You were
home to mother by then." Which, though chronologically
inaccurate, was close enough to the mark. For Carlo, son
of a fisherman, had left the sea once to set himself up as a
house painter, in which capacity he had enjoyed two
contented years in Wisconsin until, his father having
suddenly died, he had dutifully returned to the Town and
the sea to support his mother in the family home up on
Portuguee Hill. Yank did not like him; and the strain
between them was not to be explained only by Carlo's habit
of provoking people with wisecracks, nor yet his confident
manner with the ladies. It had rather more to do with
Carlo's build, which was stocky, and his coloring, which
was dark, and his origins, which lay, two generations back,
by the shores of the Mediterranean. Only young Jonathan,
making his first trip in the Boat to replace a man who had
smashed both his car and his legs, wondered why the
needle had just gone in.

They were now among the marker buoys of the inshore
lobstermen, brightly colored corks on spindles which
bobbled and swayed around the doorway to the harbor,
for shellfish lurked near the breakwater, though few of
them ever had the chance to grow much bigger than the

minimum size permitted by state fishery regulations: the inshoremen were out every morning, to haul their traps and set them again, in small boats that were often worked single-handed. It astonished Jonathan that the Skipper made no attempt to avoid these trap markers, for he had visions of them and the rope hanging down to the seabed, fouling their screws and causing them to turn back for repair — which would have been a sore disappointment to him, who had never been deep sea before. But the fragile buoys seemed to be swept aside by the bow wave, vanished for a moment or two, then reappeared drunkenly in their wake. The Skipper's eyes were set only for the turn round the big Number 6 Buoy, which was anchored off the end of the breakwater, that great monumental door swinging out the best part of half a mile from the shore. At its junction with the land stood an emplacement of coast guard buildings, the most vital of which was the stubby lighthouse whose beam carried thirteen miles out to sea. It also had a foghorn which had only just finished moaning; for, although the sun had beaten down unhindered over the Town for some hours already, a bank of mist had hung soggily over the sea a few miles offshore, as it frequently did in summer. But now the day was sparkling and clear to the horizon, where a very sharp line distinguished the blue of the water from the cloudless pallor of the sky. Gulls dropping down on the breakwater, to scavenge torn-off crab legs and abandoned bait, waddled there only for a moment, so great was the heat already baked into its stone. This long barricade of granite had taken eleven years to build at the turn of the century (forty vessels had been smashed on its foundations before it rose above sea level) and the grooves left by the masons' drills were still as plain upon the surface of each block as they were on the day they had been made in the quarries of the Cape. The breakwater was a massive monument to what had once been a thriving local industry. All round the Cape vast cavities were to be found, deep in water and fringed with bush, into which many a stolen automobile was plunged after a wild night ride by some kids. But, once, these cavities had yielded granite for the buildings of Boston, New York, and New Orleans; and some of it had been shipped right round to San Francisco.

At the end of the breakwater a slim white tower was poised upon a high and stilted platform of iron. It carried the red light that dotted the night every four seconds and pointed the way through the half-open door to the Town. Lovers, having by stratagems of their own eluded the pith-helmeted guardian of the Point, would sit close together below this platform and watch the fishing boats put to sea and come home again. Photographers would scramble out there with their zoom lenses and telescopic sights, to take pictures of the distant Manufactory, the island, the inner harbor mouth, or the wooded shore just across the bay. Townsfolk would walk their dogs as far as this tower, scrutinize the familiar sea, then turn away from it. Others would tramp out with fishing rods and angle for flounder, pollack and mackerel. Two anglers were there now, by the lapping water's edge, as the Boat came round the breakwater. At the sight of them, Big Boy exploded with recognition and rushed out of the wheelhouse to stand by the port rail. "Hey Robbo," he yelled, "caught'ny crabs yet?" And, unhitching his belt buckle, he dropped his shorts and his underwear in one practiced fumble, bent over and flourished his bare ass at the anglers. Robbo, who had been contemplating his line, looked up, flexed his arm, and thrust his fist in Big Boy's direction. In the wheelhouse they could hear nothing of his reply: only Big Boy's bawdy cackle as he stumbled back inside, drawing up his pants. His face was creased with enjoyment. "Crazy bastard, that one," he said.

Gently the sea took the Boat in its arms as she made her turn southeast. The faintest of airs stirred the water, which breathed with a gradual swell, but nothing more. Jonathan went out to the rail to savor this time and to enjoy the cooling movement, for he had been greasy with sweat in the muffling humidity around the dock. As they went full ahead down the outside of the breakwater, then past the coast guard emplacement, he looked for signs of life along his home shore. But there were none, apart from the two anglers, now dwindling in the distance. Just a huge buttress of rock at the turning of the Point and, beyond that, a long and slow ellipse of sand with bush above the tidemark, from which the occasional roof of privilege emerged. No people on that beach, for it was private, too. The sea, and those who sailed upon it, were held at a distance; whereas around the inner harbor, in spite of urban renewal, all was organically whole. Jonathan had caught himself regarding the Town as a strange place when they were coming down the harbor, casting his eyes about on all sides and seeing things he had not spotted before — or had not seen in that way. It had looked to him as though it all belonged. But none of the others had looked back once. They were headed 145 degrees now, and sometime tomorrow they would reach their fishing ground on Georges Bank. Then they would start to earn money.

Fishermen had been going this way out of the Town for 150 years. They had been putting to sea since before the Revolution, harvesting the waters between Cape Cod and the Bay of Fundy, never straying too far from home. Gradually they went farther afield, creeping up the coast of Nova Scotia, heedless of fishing treaties that were made after the War of Independence. By the beginning of the nineteenth century, Britons were wryly remarking that these New England fishermen were swarming like flies around the Gulf of St. Lawrence; and they were soon to settle on new grounds to the northeast, where the Grand Banks lay to the south of Cape Race in Newfoundland. All these waters were teeming with fish; above all, they were filled with cod, a creature so bountiful of oil as well as meat (it has been known to grow to six feet long) that national economies have been sustained by it on both sides of the Atlantic. In 1784 a Boston merchant stood up in the Old State House and moved that "leave might be given to hang up the representation of a Codfish in the room where the House sit, as a memorial to the importance of the Cod-Fishery to the welfare of this Commonwealth." The motion was allowed and a wooden emblem was carved, and hangs to this day opposite the Speaker's desk on Beacon Hill.

The men who fished the cod and the other species of the western Atlantic made their earliest voyages to the Grand Banks in barrel-bottomed schooners with low waists and high quarterdecks, which were consequently called "heel-tappers." They rolled like pigs, particularly when they were required to beat home from Newfoundland, as they invariably were, against perpetual sou'westerly winds. But they carried a weight of cargo salted down in their holds that justified all discomfort and almost all hazards. When they reached the Town and the other ports along New England, the fish were laid out on flakes, platforms of alder a couple of feet above the ground, and slowly cured by the weather. Thus economy flourished.

The drawback to fishing the Grand Banks was its great distance. Bankers made only two or three trips a year from New England, though some fishermen were away from home even longer than the Americans. British and Portuguese crossed the Atlantic to get at the Grand Banks and saw their families for little more than the length of winter. The New Englanders had never abandoned closer waters when they discovered the riches off Newfoundland. They were still putting out in their Chebacco boats — double-ended craft with sharp sterns and two masts — to find cod, halibut and pollack within a hundred miles of home. Their charts were littered with the names of the most fruitful grounds: Old Man's Pasture, Kettle Bottom, Cashe's Ledge, and Matinicus Sou' Sou' West. They were aware of Georges Bank, but they feared it dreadfully. It was enormous, extending across most of the horizon beyond the Gulf of Maine. Many generations later, more knowledgeable men were to recognize it as an upland on the edge of the continental shelf. What the fishermen feared was its shallowness and its weather. It was scarcely possible to fish the Grand Banks without having at least thirty fathoms under your keel. But on Georges, a few speculative heaves with the leadline almost anywhere within a thousand square miles could reveal horrifying shallows of five fathoms and less. Even in calm this was liable to produce fierce tidal rips. In filthy weather from the northeast, a frequent occurrence at any season but especially in winter, it resulted in a battering surf upon the shoals, as the full weight of the Atlantic ocean drove into this submarine upland with a momentum that might have been gathering force all the way from Europe. Nothing made by man, caught to windward of Georges in such a storm, could possibly survive it. Effectively faced with a lee shore, a hundred-odd miles from the nearest land, any vessel would be annihilated swiftly. Yet this awful place, the fishermen knew from their nervous circumnavigations, was alive with their prey as were few other seas within their reach. And in 1821, three crews hoisted sail from the Town and dared to tackle Georges Bank in cold blood.

As a nineteenth-century annalist records it: "During the month of June . . . Captains Samuel Wonson, of the *Three Sisters*, Elisha M. Oakes, of the *Eight Brothers*, and Robert

Marston, of the *Two Friends,* held a consultation, and resolved to run the risk of making a trip to Georges Bank. At this time it was related as a positive fact that, if vessels anchored on Georges, the current would surely run them under. The three vessels sailed, keeping close company. They did not dare to anchor at first, but drifted about and caught a few fish. Finally one of the skippers proposed to run the risk and anchor one of the vessels. This, after some discussion on the part of all hands, was agreed upon, and two extra men were put on board the vessel, as a reinforcement, to assist in getting the anchor quickly in case of any difficulty. All preparations being completed, the anchor was let go, and shortly catches the bottom, then slip goes the cable around the windlass. 'Now check her a little,' was the order. Soon it got a good hold, and the vessel started in apparent motion through the water, at about 3 knots an hour. In the meantime, the other two vessels, having taken the current, are fast leaving the anchored craft, and those on board begin to get alarmed. The order to heave up anchor was soon given, and after an hour and a half's work this feat was accomplished. Before dark a little breeze sprang up, and the vessels all met again and started for home. Thus ended the first cod fishing trip to Georges. . . ."

More than a decade passed before fishermen sailed out there in fleets. But from the 1830s onward, vessels were to be found by the score at almost any date on the calendar, their numbers varying from season to season in response to the mysterious movement of the fish, which would be present in great abundance for a while, then vanish altogether for a number of years. Halibut, no more plentiful than cod in 1835 and 1836, became almost the only support of the Georges fishery for some years after that; but by 1848 the seamen of the Town were seeking halibut in vain. There were cycles in the life of all fish, and in their whereabouts, and there was evolution in the craft that went in search of them, which basically were all schooners; that is, boats with two masts, rigged fore and aft. It was legendary in the Town, indeed, that the schooner had been invented there, though naval historians will say that Dutchmen sailed such craft in the seventeenth century. But to this day the townsfolk proudly tell how, in 1713, Captain Andrew Robinson launched a two-master of his own design from a slipway in the cove behind the Neck where, being so delighted by the way she took to the water, an onlooker exclaimed, "See how she scoons." Whereupon her owner replied, "A scooner let her be." Whatever the lineage of the schooner, the fact is that nowhere in the world was it ever made more at home than upon the waters of this Atlantic coast, was it ever more thoughtfully adapted by the combined wits of seamen afloat and craftsmen ashore for the subtle intricacies of fishing. After the heeltappers came the smacks, with wells between the masts so that the fish could be brought home alive in salt water. After the smacks came the sharpshooters, built for greater speed, because the ice age had arrived and it was vital to make port with all haste before the preservative melted round the catch. No sooner had the sharpshooter come, than the clipper schooner followed, and she was the swiftest and the nimblest of them all. She was yare. She herself was to be modified over the decades after her introduction in about 1852, with mackerel schooners, clipper bankers, Georgesmen and other mutants emerging for specific tasks on different grounds of the western Atlantic. But in common these vessels were longer than their predecessors, they sat lower in the water, and they had lines of a grace and delicate rake to make you swoon. They were fast and they were handsome and they required superb seamanship for their handling in the rough and tumbling waters where they sailed. It is possible that the men who drove these craft into a third of the twentieth century were the finest boat handlers the world has known. They did not need to be great navigators, as did so many Europeans who wandered the globe. Nor did they need the stamina, moral as much as physical, that is demanded of the long-distance voyager. But for the reflex working of a craft in any conditions, for the instinctive judgment of just when and how and where to pit her within an inch of her life against the ocean's force, and for the sheer courage to apply it, there has probably been nothing like them. Their fathers had gone to sea in sheepskin jackets, leather aprons, baggy calfskin trousers, yellow cowhide boots, and tarred canvas hats. They went fishing in the new costume of oilskin, under sou'wester hats, and their seaboots were presently to be a clumping rubber. But underneath their gear, they were of a distinctive breed of sailors who had matured here from the days when their forefathers had first dropped anchor off this continent. Their names are rolled like a litany down the histories of this coast with great tenderness and pride, even today. So are those of their ships. *Grace L. Fears,* whose doryman Howard Blackburn, having gone astray in a gale, rowed for five days and nights without food or water but with hands gradually freezing to his oars, until he reached land with the dead body of Thomas Welsh lying in the dory with him. *Nannie C. Bohlin,* which came home to the Town one day in 1894 rigged like a sloop where she had sailed as a schooner, her foremast having carried away off Sable Island, the wreckage having been cleared and the jury rig mounted all in the full blast of an October gale. *Indiana* (Captain Almon Malloch), which came home from Newfoundland in the unparalleled time of eighty-eight hours, in spite of being hove to for eleven of them in a snowstorm off the Cape. *Helen B. Thomas* (Captain William Thomas), built without a bowsprit, the first of the knockabout schooners; so easy to handle, according to her crew, that you could turn her on a dime. *Esperanto* (Captain Marty Welch), which accepted the Canadian challenge to an international fisherman's race along the shores of Nova Scotia and beat the men of Lunenburg twice; the second time, according to an eyewitness, "when the *Esperanto,* facing almost certain destruction, cut through *Delawana's* weather and went on to win the race by seven minutes and 25 seconds." *Gertrude L. Thebaud,* which never managed to win that Fisherman's Cup from the Canadians and was not even very successful as a fisherman but, being launched in 1930, is remembered as the last of the fishing schooners. There had been very many of those in the century before her, marginally but significantly different from each other, changeable in this or that particular of rigging or line; but a constant life force in the being of the Town.

What had never changed at all was the character of Georges Bank, and the weather that could turn it into a deadly maelstrom. Some years were deadlier than others, though. On the night of Monday, February 24, 1862, some seventy boats were riding at anchor on the bank when a northwesterly gale struck. Fifteen vessels went down, taking one hundred twenty men with them, leaving seventy widows in the Town and one hundred forty orphans. A storm that blew up on August 24, 1873, took nine vessels and one hundred twenty-eight men. Between 1830 and 1873 alone, 281 fishing boats with 1,252 men aboard sailed from the Town and were lost at sea. The losses were never as heavy as that when the time of sailing ships passed and the time of steam vessels came, to be superseded by the age of the diesel engine. But they happened. And, like the high buccaneering spirit of the fishermen themselves, they were part of the Boat's inheritance.

As she began to draw away from the Cape, her crew sloped out of the wheelhouse, leaving only the Skipper there to set the automatic pilot on course, to plot a few lines on his chart and then to settle in the helmsman's high swiveled chair to several hours of dreamy boredom. His legs sprawled at eye level on either side of the compass, his pork-pie sunhat pulled down to an angle that would shade him from the strongest glare, he contemplated boat mortgages and wondered whether he could afford to take a winter month out in Florida, and vaguely enjoyed the soothing dip and lift of the vessel under his command. He would have been hard pressed to explain why he had turned to the sea for a living, for he was not an articulate man in spite of his college education; but his stumbling effort would have contained some attempt to say that he sought freedom from the clerical drudgeries of the land; a less likely hint that he prized, in some embarrassed corner of himself, the Yankee traditions of the sea.

The other four men went down into the galley and raided the pantry for peanut butter sandwiches and plastic cups of milk, though Carlo, who had a sweet tooth to satisfy, also crammed down a couple of cream doughnuts. Yank said nothing, though he marked this well, for the Guinea was a greedy bastard on top of everything else. Thus he would have answered for his animosity; in terms of greed and slyness and a flashing manner. The truth that he didn't belong would have come as a pointed afterthought. Big Boy was just as hostile (he was capable of swearing to the fact that burr-heads — by which he meant blacks — were never to be seen at sea because they were frightened of it and couldn't swim anyway) but he kept his antagonisms more carefully to himself, preferring to avoid conflict by use of the ambiguous twinkle and the ribald quip. Never one to look for trouble, or even to notice its source half the time, he was rummaging in the forepeak, beyond the galley, for the tackle the lot of them would need to make some running repairs. He was a busy man by nature, endlessly finding work to do and quite uncomplaining at its volume unless he thought he was being put upon. "C'mon, let's go then," he said, dragging two huge hanks of yellow rope back through the galley with him. He jerked his head over his shoulder as he passed the newest member of the crew. "You'll find a pair of balloons in there; bring 'em, will ya."

They paired off to start with, Yank with Big Boy, Carlo with Jonathan, and cut the rope into lengths of six feet. With a small iron G hook knotted onto one end, these were known as gadgets and the lobster traps were attached by them to the trawl line at regular intervals. On the Boat's last trip, some of the gadgets had shown signs of fraying after being rubbed and dragged across the seabed for over a year and would have to be replaced as soon as they surfaced again. You couldn't afford to lose a trap when they cost thirty-two dollars or more apiece; much less their contents, when lobster this summer was selling at $2.35 a pound off the boat. So the men worked carefully on the replacements, binding the ends tightly with black plastic tape so that there should be no unraveling either. Quickly they slipped into a rhythm. One man measured the length with his arm span, then twirled the roll of tape in place; his partner sawed away in the middle of each taping — two finished ends when he'd done — and swiftly blunted his knife blade in the process, for although these were razor-edged to start with, the nylon rope was exceedingly tough. Jonathan, cutting feverishly to keep up with Carlo, felt blisters beginning to rise on his hand. He was no pushover (he'd played tight end in the high school football squad) but his laboring had been limited to packing groceries at the supermarket which, though backbreaking work on a Friday night, had left his palms uncallused. He was full of curiosity and attempted to draw Carlo on the needling from Yank. "Somethin' runnin' between you two?" he asked. Carlo guffawed with bravado. "That guy!" he said. "You just watch him when he ties the gadgets on. He only knows one knot and that's the bastard he gets himself into every time he comes to sea." The last verb was pointed and proprietary. Carlo belonged with the sea, his two years in Wisconsin notwithstanding, as the ex-Marine and ex–meat cutter from Boston did not. Only Big Boy's credentials were a match for Carlo's, for he, too, was descended from fishermen. "You ever worry about it?" Jonathan inquired, gesturing over the side. The land had receded to a thin dark line behind them and even the Hancock Tower and the other skyscrapers of Boston, which on clear days could be discerned from the breakwater, poking oddly up from the waves, had now disappeared from view. "The sea, I mean. When it gets bad." He was beginning to thrill to the emptiness of it himself, half-hoping that it might cut up rough this trip; though not too much. "Me? Nah. Don't go in for that shit," said Carlo. "If it's gonna get you, it's gonna get you. Ain't nothin' you can do about it."

Big Boy had detached himself from Yank, who was finishing gadgets by himself. Big Boy was now making new trawl marker buoys, one of which rode the surface at each end of a line that could be anything up to a mile and a half long. These were hollow steel poles, six inches long, sunk into concrete blocks to keep them upright, their shafts festooned with large balloons made of heavy-duty PVC and colored Day-Glo pink, so that the buoy would float and be visible at some distance. At their tips they had contraptions made of unpainted tin, which would show up on a radar screen in fog or when the seas were so rough that you wouldn't expect to spot a balloon until you were almost running it down. Handling one of these buoys over the open stern when shooting a trawl called for a combination of circus skills, for one man had to do the job alone, staggering under the lopsided weight like a pocket Hercules on the tightrope, until the precise moment to heave and let go. This was hazardous with any sort of sea running. Even in the calm of their present passage Big Boy, when he had finished lashing the balloons on and taping the reflectors to the poles, called for a hand to help him cart the things across the deck and stow them against the fo'c'sle rail until they were needed.

He had been working in T-shirt and shorts, with rubber boots cut low enough to expose the tattoo on his leg; and the others had been either stripped to the waist or clad only in T-shirts and jeans. The sun was blazing down on them and the high fo'c'sle blocked the breeze created by the Boat's movement. The deck smelled faintly of hot metal, embedded brine, fishy remnants, and a trace of diesel fumes. Presently the men reached for rubber aprons and fabric gloves; all but Jonathan, who gladly seized the chance to struggle into his Helly-Hansens for the first time, the set of yellow oilskins he had bought for this expedition into his manhood. It was time to start baiting up, and that was a messy business.

The bait was capsized around most of the deck behind the hatch, great blocks of frozen carcasses that had come aboard packed in cardboard boxes, though under the heat of the sun some melting had happened and the cardboard had turned soggy and highly disposable. The carcasses were those of redfish, a creature that lives near the seabed and rarely reaches the surface alive because its internal organs cannot stand the change in pressure. There was a time, during World War II, when the fishery of the Town was almost wholly based on huge Army contracts for the procurement of redfish; but the refined tastes of peacetime had found it less appetizing, and it was now caught

only to be filleted in a factory and turned into fish sticks.
The mutilated bodies of these creatures were a profitable
sideline from the factories, for only skate, flounder, or
yellowtail made better bait for deep-sea lobstering and
they were harder to come by. What you needed was raw
fish that would stay intact inside a submerged trap for a
couple of weeks if need be, to entice any lobsters in the
vicinity. Lobstermen cursed when the redfish ran out and
they had to buy herring, mackerel, or menhaden instead;
for these would last only a day or two before their softer
flesh disintegrated and was carried away by the currents.
Menhaden was the worst of the lot, being a very oily fish
which stained the arms indelibly when you were baiting.

Redfish was bad enough, for it carried a row of spines
along its dorsal ridge, sharp enough to penetrate a gloved
hand and toxic enough to poison an arm so badly that the
painful swelling could only be relieved by great doses of
penicillin. But it was, above all, messy when it came to
handling all the slithering bits and pieces of this factory
garbage for several hours at a stretch. It would be even
worse as the voyage wore on, as each trap had to be baited
with a bag of something so putrid that it was alive with
maggots, so completely nauseating that the men would
gulp for fresh air as they worked and even the impervious
Big Boy would spit over the side and say, "Don't know how
the fuckin' maggots stand it!"

They dismembered the cardboard boxes and hurled
them flapping over the side, then shoveled the thawing
fish onto the banding table above the hatch. The four men
stood around, each with a wad of porous plastic bags at his
elbow and, behind him, a large empty oil drum. There
were twelve of these and, when baiting was finished, all
would be so full of bagged gurry that it was as much as a
man could do to roll one drum across to its place along the
starboard rail, where all of them would be lined up ready

for the trawling. But first there was the interminable reaching into the heap of hacked flesh, exposed bone, trailing guts, and extruding eyes; the thrusting of these handfuls into the bags (five pounds to each); the shaking of the bonier bits down to the bottom of the bags; the tightening of the drawcords to leave a loop that would be snagged inside the trap; the tossing of the bags into the drum; and the reaching again.

It went on for five hours as the Boat plodded on to the southeast, and in all that time the men scarcely paused to do more than light cigarettes. They talked intermittently — girl talk, acquaintance talk, company talk, and talk about the price of fish — but mostly they worked in silence, mechanically concentrating on not getting redfish spines into their hands. Big Boy's pale eyes flicked up to take in the sea from time to time and once he dropped a half-filled bait bag and strode over to the rail to peer at something more intently.

"Come and look at this," he called to Jonathan after a moment. "See 'em?" And when the youth saw nothing at first, Big Boy stretched his arm and pointed toward the starboard bow.

A black thing, bow-shaped, rose out of the sea in an arc and curved back under the waves again with something between a slap and a slither; then another and another, eight of them in the end. Jonathan thought they were dolphins but, no, said Big Boy, they were young whales. And Jonathan, after watching the creatures rise and fall half a dozen times, could see how those heads were far too heavy for dolphins, sending bow waves out from their sides each time they plowed back under. "Beautiful, ain't they?" said Big Boy, smiling at Jonathan as though he had arranged the whole show in person. But, then, a school of dolphins did appear, some distance behind the whales, leaping with energy where the whales had been ponderous with power. They cut into sight across the bows of the Boat and careered away in pursuit of the larger mammals, rising clean out of the water with every ejaculating spurt to the surface. Then they vanished, and Jonathan was about to turn away from the rail when a sudden movement almost alongside the Boat caught his eye. Only yards away, and a few feet down, a dolphin squirmed past, half turning on its side as it did, so that its mouth seemed to be grinning up at the watcher on deck. It had overtaken the Boat in a flash (and they were making a good ten knots themselves) and in a moment there were half a dozen dolphins leaping and plunging in great spasmodic play where the vessel's bow wave fell back and merged with the lolloping surface of the sea. It was only then that Jonathan, looking down to see if any more of the school would shoot past, realized that the ocean here was so clear above its dark green depth that you could see the salt crystals hanging in it, millions of them gleaming like globules of fat.

"D'yever hear about Joe Stevens, George's old man?" Big Boy asked the others when he ranged up at the banding table again. "They were up Bay of Fundy somewheres and this fuckin' whale came up near the boat and stayed there on top for 'bout twenty minutes. And Joe, he says, 'Get us alongside that motherfucker cos I'm goin' to board him.' And he did. He jumped off the deck and stood on the bastard's back, just so he could say he'd done it. Course, he held onto the rail while he did it. Cock-sucker, he was."

The sun was sliding into the sea before they finished work, though Yank had left off before the others because it was his night for making supper. By the time they had trundled the last drum of bait into place, hosed down the deck to rid it of slime, and washed themselves up, the glaring light of the day had collapsed through a final cascade of brilliance into a deep and dull blue that would soon be absolute blackness. A wind had freshened from the east as the sun declined in the west and a rime of froth upon the waves palely answered the feeble glimmering of the first stars. But the Boat was still moving with pleasure-cruising ease, rolling very slowly from side to side and nodding her head so gently to the sea that it could not even be called the intimation of a pitch.

The galley was steamy with cooking, for Yank had four different pans boiling on the stove, as well as two chickens spitting and basting on trays in the oven. He was a methodical man (the Marines had seen to that) and, though he didn't exactly enjoy cooking, he had made it his business to watch a long series of girl friends throw something together after sex and (if the affair lasted long enough) to try it himself under their sensuous tutelage. This is not something he would have done when he was married; which was one reason why, when he returned from the awful squalor of Hue and the sleazy ecstasies of Saigon, he found that his wife had fled from Boston with a mechanic from Brooklyn. Yank could be bitter by nature, coming from that raddled side of the Hub where Irish and blacks, having no other scapegoats but each other, turned their urban resentments into race war, which had lately become truce because of a counterattraction in the improbable progress of the Red Sox towards the World Series. The departed wife had left him morose, so he had abandoned butchery and come to the Town, where his sister had a boy friend on the boats, and soon found himself a place on the company payroll. He was a strong man and an adaptable one, who picked things up fast. He was also, besides being methodical, a stalwart man. It would not have occurred to him, as he mashed the potatoes, opened cans of sweet corn, carrots, and beans, made some salad-on-the-side, and turned over those spitted fowl, to have served Carlo differently from the others, or to make his working life difficult; even without the watchful presence of the Skipper. For the Guinea was one of the crew; better he weren't, for the bastard had it coming to him, for sure, but he was, and they were earning a living together. So, as well as the plastic carton of milk that sensible men drank, Yank brought from the fridge the can of Hawaiian Punch, which tasted like all the fruity concoctions of childhood spewed into one and to which Carlo was powerfully addicted.

The galley was a misleading name for an area which might have been designed for a low-budget vacation cottage, or for a rather grand home on wheels. On almost all the other, and much older, fishing vessels of the Town, the galley was palpably nautical from the moment you stepped into it. In the most ancient boats still afloat it was generally located in the same space as the crew's sleeping quarters, down in the forepeak, with the bunks curving round the two sides of the hull until they met in the sharpness of the bows. Elsewhere, on vessels where individual bunks were stuck in odd and otherwise useless corners of the deck housing, the galley and the mess table would have a compartment to themselves. Invariably there would be a Shipmate range of cast iron, fired with solid fuel and roaring with flame, with a long and wide top for the cooking and a rail above for the drying of clothes. The mess table would be hemmed in not only by the wooden benches on either side but also by the long tray hanging above it, with slots for the stowing of coffee mugs and a selection of seasonings, so close to the eaters that they were liable to bump their heads as they leaned forward to take their food. The Boat's galley was almost sybaritic by comparison. It was part of a crew space that was completely situated beneath the wheelhouse, which could be reached up a steel ladder that began just inside the heavy metal door opening out onto the deck. Along the starboard side were two bunk rooms, but the rest of the space, until you walked through to the forepeak where working gear was stowed, was for cooking, eating, and lounging. The for'ard end of this space was occupied by a table, with a padded couch round three of its sides. The after end and the port bulkhead began with a refrigerator and finished with a cupboard, with electric stove, working surface and sink in between. The entire space was veneered in walnut, illuminated by fluorescent strips and two portholes, warmed by central heating, and embellished by a couple of bookshelves laden with paperbacks. A chart of the eastern seaboard was on the bulkhead above the couch and there was linoleum on the deck. Someone had tacked a couple of printed slogans onto the paneling by the for'ard bunk room door. One said, "Fishing is the art of almost doing nothing." The other advised that "Nice girls do it, too." This was more restrained than the reflex aboard some vessels working out of the Town, which religiously maintained gimcrack altars dominated by the Blessed Virgin and, within a few feet, a selection of pulchritude from the magazine trade, asprawl with invitation, nipples erect and hairy pudenda gleaming suggestively with oil.

Big Boy, ample in all his ways, was wont to be highly sentimental about these quarters when, as frequently happened, he had invited visitors aboard at the dock. Appreciating their curiosity and wonder, he would gesture expansively around the galley and say, "Welcome to my home"; then, catching their startled looks, add with exquisite satisfaction, "Well, this *is* my home. It's the only one I need." Now, having called the Skipper down from the wheelhouse, he was hunched over his disposable paper plate and thrusting quick forkfuls of food into his mouth. "How we doin'?" he asked between mouthfuls.

The Skipper, taking his chicken and corn more slowly

between sips of milk, nodded approvingly. "Pretty good," he replied. "Should be on Gilbert Canyon before ten tomorrow."

"Whatsa weather doin'?" asked Carlo, his mouth crammed, from across the table.

"Sounds okay. Forecast says maybe a bit of fog tonight. Might have freshened a bit by morning. Better keep an eye on the radar, though. Looks to me as if it's goin' on the blink again. It's been fading and coming clear on and off this past couple of hours."

"Shit," said Yank, glaring with a contempt aimed at maintenance men ashore.

"Fog and no radar," chortled Carlo. "Could be fun and games tonight." And he beamed happily round the table.

"Well anyway," said the Skipper, "just keep an eye on it. If it freaks out give me a shout, though I doubt I can do anything about it. Watch list is on the notice-board. Big Boy's first and you . . ." (to Jonathan) ". . . you stick with him tonight. Tomorrow night you'll be on your own." The Skipper inched his way off the couch, stood up and tossed his plate into the garbage bin. "Good grub, cookie," he said. "Well, I'm goin' to hit the sack," and took three paces into the smaller of the two starboard rooms, which he had to himself, though there was another bunk besides his own. Carlo belched loudly and went into the other room, while Yank began to clear the work surface for washing up. With a jerk of his head and "Let's go, then," Big Boy led Jonathan up the ladder to the wheelhouse.

On most craft, four men would have been hard put to squeeze themselves into the space around the wheel and, although sometimes the captain's bunk was set into a recess at the back of the cabin, to get to the crew's quarters more frequently meant a dash down an outside ladder and across some distance of open deck. But the builders of the Boat had here, as in the living space, declared an interest in some degree of comfort. Not only could the crew move from one area to the other without even seeing the sea, but a dozen or more men could have stood quite comfortably in the wheelhouse, in spite of its chart table and its helmsman's chair. The first was really no more than a deep ledge by your right ear as you came up the ladder from the living space. The chair was bolted to the deck behind the wide windscreen (complete with wipers) and behind another ledge that ran the whole width of the wheelhouse and resembled the dashboard of an outsize automobile. The wheel itself, steel and spokeless, was no bigger than some truck drivers might handle. To its right, on the dashboard top, were two flimsy-looking engine levers, one a clutch to control the gears, the other a throttle to vary the speed. Beyond the levers was a small box bearing dials which recorded revolutions, oil pressure, and such like, not all of which worked. The only thing on the dashboard top unmistakably nautical was the compass under its glass dome, set high upon a wooden base and a black metal cylinder. If the helmsman stood at the wheel, his right hand could reach to the ceiling and tune in a radio to the coast guard, weather service, and other marine frequencies. If he turned a little to his left he could manipulate another radio, which provided all the commercial wavelengths. But he would have to move his head a fraction to avoid banging it against the radar set that projected at an angle from above, set very carefully so that he could glance at its screen if need be while still within reach of his controls.

At the back of the wheelhouse, above the chart table and its drawers, the Loran apparatus was clamped to the bulkhead in two cabinets. At various points on the earth's surface, of which Nantucket was one, Bermuda a second, Cape Race a third, radio stations emitted perpetual signals which, being received simultaneously by ships at sea, would tell them to within fifty feet just where they were. Radio navigation had thus rendered the sextant and the chronometer obsolescent and the Skipper, indeed, would have conceded (quietly, for he had a care for the old traditions) that he had but the haziest idea of how to obtain a fix from the stars or any other heavenly body. At any time, all he had to do was look at his Loran, understand the significance of the green impulses jerking across its screen, and read off the figures which were constantly revised as the vessel shifted position and they flashed upon its computerized nerve end. True, he did have a chronometer aboard. It was fixed in its brass mounting alongside the almost identical barometer just inside the lintel of the wheelhouse's starboard door. But its precise timekeeping was no more necessary aboard the Boat than it would have been to a shorebound commuter, who can make do with an alarm clock.

It was completely dark when Big Boy and Jonathan climbed up to the wheelhouse, and it was minutes before their eyes adjusted to this gloom after the glare of light in the galley. It would be a couple of hours — almost the end of their watch — before the moon rose, but this at least made it easier to spot the lights of any other vessels in their vicinity. There would be such a flickering brilliance upon the waters where the moon's beams fell that you would have to stare hard and long in that quarter to distinguish those few pinpoints that were artificial and warned of potential danger from the thousands that were natural and meant the open sea. The radar plotted everything within six miles, which was warning enough, but its whining was an irritant and the set was usually switched off unless visibility was bad. Tonight, once the eyes had accustomed themselves to the subtleties of darkness, it was possible to detect that fine boundary between the deep leaden hue of the sky and the more substantial blackness of the sea; and that was more than twice the distance covered by the radar scanner. But to see anything clearly the eyes had to range themselves consciously some way beyond the Boat and the luminous arcs created by its navigation lights. There was also distraction from the Loran, with its own green and red illuminations, which reflected in the wheelhouse window and could startle a drowsy lookout with their likeness to the starboard or port lights of a craft crossing the Boat's course.

You had to keep from getting drowsy, as Big Boy explained to the young man. It was no good spending your watch in the chair, listening to the all-night disc jockeys on the radio; that way you might drop off in no time. You didn't have to touch the wheel with the automatic pilot switched on, and there was no call for switching it off and steering manually unless you needed to avoid another ship. You had to keep your eyes peeled, first at this side of the wheelhouse, then at that, not forgetting to look astern every so often to see if anything was going to overtake. Then you could sit down for a spell. But every hour, mind, you had to go down to the engine room, below the galley, to make sure everything was okay down there. Big Boy led the way down the two ladders, into the roaring cavern where the yellow Caterpillar diesel thumped and pounded from one end of the voyage to the other. It was not very large — it occupied no more than a quarter of the echo chamber in which it was lodged — but with its tappets and its pistons, through its thin brass tubes and its heavy steel valves, it could translate five thousand gallons of treacly fuel oil into enough energy to keep the Boat at sea for twenty-five days; which, in fair conditions, would have almost taken her to Europe and back. It needed no help from the crew to accomplish this, just a watchful eye every hour on a couple of dials, to make sure that nothing was overheating and that oil pressure was steady, and a careful glance at the bilge beneath, to see that the filthy mixture of oil and water, sloshing back and forth along a trough in time with the Boat's movement, never rose above that beam there.

After the engine room's racket, the noise in the wheel-house was scarcely more than a chatter of vibrations transmitted from the diesel through the steel plating of the hull; and a low seething rumble from the wind and the sea outside. It pleased Jonathan to be up there, his legs braced to absorb the rocking of the deck, his elbows resting on the dashboard ledge, his eyes very deliberately searching the sea to port for any twinkle that would at one and the same time be comforting and cautionary. He much wanted to spot another vessel, to do it before Big Boy's practiced gaze took it in, because that would stamp him a member of the crew much more than anything that had happened so far; it would start the word around that he was reliable. But he also wanted to know the companionship of another ship out here, to relieve the awful loneliness of the deep sea. This was not a fear of what terrifying things the sea might do in time of storm. It was simple unease at the boundlessness of it all; you could not sense its limits and therefore you might become lost. But there was no companionable twinkle out there yet, and the occasional gull wheeling through the pool of light provided by the Boat itself seemed only to emphasize the emptiness of the waters beyond. Appearing suddenly from that outer space it vanished just as quickly, as if it were a phantom. There were other birds about, though Jonathan was unaware of them until Big Boy, having shouldered his way out on deck to empty his bladder at the lee rail, shouted to him to come and have a look. He pointed to a dark corner behind the wheelhouse, where there was shelter from the wind and some warmth from the engine-room exhaust pipe. A small black bird was crouched there, but began to flutter and hop at their approach, though it made no effort to fly away. It had the most curiously long webbed feet Jonathan had ever seen, so much longer than the leg above the joint that it looked as though it were standing on elbows. "There's more of them," Big Boy said, and showed where half a dozen were scattered around the outside of the wheelhouse, all of them steadfastly facing an upright surface of superstructure, never facing the open. "Petrels," he said. "Poor little buggers get exhausted and come aboard for the ride. They'll stay there all night, too."

They were still there (Jonathan went on deck to check) when the watch with Big Boy was done and Yank came up to relieve them. The two older men exchanged a few words before Big Boy indicated that sleep was his chief priority now. It wanted another hour to midnight, and in the Town the bars and the harbor cafes would still be babbling with trade. But their back was turned on the Town, and its nocturnal rhythms were no longer theirs. When you were not working the Boat, or hastily taking food to keep you working strongly, you slept. It was the only way, even at the start of a trip, for, by the end of it, the working of the Boat would have drained its crew to weariness. So Jonathan obediently followed Big Boy below and clambered into an upper bunk, opposite the one where Carlo lay flat on his back, his right leg raised at the knee, his arm crooked above his head, his blue stubbly chin slack and his mouth wide open, so that his snores seemed ridiculous as well as resonant. Jonathan grinned at this spectacle, wrapped his blanket into a cocoon and turned toward the bulkhead, now feeling the lift and settle of the Boat along his entire body. Two stars revolved around the circle of the porthole by his face. He watched them for a moment; then he was gone.

He awoke with a start as some strange sound bore into

his sleep. He blinked for an instant, trying to focus it, but there was nothing to be heard for a while. Then it came again, a high-pitched wail from somewhere above. Instinctively, for he had never heard it before, he turned his head toward the porthole to confirm his sudden recognition of the sound. There were no stars to be seen now; nothing but a gray blankness. Quickly Jonathan squirmed round in his bunk and looked over its sideboard. Big Boy was down there, in a heavy heap of stillness, and Yank was sleeping opposite him, across the narrow gap between the bunks, both of them with their backs to the space, just like the petrels. But Carlo had disappeared from the other top bunk. A primitive alarm as much as sheer curiosity slipped Jonathan out of his berth, groping for his shoes on the deck, his mind slowly clearing from the fuddle of his sleep. When he reached the wheelhouse, he found Carlo leaning against the starboard corner of the dashboard, his eyes fixed on the chronometer, his hand over the button of the siren. He was not relaxed and for once he did not grin at Jonathan's approach. He pressed the button and the siren wailed again at the blankness that had fallen upon the world. It covered everything, and only by putting his face up to the windscreen could Jonathan make out the junction of port and starboard rails at the bows, with the long harpoon lashed to the starboard side, together with its attendant tub of line: cocky armorial bearings which, Big Boy had explained, they carried just in case they came across swordfish or shark; for in swordfish there was profit and in shark the opportunity to savage an old foe. There would be no seeing whatever swam in the sea this night, however, and precious little chance of spotting anything that sailed upon it until it was too late to avoid a collision. In his inexperience, Jonathan had not instantly noted the full extent of potential hazard the moment he climbed into the wheelhouse, but Carlo's first words told of the great

anxiety he himself felt and showed in the tightness of his body. "Goddamn radar's gone," he said. Jonathan glanced up at the set projecting above the dashboard and saw that it was motionless, heard that it was silent. Where there should have been six golden circles and a golden band steadily sweeping through them like the second hand of a clock, with at least fuzzy patches of light appearing sporadically when the scanner covered tumbled water, there was nothing but a black blank screen. Not a buzz out of it, let alone a whine. "Went off half an hour ago. Skipper came up and messed about with it but he reckons one of the contact breakers has gone. So that's it, baby." Carlo paused, aggrieved, and pressed the button again. He had not yet, since Jonathan came up to join him, taken his eyes off the chronometer in his anxiety that the Boat should wail its warning for ten seconds precisely every two minutes. The back of his head was facing the bows. In the thickest fog imaginable, the Boat was quite without a lookout. "I reckon they ought to have two-man watches in this sort of weather," said Carlo, inclining his head to listen for anyone else's answering wail. "Specially when we're coming into the shipping lanes." It was only then Jonathan realized that the engine throttle was still wide open. They were steaming their best ten knots and somewhere to the west of them by now would be the Nantucket lightship, insignificant in itself for they would go nowhere near it, but marking the confluence of shipping lanes into New York and Boston. The waters they were now crossing might, for all they knew, be crawling with tankers, container carriers and all the heavy vessels of the high seas bound between Europe and two great American ports. Not the sort of traffic for a blind fishing boat to be mixed up in even if it were to be assumed that everyone else's radar was functioning properly that night; for the watch-

keeping on some supervessels sailing under flags of
convenience was notoriously sloppy.

"Christ," said Jonathan, having been struck by the
possibilities inherent in their situation, "why don't we stop
or something?"

A touch of bravado returned to Carlo, and he shoved his
woolen watch cap dramatically down from his hairline,
halfway toward his eyebrows. "If you gotta go, baby, you
gotta go. May as well do it in style." And, squinting
carefully at the chronometer through a haze of smoke, he
plucked his cigarette from the corner of his mouth with
two careful fingers, his elbow raised to the high port in a
gesture that he intended to be both nonchalant and
flippant.

But Carlo was comforted by Jonathan's arrival and
greatly relieved when he volunteered to go out on deck
and try to see what might be seen from the open, without
the distracting reflections from Loran and compass light
on the windscreen. Not that you were much better placed
standing by the harpoon, Jonathan thought, when he had
gone below to collect his oilskin slicker and then taken his
self-appointed post in the bows. There was something
grand about being there, to be sure, with the moisture of
the mist beginning to rinse your face, with you standing
up to the elements like a seaman, the fate of the Boat at
least partially in your hands. But there sure as hell wasn't
much to be seen, and Jonathan was conscious of his blood
pulsating as he tried to peer through the swirling fog
ahead and on either side. He wondered anxiously what it
would be like if another vessel suddenly loomed out of that
lot; how far away would it be when you first got a glimpse
of something solid and dangerous; and how big would that
threatening shape be? Would you be able to see some glow
of light as a very late warning that the worst was about to

happen unless someone did something very quickly? And if he saw something like that, how would he tell Carlo fast enough to do something to stop a crash, to spin the wheel or stop the engine or whatever was the best thing? Shit, the man couldn't even see him, the way he was standing with his back turned. Jonathan turned himself and looked astern along the deck, measuring the distance from where he was to the wheelhouse door: or would it be better (it would be fractionally quicker) if he simply thumped on the windscreen to attract Carlo's attention and hoped to Christ he saw his signals in time? Why the hell didn't they stop or slow down? What sort of a bloody skipper was it that left a man alone with a busted radar on a night like this with tankers about, and still going full steam ahead? Jesus, the man must be nuts. You couldn't see anything at all, beyond a few feet, because the glare of their own lights only shone that distance and then bounced back off the fog; and, at the same time, rendered the entire world beyond that gray wall of vapor utterly invisible. Jonathan craned his neck over the bows and could just make out two waves cascading on either side as the Boat clove the waters sightlessly. It was twelve feet from foredeck to waterline, and that was very close to the limit of visibility. He raised his head and gripped the rail and stood there with his legs braced apart and wished he were back ashore.

The worst didn't happen. Nothing at all happened but their headlong plunge to the southeast, through fog that billowed along the decks and gusted in swathes past the masthead light and occasionally revealed pockets of black clarity before enveloping the world in gray again. Every two minutes their siren wailed its nervous message through the mist, but no one ever answered. Before the watch was half done, the young man's legs were soaked through the denim of his jeans and his hair was plastered around his forehead, where the fog had swept in under the hood of his slicker. He was glad when Carlo shoved his head out of the wheelhouse door and bellowed at him to go and make some coffee. After that he went up to the bows only once or twice, contenting himself with a few stamping turns round the fo'c'sle before returning to the sanctuary of the wheelhouse where, he now told himself, you could see almost all there was to see anyway without getting drenched to the skin.

At ten to five in the morning, Carlo told him to go and waken the Skipper, who seemed unsurprised at the presence of two men on watch. "She's still thick, eh?" was all he said when he joined them and, after a quick look at the compass, went to check the Loran reading and make some calculations on the chart. Carlo stopped applying himself to the siren, stretched his arms and yawned loudly. "We're making good time," said the Skipper, as he came across to the wheel, switched off the automatic pilot, and changed course a few degrees. "Should be at the first buoy about ten." He seemed blandly unconcerned about their inability to see where they were going. He appeared to take no notice at all of the sudden silence from above. He reached up and switched on the marine radio and, through much spluttering static, punctuated by sharper and louder cracks, a voice was saying ". . . winds westerly light to moderate. Seas will be three to four feet high in most places and five to six feet over shoalwaters. . . ."

By the time the forecast was done, Carlo had disappeared without a word and Jonathan, feeling quite unnecessary now but wishing to have his contribution marked, mustered an artificial yawn and said, "Yeah, well, I reckon I'll turn in now." The Skipper never even turned his head from his watch on the compass card. "Okay, see ya later," he replied.

It was broad daylight when Jonathan awoke again to a sudden cry of "C'mon then, let's go." He had been dreaming restlessly of thick fog and narrow escapes and sat up with a jump, turning to the porthole as he did so. But there was not a trace of fog now. There was a clear blue sky and a climbing sun and, as far as you could see, low sloshing waves dancing with light. It looked very healthy out there. The voice had been the Skipper's, but he had already gone back to the wheelhouse and the other three men in the bunk room were slowly heaving themselves upright, their faces foolish with sleep. One at a time (there was scarcely room for more than that) they levered themselves to the deck and fumbled their way into the few pieces of clothing they had discarded before taking to their bunks. Big Boy clumped out first and, by the time Jonathan got into the galley, he had made himself a thick sandwich spread with peanut butter and was dragging the milk from the fridge. The others made sandwiches of their own as soon as they appeared but, before eating, cast around for seaboots and struggled into them, ready to stride out on deck with their breakfasts in their hands. It was almost ten o'clock and they would not make such a late start again, but after twenty-six hours at sea they were only just coming up to their fishing ground. Big Boy was into his third mouthful of peanut butter and bread when a buzzer sliced through the sound of their digestions. "He's on to it," he mumbled through his mouthful. "Let's get movin' then." And, with a quick gulping of milk and tearing bites at sandwiches, the four men followed each other out through the great iron sea door and into the sunlight.

There was a breeze but it was pleasant, for the day was already warm, and it seemed to Jonathan as he came into the fresh clear air that there was no place he would rather be. A thick boiling wake trailed in an arc behind the Boat, for the Skipper had sighted the end of their first trawl on his starboard bow. Big Boy motioned Jonathan over to the rail and pointed out the buoy, its steel pole with the radar reflector on top swaying jauntily in the low sea, its big pink balloons bobbing in the waves, the hieroglyphics identifying it as theirs sprayed inexpertly across the round surfaces with black paint. Somewhere below, in seventy-odd fathoms, the first collection of lobster traps lay scattered upon the rocky floor of the sea.

The Boat had crossed Georges Bank in the fog and was beyond its shallows now. This first trawl had been set on the very edge of Gilbert Canyon, which marked the jagged limit of the continental shelf, before the greatest deeps of the Atlantic Ocean. Range after range of these canyons lay along the edge of the shelf. Lydonia was somewhere miles away to their left, Oceanographer a similar distance to their right, all giving more or less the same soundings. As the seabed slid into Gilbert Canyon it descended from seventy-odd fathoms to three hundred sixty-seven fathoms, quite abruptly. Then it ran downhill a long way, until it dropped off the shelf onto the floor of the Atlantic. The water was a mile and a half deep there.

This was where these five men had come to earn their living.

Jonathan came back from that trip much more of a man than could be measured by the ten days he had actually spent at sea. Yet he had faced nothing more of hazard after that first night out in the fog without a working radar, for the fog did not return. The wind had never been more than moderately breezy, the waves had not risen to more than a playful chop. Indeed, their last day before landfall had been spent steaming across an expanse of sea so utterly silent and motionless, its surface as still as a pool of oil, that any sound at all carried a marvelous distance. They had to change course in the late afternoon to give way to a huge tanker bound in ballast for New York and, as they curved around its stern, about a mile to port, they heard, above the steady beat of the Boat's engines, the sudden crash and rattle as someone aboard the tanker allowed a length of heavy chain to slip loose from some machinery and drop a few feet onto its gigantic hollow drum of a deck. The next day, as the sun was setting, found the Boat running up the coast toward the Town. As it came near a point within sight of the winking red light on the end of the breakwater, a gentle air off the land brought a delicious fragrance with it, a bouquet of jasmine and rose and dogwood and many other blossoms, that fell headily upon nostrils cleansed by the antiseptic void of the sea.

It was that sort of trip: blessed by the elements after the fog and finished in tranquillity. It was also fruitful, for they had landed 15,000 pounds of lobster by the canal, deep inside Cape Cod Bay, which is where they always sold their catch. Being so much nearer the profitable appetites of New York (not to mention the tourists flowing between the mainland and Cape Cod), the lobster mart there offered prices significantly higher than any that could have been obtained at home in the Town. The Skipper was well pleased with the addition to his bank balance, the step toward the fulfillment of his ambition to be an owner himself; as he revved his pickup at the town dock for the drive home to Rhode Island, his pleasure at the prospect of two nights in bed with his wife was not even dimmed by the thought that the maintenance men might still be messing about with the defective radar when he returned, a circumstance which would unsettle his normally benign good nature: having at college decided with navigational precision just where he wanted to go and at what pace, he tended to become surprisingly edgy when faced with delay. As for his three experienced crewmen, the trip they had just finished was so much like scores they had already made that most of its details would be forgotten within the week. Big Boy, on the run home from the canal, had worked out that he would collect two hundred and fifty bucks as his share of the catch and, having done so, announced expansively to Jonathan that it was "enough to get drunk on; not enough to put in the bank." And the money would, for sure, be spent on forty-eight hours of varied pleasure whose purpose as much as anything was to forget the fact that the Boat, much more than the room he occupied in his mother's house, was the place he most felt like calling home. Carlo, more congenially anchored to maternity, would divest himself of half his paycheck to pay his filial dues and, in spending a portion of the other half, might very well collect himself a black eye after inebriated conflict with some bar bouncer in the course of defending or notionally assailing an aspect of female honor. He would not be tangling with his regular adversary, for he and Yank kept well out of each other's way ashore and, besides, this particular trip had left Yank less well equipped for combat than usual. On their fourth day out he had misjudged the agility with which a lobster can move that pincer which nature has designed for crushing its prey rather than for holding it helpless until the crusher is in a position to grip. Yank was struggling to get the thick rubber bands onto the holding pincer of a very large lobster, a fifteen-pounder of armored muscle, succulence, and ill-temper, when its crusher lunged round and seized the fisherman by his left thumb. In a flashing reflex of agony, Yank had dashed his hand against the banding table's edge and the lobster was almost instantly shaken loose. Had it not been, the thumb would have been crushed beyond repair and possibly severed at the joint. As it was, it merely throbbed with pain under the dressing Big Boy had applied, was swollen to twice its normal size, would lose its nail within a week or so, and would take a full thirteen months to recover its customary appearance.

Jonathan, hearing Yank's roar of obscenity, had felt his stomach turn when he saw what was happening, for there was something primevally vicious about that great brute of a lobster, something powerless about the man's whole posture in that split second when the pincer closed upon the bone: his mouth agape with horror, his shoulders heaving with tension, his eyeballs rolled up with pain. In another split second the positions were reversed for, as the lobster fell to the deck, Yank kicked it furiously into the scupper, where it lay on its back, its tail threshing wildly to obtain purchase, its two enormous pincers (the crusher as wide as a man's handspan) circling powerfully to fasten onto anything within their reach. For a moment, Jonathan thought he was going to be disgracefully sick, but took a deep breath and forced his rising stomach contents back where they belonged, and came out in a sweat instead. It was a fractional move toward manhood; he would not be so disturbed by such a thing again. Nor would he again, after that trip, experience quite the same exhilaration as his awareness, after three or four days, that Big Boy was no longer chivvying him to keep up with the others in the laborious teamwork of hauling a trawl aboard. But the greatest pleasure of all, a sharp turning point in his life, came on that second night when he stood his own watch for the first time. True, the Boat was laid-to from dusk to dawn, for the first trawl to be hauled in the morning was but a mile or two away from their position at the end of the previous day. All Jonathan had to do was to keep his eyes open and check the bilge occasionally as they wallowed comfortingly in low swell, for the night was clear and their stationary lights would be visible for miles to anything that passed their way. But the fact was that, for more than a couple of hours, he and he alone was in charge of the Boat; only his character and horse sense

could make the first vital move toward safety, should peril
suddenly threaten the lives of four shipmates sleeping
carelessly below. He was deeply conscious of this as he sat
in the helmsman's chair and meticulously surveyed the
horizon. He was thrilled by it when he took a turn on deck
to enjoy the sparkle of moonlight on the water and the slap
of waves against the floodlit stern. He was reluctant to go
below and get some sleep, even though the day's work had
dog-tired him, when Carlo came up to relieve him. There
would never be another night quite like it.

The Town was still sweltering through its long summer
when the Boat returned, still swollen beyond its normal
size by the seasonal incursion of tourists. Droves of them
came each year, although the Cape lay to one side of the
most attractive parts of New England, which drew people
from all over America and beyond, partly because here the
continental taproot was to be found, but mostly because
here that rarest of all things had happened: a very
beautiful land had actually been enhanced, rather than
spoiled, by the care and the love and the passionate desire
to belong with which man had settled himself upon it. His
clapboard and his boxcar red had been built upon this
landscape with organic sense, and the white-walled townships with their ruddy outcrops served only to give it a
tranquil scale just as, in Europe, villages of ancient stone
seem to breathe in harmony with the hills and the valleys where they are set. The Cape was not devoid of such
harmony itself, though the Town certainly had its ugly
moments down by the harbor. The tourists came each year,
in spite of the detour involved, for the sake of its history and for the vicarious adventure they got from a
whiff of its sea; and some of them, the ones who would
follow any trail so long as it was comfortable and clean and
notorious, because they had seen its prettiest pictures in

some glossy publication and had vowed they would go to New England some day.

Whatever had drawn them to the Town, these people spent most of their time near the harbor. Apart from the sprawling variety of life there, the Town could offer few other tourist attractions if you excepted its excellent local history museum (not much noticed by the visitors) and the folly erected fifty years ago by an eccentric and wealthy inventor, in half a dozen wildly clashing European architectural styles (including a Roman bath complete with artificial rain), which was heavily patronized for its organ recitals as well as for its fantasy. The waterfront could outbid everything else simply because it was so full of vitality. It was also, in the nature of its shape and surroundings, extremely picturesque. So the pleasure boat *Dixie Belle* did a roaring trade all summer, its three hulls pontooned together to make a platform for rows of seating, its corrugated plastic roof colored emerald green to keep the sun from barbecuing the passengers, its two Stinger outboards puttering exhaustively as it tacked around the harbor with a running commentary from the captain thrown in. Some of the passengers subsequently investigated matters further and more closely, if not usually on their own two feet, then at least under their own power, cruising almost every inch of the way to their quarry upon the swaying suspensions of Pontiac, Plymouth or Olds.

A small crowd gathered at Fisherman's Wharf, where narrow thoroughfares would still have descended from Main Street to the water's edge if the urban despoilers had not had their way. There were many wharves in this segment of the harbor and, by some communications system known only to tourists, sightseers invariably picked the right one even when an approaching vessel was still half a mile away and might just as well dock at a

neighboring jetty, across some width of water. The people
at Fisherman's Wharf, sublime in this intuition, watched
patiently as a dragger came slowly into the inner harbor
and curved around to where they were, its skipper leaning
from the side window of his narrow wheelhouse so that he
could judge exactly the moment to reverse his engine and
avoid bumping the piles of his dock. These were a residue
of the better days the Town had known, before the
planners' vision of renewal. The piles were whole tree
trunks, driven deep into the silt that thickly covered the
granite bed of the harbor and bolted strongly to the
planking of the wharf. At the top of the harbor, and even
at some wharves inside the Neck, where deep-sea fishermen were not so plentiful, there were jetties whose
planking was collapsed and whose piles were rotted into
surrealistic shapes that would have given way entirely had
any craft been brought alongside smartly. But down here,
at the business end of things, the tree trunks still stood
firm under their barnacles and their slime, their tops
capped with canvas and gum to stop the weather from
penetrating and demolishing them from within.

Some of the sightseers leaned against these fortified
trunks as the dragger tied up and two crewmen leaped
ashore; and a couple of lumpers emerged from a shed to
stand by their great iron weighing machine. The skipper
came down from his wheel and joined the lumpers, to
keep tally with them on the amount of fish landed: for,
although they knew each other well and would split beers
this night in St. Peter's Club, a fisherman never really
trusted a lumper to give him his due and was always
vigilant for the boxful of fish that missed the weighing
machine in the bustle of a landing and was slipped into
some dark corner of the shed.

To the sightseers, however, fishermen and lumpers
were almost as one, brawny men handling a cargo from

the sea, the first watched more keenly perhaps because they had come out of the sea and because they surely went well in Kodacolor in their yellow oilskin overalls. "And you would be amazed, you really would be amazed, at the fish they landed. There were whole boxes *full* of flatfish coming out of that fishing boat's hold, one after the other. It never seemed to stop, not while we were there; just came up, on the end of that winch hook, one after the other. And the things they were doing to some of that fish! Some of those boxes had more fish in them than others and they had to even them up. And you know what? They just took pitchforks to them, stuck them through and pitched them out, like they'd never heard of food poisoning. Because those forks, they were not clean; they were old and rusty."

The winch hook, swinging loose from a lumper's grasp, dangled elusively above a deck pound full of disagreeable monkfish that were still alive long after leaving the ocean, wriggling and gulping and trying to make themselves a bit more comfortable on top of a huge heap of other creatures. A crewman balanced on the edge of the pound but, finding the hook still beyond his reach, took one oilskinned and seabooted stride into the middle of the heap and sank into it up to his thighs. Several women pulled faces, a small boy looked as though he was going to be sick, and a man in tartan trousers and blue T-shirt gazing down at the morass of browny-yellow creatures, exclaimed, "Jesus, what sort of fish is *that?*" Neither fishermen nor lumpers replied. Goddammit, you'd go crazy answering all the questions the tourists asked. And, by the time they had finished their landing, there was no one left to ask questions. Their curiosity satisfied, their Kodacolor expended, their anecdotes comfortably incubating, the tourists had moved off to see what else was to be seen.

Most of them worked their way around the harbor,

pausing at its vantage points to inhale some fresh view.
Not many found their way to the state fish pier and the
dock where the Boat lay between trips, because the
obvious route to the East Town swept around a hillock,
well settled with dwellings, and the byway to the fish pier
ran uninvitingly past the crushed beer cans and the deep
ruts of the gritty plateau where the refrigerator trucks
were parked. Once the top of the harbor had been
negotiated, however, the winding route through the East
Town was an invitation to relish without regret, for the
awful writ of urban renewal had never run thus far. The
road could be a nightmare to the driver, for it followed the
twists and turns of the water's edge and was as narrow as
any rural road in Europe, a combination which was never
intended to accommodate the cumbersome automobiles of
America. In exchange for this disadvantage, the tourists
could roll cautiously past cottages of wood that had been
placed carefully to keep an eye on the water and to be on
easy terms with their neighbors. They were in small plots
of their own ground, sometimes vivid with flowers, sometimes only green with grass, tree, and shrub. Occasionally
they grew flagpoles besides, from which the Stars and
Stripes drooped in the sultry air, or at least they had the
Republic's bald eagle in gilded wood or weathered bronze
mounted above the door: these were proud and patriotic
homes. Such commerce as there was in the East Town did
not often violate it. Generally its tradesmen were slipped
unobtrusively in-between the homes, as organic as the
wood from which everything was built. There was an
awkward right angle in the road, which the East Townsfolk called a square, and within a hundred paces there
were premises in which you could buy food, post packages,
hire bicycles, do your washing, purchase medicines, eat
meals, and obtain houseplants. There was nothing special
about these premises, except that they gently helped a

community to live decently and well, and they mocked the ruthlessly supermarketed, expensively packaged, utterly calculated image of the American dream: people could experience delay in those shops because the guy behind the counter liked to gossip with his customers. A little farther along the road, at the Yankee General Store, they could wander around a crammed and haphazard collection of utensils and bric-a-brac, where something precious had managed to stay still since the turn of the century. There were all manner of knives, keen and shiny, and other kitchen implements besides. There were ancient blocks and tackle, duck decoys with chipped beaks that needed repainting, mildewed books that only obsessed collectors would read, incense sticks to tickle the nose, cribs made for infants who were now grandparents, and soaps smelling powerfully of balsam and cranberry, to bring back memories unknown to the suggestive refinements of Revlon and Rubinstein. There was much else in the store's hoard of bygones and utility; and, in its front window, an obliging notice told where (up the hill, in the yellow house set back from the track) to find the man surrounded by wood and tools, who made model ships and didn't mind if you watched while he did so.

All this was manna to the tourists, as was the adjacent colony at the Neck, with its self-conscious artistry, its arch commerce in handmades, its seafood eating houses and, finally, its repair yard for fishing boats and the row of sturdy wharves where draggers docked. Any visitor who strolled down those wharves after enjoying the quiet pleasures of East Main Street and the studied mannerisms of the Neck, anyone ignorant of the social texture of the Town, was in for a small culture shock if he poked too inquisitively around the boats tied up there. In the midst of the utterly Yankee New Englandness of these surroundings he might, if his questions had gone on too long, and if his ear was finely tuned, have heard one fisherman mutter to another, "*Sta minga?*" — which is a Sicilian vulgarism meaning approximately "Why's the guy shoving his nose in here?" The visitor might well have heard the same phrase at Fisherman's Wharf, or on any of the other jetties on the Town side of the harbor. The chances were somewhat higher over at the Neck only because there the dockings had become by habit the almost exclusive preserve of the Italians.

There had never been a more downright Yankee province than the Town, from its origins and for much of its history. It had been instinct with Old World Puritan virtues of diligence and robust independence from its start. This strain had continued to run deeply through the current of its life, but from the middle of the nineteenth century it had been joined by others alien to this British source. Portuguese, ever the most restless of Europeans, had settled into the fishery here after generations of working these waters from their homes by the Tagus and in the Azores. Finland contributed much of the manpower that was to work the quarries of the Cape, strapping fellows with a taste for knife-fighting and incendiary politics, who settled into a coastal village just outside the Town. Irish came, of course, as they came everywhere in America. But the biggest wave of immigrants was Italian, and swept in between the end of the century and the 1920s. At least, everyone already in the Town thought of them as Italians, though most of them were from Sicily. Precisely, they came from one of two places on the island. One was the fishing village of Terrasini, which lies just around a headland from Palermo. The other was the town of Sciacca, whose white terraces drop down to the Mediterranean on the far side of the island, where the Sicilian shore faces North Africa.

These Italians did not come straight to the Town from

Europe. In the beginning they had settled in Detroit,
where the car-makers needed much labor in exchange for
which, besides wages, they would teach the Italians to
speak the new language, starting with the sentence "I am a
good American." But presently, having accumulated some
money and having learned to say things not necessarily
patriotic, and being fishermen or at least seasiders by
birth, they drifted down their new continent to the shores
of New England. The Portuguese were well established on
the Cape by then; so were the Finns and the Irish. The
latecomers began to settle down at the Fort, a knob on the
harbor downstream of Fisherman's Wharf, which had
once mounted gun batteries in the Civil War, but which
since then had gradually become a haven for the poorest
of the citizens. The Irish had preceded the Italians there
and grudgingly yielded to them this ghetto at the bottom
of the social heap. Life at the Fort was always hard to start
with; even in the 1940s some people living there would go
to the cinema not so much to see the movie as to collect the
free china that was given away by the management to
attract trade from a rival establishment. Poverty-stricken it
might have been, but it was thoroughly Italian, where folk
would sit down to *merluzzo a bianco* before they would
consider chowder, and where they could obtain real
parmigiano instead of glutinous Kraft because some
enterprising fellow had established their own kind of shop
in the basement of a rooming house.

Recalling hard times in those early days at the Fort, and
the prejudice they encountered from some of the older
settlers in the Town, senior Italians might still say, "We
was made to feel like niggers! We had to stay down in the
Fort or we got our asses kicked. Even the police!" Some of
the prejudices lasted a long time. It was not until 1927 that
the local newspaper, in its daily list of fishing boats which
had come to port that morning, actually named a vessel

and detailed its catch, if it was crewed by Sicilians. Until that year, such craft were merely noticed as "Italian boat, seining," or whatever. By then, the Italians were beginning to overhaul the Portuguese as chief competitors to the Yankees in the fishing of Georges Bank. From the moment of their arrival they had put the acquisition of a boat before everything else, in spite of the desire to move quickly from the ghetto slums to clapboarded respectability higher up the Town. "First we get a boat," the men would say to their womenfolk. "A boat will buy a house, but a house no buy a boat." So they grafted and clubbed together with clannish devotion and they acquired their boats and they ran them on family share systems, which were so embedded in their natures that, on the birth of a new child, a seagoing grandfather's first response would be "Ah, *bene!* A new share for the boat."

Presently these Italians began to move out across the Town from the indignities of the Fort. As they prospered at sea, so they shifted into some of the grandest homes in the Town: places on the urban hilltop above Main Street and elsewhere, as impressive as any of the old Yankee sailing masters' homes, complete with widows' walks; homes that surpassed anything else in sight if you excepted the mansions ordained by the Almighty for the Aryan fastnesses of the Point. By and by, the telephone directory was littered with columns of Aiellos, Ciaramitaros, Favazzas, Frontieros, Orlandos, Pallazolas, Parisis, Taorminas and the rest, as more and more people came from Sicily to join their kinsmen in the Town and, like the kinsmen themselves, fruitfully multiplied. With their coming, the predominance of the Italians in the fishery was established. As the last quarter of the twentieth century began, sixty percent of the vessels sailing out of the Town were in Italian hands, twice as many as those belonging to Portuguese. Only ten percent belonged to Yankees.

All of them, whatever their country of origin, were intensely proud of their race, and of its inherent superiority over others. A large proportion of the automobiles in the Town bore the red, white and green shield of Italy on their rear windows; others had the Irish emblem, and there were even a few stickers proclaiming "Finn Power." None was more ardent in its consciousness than the Italian community, however, which no longer lay at the bottom of the Town's social heap. Had there been blacks around, they would doubtless have filled this role, but almost the only black face ever seen upon the streets belonged to the driver of a refrigerated truck that regularly came to pick up fish sticks and carry them back to Maryland. (There was, though, a group of little plaster black boys, instead of plaster gnomes, in the front garden of an Italian home on the road to the Stop & Shop.) The bottom of the heap by now was a mishmash of white people who, through sickness, indolence, or an unfortunate failure to accumulate enough substance before old age, existed on welfare and were much despised by everybody else for doing so. The Italians did not often fall into this predicament, for they had their clan system to support them. This was so meticulously structured that not only did it care for the most distant relatives of a family, but ran to sharp little rivalries between those whose ancestors came from Terrasini and those whose roots were in Sciacca. "A Sciaccatani," to a Terrasinian, was another way of saying the guy was flashy; and "Sciassino" in the argot meant troublemaker. These roots mattered and were never completely torn up. They could never be forgotten, when it was possible, in any supermarket in the Town, to see a handful of young women, clad in black, so recently arrived in the New World that they could scarcely muster enough American to understand how much the girl at the checkout was demanding of them. But the traffic across the

Atlantic cut both ways. Some people went home to Sicily after a lifetime in the Town; like Antonio Orlando, who died in Terrasini at the age of eighty-six after rearing a family on Columbia Street, fishing Georges year in and year out, retiring to the place of his birth, but leaving behind in the Town and elsewhere in the States three sons and a daughter, together with many grandchildren, great-grandchildren, nieces and nephews. Many more Italians would go the same way. But meanwhile they worked the deep seas of the Atlantic, they played their games of biscula (which demanded even more bluff than poker), they drank their coffee weak to stave off the heartburning *agedu*, they sometimes had plaster black boys in their gardens to remind them of how they had grown, and they muttered *"Sta minga?"* to each other when interlopers were about.

June was the month to be a visitor to the Town, for that was when its races displayed themselves most self-consciously, with feeling and flamboyance. The season's first flock of tourists had scarcely returned when, on the first Sunday of Pentecost, the Portuguese rejoiced in their nationality by crowning their imperator. This was a festival with antique origins in the Old Country, but it had not come to the Town until the turn of the century, as an act of thanksgiving for deliverance from the sea. There had been a fishing schooner out on Georges on a night filthy with fog when a transatlantic liner came pounding through the mist on its way to New York. In the disemboweling moment of impact, as the iron bows of the leviathan smashed through the wooden sides of his boat, so that two halves dropped straight to the seabed like stones, Captain Mesquita (he was Smoky Joe along the waterfront) vowed that, if he lived, he would revive the devout custom of his ancestors in the parish of his new home. Each year since then, the Portuguese of the Town had acclaimed a worthy and God-fearing man of their own as imperator. They had led him through the streets in a long procession of Silvas and Pereiras, Araujos and Amarals, Souzas and Costas, himself attended by maidens in white, with a brass band thumping in his ear, to the steps of the Portuguese church, where Our Lady of Good Voyage cradled the schooner in her arms. Inside, in the deep-sea blue of the sanctuary, beyond Stations of the Cross which were also marked by fishing schooners, priests placed a crown on the imperator's head as a symbol of his worthiness and piety. Then everyone moved to the church hall or to the Portuguese-American Club across the street, and consumed vast quantities of linguica and pastries, wine and Coke; and reminisced a little about the Old Country, but talked mostly about the new.

Toward the end of the month came the weekend of Fiesta, when the Town entirely abandoned itself to fun and games and every fishing boat made sure it was in port for a few days, whether it was Italian or not and however plentifully the fish might be running out on Georges and the other grounds.

For weeks beforehand the mamas of the Town busied themselves at their sewing machines, stitching bunting and streamers and uniforms that children would wear in the parades, and preparing quantities of food for family reunions. The men, meanwhile, transformed St. Peter's Club from its regular role as a place where they could drink and play cards, take refuge from women and brag about their manhood, into a headquarters from which the annual celebration of St. Peter's Feast was organized. It cost thousands of dollars each year to mount this extravaganza, the way it ought to be, with fireworks and colored lights, musicians and Ferris wheels. Blackboards were propped up in the club, so that contributions could be marked as they came in, and this became an index not only

of the feeling townsfolk had for the event itself, but also of
the care some had for their own reputations among the
Italian fishermen, whose patron saint Peter most particularly was. The Italian boats could be relied on to muster
two hundred fifty dollars from their crews if they fished
the deep sea, a hundred bucks if they worked inshore.
But, chalked alongside these subscriptions, came the tallies
from the careful outsiders: three hundred dollars from
the Town House Restaurant, which was nearly twice as
much as its chief rival had given; two hundred fifty from
the ice company and the same from a fish processor, one
hundred fifty from a funeral home, and twenty-five bucks
from the Town's Jewish mayor. The inspiration of this
largesse, a statue of St. Peter, stood meanwhile in the club
window, so that the passersby along Main Street could
solemnly appreciate it. As the week before Fiesta short-
ened, as the crews came home from the sea, as the
blackboards became crammed with information and frantic with messages ("Volunteers needed to carry flags";
"Please pay assessment for Gaspar Palazzola"), so the
wharves around the harbor became clogged with vessels as
otherwise they were only at Easter and Christmas. In some
places they were tied up alongside each other three and
four deep. Then came out the bunting the women had
carefully sewn and, one morning, men were sitting astride
crosstrees and balancing on wheelhouse roofs, dressing
their vessels vividly overall.

The feast began on Friday night, when eight fishermen
placed St. Peter on a sedilia and carried him shoulder high
from the club down the short end of Main Street to a waste
ground on the edge of the Fort. Normally a municipal
parking lot, this was turned into a fairground for the
weekend, though most of its space was left open so that
people could congregate and pay attention to what happened at St. Peter's Shrine. The shrine had been built,

with a fine sense of theatre, where the waste ground terminated in fish packing sheds, which themselves hemmed in the dwellings of the Fort. It was so high and so wide that it obscured the sheds for, although the shrine itself was but an alcove beneath a fairylit arch, it was flanked by eight bays with Corinthian columns separating each, and in front was a platform on which priests and dignitaries and bandsmen could perform. It was a great piece of stage scenery whose ultramarine surface was tricked out with golden fleur de lis, cream columns, and a multitude of light bulbs. From start to finish of Fiesta, this would be the Town's chief reference point. And on this first night, a clutch of state politicians had turned up, to husband their votes and maybe catch a few more.

The eight fishermen carried their saint slowly, for this was a reverent act (and the statue was very heavy), down to the shrine, behind an Italian colonial band playing almost operatic music that was full of portents, foreboding, and syncopation. And had it not been for the all-American cop holding back traffic by the gas station, if it had not been for the New Englandness of the buildings rising up the hill above Main Street, this start to Fiesta might well have been somewhere at the side of the Mediterranean. Most of the people in the crowds that pressed close to the procession were Latin dark, the young marrieds tended to be handling rather more children than they could comfortably manage, the women's eyes came piercing up from their depths, and the men wore their clothes tight and dandy, not loose and casual. By the time St. Peter had reached the stage and been installed in his alcove they had massed on the wide open space and some of them were already eating; there were mobile stalls set up across the street ready for an endless trade in french fries, doughnuts, pastrami, and "real lemonade." Neither the trade nor the digestion stopped while a monsignor said his prayers in front of the saint, or while a consul from Boston said his piece in Roman Italian (which hardly anyone understood), or while a senator from Beacon Hill (coming up for reelection) declared that Fiesta meant a lot even to the Yankees. Then, somewhere down the harbor, the coast guard cutter let off six signal rockets, which took off with a thump, a flash, a puff of smoke and an earsplitting crack. Thus was Fiesta truly begun. The Ferris wheel and the dodgems began moving on the fairground. Small boys, blindfolded, began to swipe with wooden staves at a clothesline strung with bags of flour, the object of the competition being somewhat obscure, though those kids surely covered themselves with flour, and everyone else roared with laughter; as they did when another group of youngsters in a watermelon-eating contest smothered themselves in seeds and pink pulp. Couples encountered other couples as though they hadn't met since this time last year, though the women had gossiped that very morning by the dairy display in the A & P. Young fathers fussed adoringly over their infants, and stood by their wives tenderly and possessively, and exchanged greetings with similarly devoted shipmates with whom, only a few days before when homeward bound, they had dreamed glass-eyed over the girls in this month's *Playboy*, gesturing forthrightly at a Playmate's tempting crotch, sucking greedily at her art-paper breasts; and never a word of their own women the while. Young priests, acolytes to the monsignor, went glass-eyed now as old ladies of legendary morality and unsparing devotion kept them too long in conversation which did a little, just a little, to relieve the arid monotony of many years without a man. A candidate for City Hall went expansively and ostentatiously to the gas station for a cup of water with which to bathe the slightly grazed knee of somebody's little boy, who was

himself wondering what all the fuss was about by the time
the traffic cop had also turned up (he, too, had a
reputation to take care of) and applied a Band-Aid.
Teenagers eyed each other carefully, in their segregated
groups of two or three, and did nothing at all without
wishing to be watched.

Jonathan came with Ellen Fremantle. They had lived on
the same street all their lives, but she had been three years
ahead in high school and therefore distant. Her interest
had quickened when she heard he had got himself a site
on the Boat after his months in the supermarket. She was
thinking of no future (she had lately had too much past)
but the sea was a wholesome thing and he was no longer a
high school kid. He was easy and let her relax and didn't
get nasty when she said no. So she let him date her now
and then and didn't object to his arm on her shoulder
when his friends were in sight: men had to prove things to
each other all the time, but he always let his arm drop
again when the friends had gone by. She had even got to
liking this ritual, because there was warmth as well as
possession in it, and because he seemed to accept her
limits. She might not have come to the Fiesta opening if he
had not suggested it. For she was a Yankee girl and this
was a very Italian night, and you didn't want to get too
friendly with them. She wouldn't have missed the dory
race, though.

The dory race took place on Saturday and it was the
distinctly Yankee part in Fiesta weekend, being the
diminutive successor to the schooner contests with the
Canadians. Now that the schooner had vanished from the
seas, apart from that handful up in Maine which were
chartered for tourist cruising along the coast, and the few
five-masters that still came from Lisbon each year to spend
months on the Grand Banks, the fishermen of the Town
met their old rivals from Nova Scotia in the smallest craft

traditional to the working of the western Atlantic. Originally wrought as a ship's boat — and still carried as such upside down atop the wheelhouse of many diesel-engined vessels fishing Georges — it had evolved into a fishing boat in its own right by the mid-nineteenth century. Before then, the crew of a schooner on the banks would fish directly from the schooner's deck, each man lining up at the rail next to his shipmates, with a handline over the side. But shoals of fish were more easily plundered, and catches became bigger, if each man took to a small boat and fanned out from the mother ship before putting his handline down, sometimes rowing out of sight over the horizon before fishing; and sometimes never coming back if fog or a sudden storm swept in. Thus the bank dory came into its own, a flat-bottomed thing with a high freeboard, swept up to peaks at its sharp stem and its all but sharp stern. A damnable thing for a novice to manage if it was empty, for it sat high out of the water and it was narrow on its flat bottom, which made it the daftest craft imaginable for the high seas, being liable to capsize if the oarsman lacked a fine sense of balance. But once it started filling with fish it settled comfortably into the water and became more stable than a conventional design would have been. Its peculiar shape had the additional advantage of easy stowage aboard the schooner when its fleet of dories returned at night. Remove the thwarts of each dory and nests of half a dozen or more could be stacked on deck, one on top of another, like basins on a shelf.

So the rivalry that had started with the schooners *Esperanto* and *Delawana* had now come down to the dorymen, a pair to each competing craft. From early spring through midsummer, as the sun began to burn more fiercely over the Town and as the humidity made everyone sticky with sweat, as most people made for the beaches after work and as even virile boys became too

lanquid to throw a few baskets through hoops jutting over
garage doors, a handful of young men took to the harbor
and started to work out for the race. Each evening you
would see them, as the sun curved brazenly down toward
the invisible Berkshires and made the placid water molten
with its flames, crossing and recrossing from Fisherman's
Wharf to the Neck, or from Seven Seas Wharf straight up
past the state fish pier. Easily at first, to get into a swing
without splitting a gut, then frantically in bursts to see how
fast they could shift, the two backs in each dory would bow
forward in rhythm, then heave over in strain against oars
that gave like strong saplings at the deep-thrusted pull.
Trials were held as summer began. Crews were elimi-
nated. The local champions were acknowledged. A few days
before Fiesta began, the Canadians came to town aboard a
coast guard cutter of their own, bringing with them a
supporting cast of dozens, including a bagpipe band.

The starting line was a tape stretched across the top of
the harbor, where the waters oozed into the plateau of
waste ground. The two dories made for a buoy half a mile
away, beyond the end of the fish pier, rounded it, and
came back to the starting line. It was no big deal nowadays,
this international fisherman's race, compared with what
the schoonermen had sailed. Nor did it rivet the Town as
its full-blooded ancestor had done, in spite of the Yankee
pride. Only a few score showed up to line the harbor
thinly, and their cheers were not enough to drown the
Canadian pipers, blowing their lungs out on the coast
guard's poop. Even on this day, most of the action was
down by the Ferris wheel and the fairground shrine of the
Italians. It was a measurement of a drift in the history of a
people.

But Big Boy was there, as well as Jonathan and his girl,
because an old buddy of his was pulling in the American
boat. At least they had something to cheer about, against

the penetrating counterpoint of the Canadian chanters. For ten straight years the Nova Scotians had whipped the Yankees, both in their own harbor and down here. But this time it was the white dory from the Town that pulled away from the boxcar red of the Canadians, into a lead that was never to be lost. The Canadians, stripped to their bulky waists (they added up to nearly four hundred pounds the pair), were a length behind at the buoy and trailed even further on the homeward leg. The American boys both had an abundance of hair tied into pigtails at the nape, and these beat a tattoo upon their shoulders as they ducked and pulled, and the dark green of their T-shirts became darker still as the sweat spread across their backs.

"Attaway, fellas!" roared Big Boy from the pier as the white dory skimmed past its piles, adding an inch to its lead with every wrench on the oars. By the time it crossed the line it was three lengths up and Big Boy was dismembering a six-pack to share with the victors and secure his own place in subsequent celebrations; and thus his Fiesta would proceed, never more than a convivial arm's length from his old buddy, occasionally surfacing from a stew of Budweiser and food to take in momentarily some other aspect of the weekend's show. Jonathan, seizing the opportunity presented by euphoria and proximity, took Ellen to the other side of the pier to inspect the Boat, where she, declining to try out his bunk, nevertheless allowed him an excited embrace until she felt his hard want and removed his hand from almost just there and reminded him of his promise to go into Boston that night if the Americans won; so they really should be getting along if they wanted to make Jimmy's before it filled up. Swiftly the other spectators turned away from the harbor, too, leaving the exhausted dorymen to be sustained by a handful of officials and old buddies. The clapboard terraces up the hill began to doze again in the thick, smothering heat. At the moment of victory they had echoed to the whistles and bleeps of pleasure craft run by Boston weekenders and the gentry of the Point, each of whom patronized the dory race to recover something of the past, even though it had never been their own.

Nor could they ever have had more than a spectator's part in the Sunday parade. This was preceded by a mass at the open-air shrine, which filled that large space with people. The devout sat solemnly on rows of canvas chairs beneath the platform full of priests, or stood just behind with hands obediently clasped. But others strolled where the crowd was thinnest and gossiped when they would. People sat on the porches of the houses opposite and listened carefully to the prayers, with the sure comfort of cold beer at their sides. Loudspeakers relayed the mass into the streets of the Fort, where only dogs and cats moved until a woman came out of a house, a cigarette drooping from her mouth, got into her car unmindful of ceremony, and drove away. It was a pensive time, between the hurly-burly of the fair and the measured excitement of the parade; though that was a sort of religious experience, too.

The eight fishermen who had carried St. Peter to his shrine reappeared in their white drills and shouldered the saint once more. Dollar bills were by now pinned thickly to the streamers issuing from the region of the statue's neck, and bystanders offered more as the sedilia passed them, to bring themselves good luck. As the haloed head and the upraised hand bobbed and swayed to the movement of the bearers on its progress from the shrine, Minutemen mustered on the roadway by the gas station, where it sloped up past the rotary with a stiffer climb ahead. They wore knee breeches and tricorne hats and they carried clumsy muskets, just as their forefathers had when they defied the British at Lexington and Concord Bridge. It was their honor (almost their sacred duty) to lead the parade when it moved off up the hill past the American Legion post, outside whose portals Joan of Arc rode a charger which was itself improbably mounted upon a memorial to World War I. Behind the Minutemen came the bands, and there were rather a lot of them.

There was a band of high school girls, whose upper works smacked of the Revolutionary navy (striped jerseys and tarry hats) but who were transformed at the waterline into swinging Fifth Avenue, with crisp white skirts, a glimpse of bare leg, and a heavenly length of shiny black boots. There was another band, whose buglers were topped with plumed shakos, led by a buxom blonde with the panache of a drill sergeant. There was a pipe band and a fife band, and a band composed of nothing but drummers beating rhythms so dizzy that they would have put a metronome off its stroke. There was the Italian band again, no longer ponderous with foreboding but now in a gaily operatic mood. There were flagbearers. Some of them upheld national flags with grim dignity, as though it were George Washington's birthday at the Lincoln Memorial, but others brandished their staves this way and that to make the bunting billow and swirl, the way coach had seen the *alfieri* do it the year that the Knights of Columbus went on a package tour of Europe that included Siena. There were floats, on which children reclined or performed amid motifs ranging from "God Bless America" to "Little Bambino" and "St. Rosalie in the Cave." There were other children, lissome in tights and spangled with sequins, doing cartwheels along the road (Tina's Studio of Dance) or merely pirouetting delicately as instructed by the rival Gardner Perry School. There were hordes of anybodys, who fell in behind the last float and followed gamely in its wake. There was that careful bunch of somebodies with elections on their minds, striding easily along, beaming on both sides at once, with "How ya doin'?" and "Nice to see ya" to the spectators at almost every pace.

Yet for all its variety, there was something uniform in the parade and the way it moved. Instrumentalists and flagbearers all marched with the same knees-high quick step that was military by instinct yet something remote from human nature, like row after row of overtrained marionettes passing by. They were mostly pretty young and they were all very solemn, without a flash of oral charm in sight (much less a nervous giggle), and the bandsmen held their instruments as though they had been taught how to handle them by a tin soldier. The crowds loved it, though, and when the parade had passed, people went streaming along the sidewalks up the hill after it, to take just one more shot for the album, to enjoy proud parentage (which had spent so much of itself preparing for this day) and to be anxiously on hand in case Junior should collapse in the heat ("Didn't you think he was looking just a little peaky, John, just before they stepped off?").

There was only one ritual left before Fiesta was done, and that happened along the outer harbor boulevard, where the bronze fisherman at his helm stood forever looking out to sea. For hours before the event, tourists began to loiter by the statue, which was itself the best-known landmark in the Town. Presently, craft of one kind and another made their way across the harbor or came in past the breakwater from the open sea, and hove-to on the water nearby. The congestion slowly grew both ashore and afloat, until cops were marshaling traffic along the boulevard and skippers were worrying more about their glistening paintwork than whether or not they would be able to hear when the ceremony began. Eventually, a tantivy of trumpets announced the approach of the high school girls,

and they came high-stepping it down the road as freshly as
when they moved off from the Fort, the majorettes at their
head still going through their flag-waving drills with
impeccable allure. They came to a stop close to the statue,
could have gone no farther in any case, because the traffic
was now beyond the ability of cops to dislodge it and
concessionaires were doing a heavy trade from stalls laden
with popcorn, ice cream, soda, and Italian sausage. There
was scarcely room for the bishop to cross the road, let
alone for the girls to march any more along it. The bishop
had come down from Boston for the day, as he did every
year, and he had been lunching behind the lace curtains
and the screen doors of a good Church family whose
property was handily placed. Now he emerged, brilliant in
crimson and gold, and shepherded his way through the
crowd with his crozier. They closed about him when he
stood on a balustrade sticking out into the harbor, his back
to the statue, his face and his microphone turned toward
the great fleet of vessels paused upon the water. He said
prayers and he delivered a homily about the majesty of
God and how it could not truly be appreciated unless one
had seen the ocean. Then he stepped into the police
launch, acolyte priests with him, and they poppity-popped
around the fleet with vessels so that this tall, gray old man
in crimson and gold could splash holy water in the
direction of each. Some of the crews stood in bare feet or
in Topsiders as the bishop passed, others stayed lazily
where they lay on immaculate decks, enjoying the sun-
shine and the spectacle. Some of them watched motionless,
inscrutable behind sunglasses, as the bishop raised his
hand; others waved back or made vague gestures of their
own; and a young priest heartily allowed that he liked the
guys who blessed the bishop in return.
   Then the police launch made off toward the inner
harbor, where other boats were tied up at wharves, the

bunting fluttering from rigging and masts, the odor of fish wafting from battered decks, the stains of the Atlantic marking rusted sides. There were no crowds here, no high school band, no traffic needing cops, no lines for popcorn and ice cream. There were just a handful of men on some of the decks, who crossed themselves as the police launch passed. The bishop splashed his holy water in their direction, too, and raised his hand and uttered his blessing of the fleet. But he delivered no homily at the inner harbor. The fishermen were spread too thinly around its wharves to have heard it clearly, even through a microphone. And the bishop would have felt it an impertinence for him to tell them about the ocean, even about the majesty of God, when he was not in his pulpit but out here, among men whose bodies were daily committed to the deep.

FALL

THE HOT AND STEAMY DAYS proceeded through July and August and were only just beginning to flag, sapped at last by their own enervating weight, when September came. These were days that drained the energy fast and, whenever it could, the Town took them easy. Morning shoppers kept to the harbor side of Main Street, where there was shade, crossing to the opposite curb only when they had to; after midday they tacked along its narrow winding length from one protective shadow to another. In the gloomiest and most cavernous bars, young men bent early over pool tables, more than ever glad of respite from the day. At the railroad station, the Boston-bound commuters already had their jackets off, their armpits dark with sweat, when it was but breakfast-time for others, and thankfully climbed into cars which, by means of tinted windows and air-conditioned space, preserved them for one lurching but otherwise blessed hour from the exhausting world outside. Dogs loped the wastelands dully, with tongues lolling from their mouths, but more often lay on porches and panted for the dusk. Old people sat beside them there and rocked themselves to sleep, skulls shining porous through thinning damp hair, moisture trickling slowly down stubble and skin, over creases and veins, into cavities below the neck. Cicadas jingled steadily through the throbbing of the day and drugged every other creature with the monotony of their sound. Yet, for all the lassitude it imposed, summer was a season of high mobility around the Town. Impecunious youth careered along the harbor roads by bicycle, in a flash of whirring spokes and revolving brown limbs. Sinister youth roared around the place by motorcycle in long cohorts of leather and plastic, buckle and helm, beard and black goggles, sometimes twenty or thirty riders at a time. Orthodox youth took to the road in automobiles; old bangers with fenders hanging loose from battered bodies, or pretty smart numbers that Dad had dispensed with after a couple of years; and made heterosexual forays to the beach, the ice-cream parlors of the Cape, or merely to Dunkin Donuts by the A & P. Youthful, middle-aged, or elderly, whoever could afford it got the boat out and drove it or sailed it down the harbor, past the breakwater and off the rocky shores nearby. On most days of summer, the great bay to the south and all the inshore waters round the Cape were dappled with the white and pastel shapes of foresail and main. Spinnakers filled and swelled so voluptuously, whenever there was a breeze, they made you want to reach out and stroke them.

September was a hyphen between the sopping humidity of summer and the comforting balm of fall. Green leaves began to brown and curl on their undersides and berries suddenly ripened, vivid and a-shine. The days themselves became easy with warmth that was no longer fierce, with air that did not oppress. The first weekend brought Labor Day, which was tourism's final fling before America braced itself for weekday work almost all the way to Christmas. After that, the terrace of the Clam Shack on East Main was no longer filled throughout each day with idlers topping themselves up with Coke, ice cream, and hamburgers, and a perpetual line of autos was no longer drawn up at the take-out. The owner of the Yankee General Store started to unchain the rocking chair, the antique lobster trap, and other tempting wares from his frontage by 4:30 each afternoon, knowing there would be no more trade that day. Along the meandering alleys of the Neck, shopkeepers and art gallery proprietors found their commerce so declined that they could bring chairs out into the sun, sit there and gossip to each other for almost as long as they liked. A young woman had spent her summer on a landing down there, surrounded by two galleries, a silversmith's, a handloom weaver's, and an engaging view of fishing boats, while she sang ballads by Dylan, Baez, Previn and her sweetly caftanned self to anyone who'd listen and drop a quarter into her collecting bag (rotund matrons from Chicago or The Bronx, whose husbands looked embarrassed; entwined twosomes from anywhere, who dreamily knew the words but liked the confirmation). Now she sang and smiled intermittently for the curiosity of a few local kids who were reclaiming the Neck from the summer migrants, and knew it was time to move on to the city for her long season in the folk clubs of Cambridge. Behind her, across the water of the cove, sloops and yawls and runabouts were daily winched onto cradles, where they would lie beneath tarpaulin until spring; or else they were loaded onto trailers to await the morning when the boat's owner would drive up from some place inland and tow it home to be stranded for six months where the neighbors could see it, too. From all the marinas and yacht basins around the Town, there was now this daily exodus of pleasure craft which could pick and choose their seas.

Migration went another way, once the summer was done. As September turned to October, people who had sought the coast at every chance now drove inland instead. The radio stations, with spotter planes in the air and spies upon the ground, told where color was infiltrating the hills of Vermont, New Hampshire, and western Massachusetts as weekends approached, and small armies took to the roads each Friday night in response. Their marching orders had descended through generations, for this was one of the legends of their land. Indians believed that celestial hunters slew the Great Bear in autumn, causing some trees to be stained with the scarlet of his blood, others to be splashed by the yellow of his fat from the cooking in the pots. In less imaginative times, the smallest child knew that to be a New Englander in the fall was to have one of the luckiest gifts in the world. It depended on a poor soil with little nitrogen, and a warm and brilliantly lit season with lack of rain. On rich and damp ground, leaves stay green until the frost is ready to wither them with one bite; and dull days never develop pigments which, hidden by the powerful green of summer, can be exposed only if there is time and light enough when the green fades with the staunching of the sap. Even in New England, the trick is not always pulled off with the same impact, for some falls do come damp and the country is then more tawny than vivid. But no place can compete with New England in a brilliant year; not Arizona with its blazing hawthorns, not even the Great Lakes with their flaming sumacs. Even the grudging Mrs. Trollope, who did not care for the United States, admitted that this was the time and place when the landscape went to glory.

So the weekend armies rolled up the broad highways and over the northern state lines and for once were not bent, as much as anything, on plundering New Hampshire and Vermont of their cheaper booze and smokes. At any time of the year outside winter there is almost nothing up there that will not restore an empty soul, and winter is only disqualified because it renders the hills and the valleys well-nigh impassable to anyone without skis, snowshoes or snowmobile. It is a land where villages congregate neatly around the church, which is almost always a classical white with a slender spire, designed by unacclaimed men who had the flair of a Wren. Bridges of heavy timber cross wide rivers, and they have been built with pitched roofs to stop the winter's snow from weighing them down. Rambling old homes perched on hillsides call themselves inns, and in an amplitude of ticking clocks, antimacassars, paintings in oil, the odor of beeswax and the mahogany to which it is applied, manage to turn supper, lunch, and breakfast too into a regular Dickens of a feast; with central heating and "Have a nice day" thrown in on the side. There are fields where sheep graze and in Vermont you even see cows. But, most of all, there are trees rising straight up hills directly from the highways, from the fields along the byways and from the small spaces surrounding the villages. This is where the landscape goes to glory, when the time is ripe. There is an undergrowth of blueberry, which comes dark as port. Above this soars a deciduous range of pigment which is infinitely finer than the colors on a spectrum. Oak trees defy the convention of what lies between lemon and gold. Maples make nonsense of distinctions between scarlet and red, for they go half a dozen kindred shades as well. Sumacs are vermilion when they aren't aflame, and sometimes they are something else that no palette ever caught. Yet the glory is not only in the colors themselves, but also in their disposition. Not one of them gaudies a hillside entirely on its own. They seep and merge and blend together, and silver birch trunks poke up here and there to stripe their dazzling effect. At a distance they bewitch with the wild variety of their rhythms. Close to, the human being is spellbound by the waxen texture of individual leaves, and by the evolution of a color across the graphic filament of the veins.

The people of the Town joined the fall migration, too, being no longer objects of curiosity themselves and being more attuned than most to the ebb and flow of seasons. They took the highway across their bigger bridge, whose cantilever arched high above the tidal mud flats of their river, where pleasure boats were no longer taking short cuts up the coast. This highway eventually led to the city and scores of people used it throughout the week, for many commuters preferred the competitive independence of Route 128 to a daily bouncing in the air-conditioned fellowship provided by the Boston & Maine. Just after the bridge, however, there was a turnoff to the north, and this was the way to go in search of the fall. The road wandered from here, for it too had grown organically out of the land, in days when traffic was measured in horses and carts. It was a gentle road, which slipped across creeks and was embanked over marshes, and was constantly twisting and turning because simple New England homesteads had grown there before it and obstinately stayed put to produce a long succession of bends. It was a road to take easy, for it was kind to the eye and the traveler never knew when he might want to stop and rummage in the occasional commerce by its side. Down Route 128 the commerce was brash and bawling from Peabody on, a psychedelic show of eateries and nite spots, gas stations and auto marts, Hockey Town USA and Howard Johnson's: all tricked out in neon and billboard, so crammed together in its desperate desire for attention that you had to know what you were looking for to stand a chance of picking one loud salesman from another. But the commerce of the byroad was quiet and it had style. There were homemade notices on front lawns, which proclaimed "Garage Sale" at the back of the house. There were dwellings which had been transformed into antique shops and seemed to have put the whole of their stock out to air, so that anyone could see what was going in the way of sideboards and wardrobes, lanterns, and butter churns. There were farms which had set up stalls outside their white post fences, where you could get vegetables straight from the earth—and Lord knows they were worth driving a long way to have. Now, in the fall, there were stalls which offered cider, just pressed off the tree. And golden pyramids of pumpkin, huge glowing spheres that echoed faintly when they were tapped. All this beneath a warm blue sky; and curls of woodsmoke drifting above the scattered homes.

The fall was never spectacular around the Cape, which is why its people had to take the byway north and not expect much excitement until they were well on the other side of the Merrimac. There was always too much sea-damp in the air of the coastal fall, so that, although the days were warm, the light was never quite brilliant enough to produce the most glorious effects. For those, the townsfolk had to head for the hills.

Otherwise, they contented themselves with barbecues amid the stony vegetation of the park beyond the boulevard where the fisherman's statue stood. In high summer it was noisy with the shrieks of Little Leaguers slogging flyballs from the sand of the baseball cage and setting their juvenile faces into determined imitations of Yaz or Carleton Fisk, as they scowled at umpires and pitchers both. But now came the softer sounds of family weekends, with steaks spitting on grilles in the lee of rocks, bags of charcoal being torn open to get at more fuel, and parents chiding children for leaving trash on the ground.

Some people came to the park now simply to lie on the rocks by the water's edge and enjoy the last warmth before the cold weather set in. Others still sought out the beaches accessible to the Town; not that there were many of these, which is why they were so hideously packed with humanity between spring and fall.

Though the Cape was ringed with sand as well as rock, most of the shoreline was in strictly private hands only marginally less powerful than those which controlled the interests of the Point. If you could afford a home overlooking the sea, your ownership extended to the lower tidemark as well, and you tacked a "No Trespassing" sign on the roadway above. This was not a peculiarity of the Cape; it was merely the way of the world in the land of the free. From Maine to Connecticut there were six thousand miles of shore, and on only three hundred miles could anyone wander where he would.

Jonathan and Ellen had been thinking of a beach when they cycled over to the bar on East Main. He was hoping that a walk by the sea, away from crowds, might by its elemental nature induce her to let go to him. Since working on the Boat, he felt he had acquired an aura from the sea, that some of its power had transferred itself to his person. He was more confident, now that he stood in the company of unmistakable men, and he swaggered as they did when he spoke of the few trips he had made. He sensed that she was susceptible to this, she who had always been beyond him before, both in age and experience.

How many guys did they reckon she'd had before she was nineteen? Six was it, including that Finn whose reputation was for taking it all ways except straight? She was really something, and she had come within his reach. He thought he had nearly got there, a couple of weeks back, when the family car had been released for the afternoon and they had driven miles up the coast to a public beach where the Atlantic rolled into a long ellipse of sand that stretched far enough to offer a modest privacy. They had walked a while where the sand was wet and firm, she searching it for telltale traces of clam, he pausing every now and then to scrutinize the horizon with screwed-up eyes and make almost monosyllabic observations about the habits of the deep sea. But when he had said, "It's chopping a bit out there" for the third time, she had laughed at him as though he were a small boy again. So he had chased her irritably until she tripped and fell full length, and his crossness had gone in a spasm of concern. They had walked quietly then, and she had allowed him to steer them to a dune, but not over the other side where they would be hidden from sight behind the grasses on its ridge.

He had played the game of lying side by side, backs flat on the sand, eyes blankly on the sky, enough to make you sneeze. But then, when he felt the gesture had been made, he turned onto an elbow and looked seriously at her face. It wasn't exactly beautiful, he thought; the chin was too small for that. But it had a lot of merriment in it and, although she was a tease, for sure, there was a suggestion in those brown eyes of someone who would give anything away if she liked enough and the asking was right. Right then, as he bent over her, she had cleared away some hair that had blown over her eyes, which seemed to him to be waiting for a move to happen.

She had, in fact, been hoping that he would simply talk to her gently, as he could; which was why she had let him come this close already. Though she could not prevent her body bracing when his face came slowly down, she did not put her hands up to hold him back. So his lips came onto hers and plucked at them softly, but even that did not make them part. He had stroked the crown of her head, where the parting ran finely between the billows of black hair, and now shifted his face to nuzzle her at the neck and slide his nose upon her ear. Her head had turned sharply when he did this, exposing the nape of her neck, and he, feeling passion in her move, had brought her face back toward him in his surge of wanting to be there. Her mouth was open now and her eyes were large with something he had not seen before and could not have known for what it was. It was past and present melted into one, a primitive urge and an abiding pain. He saw in it what he wanted to see and plunged his tongue inside the slippery opening of her lips. For an instant she clung to it, drawing it on, and his hand began to move to the buttons of her shirt. But then her fingers reached for his and dragged them off, her head jerked willfully away, and she was sitting up and looking out to sea while he was still there with his tongue half hanging out. He was bewildered even more than he was humiliated, with the shock of transformation.

His voice was plaintive as well as edgy when he looked up at her and asked "So what did I do?"

"You got too far out front, that's all," she said still seeing something distant. She rose abruptly and dusted sand off her jeans. "I think it's time we were moving." And they had walked back to the car, through the deep soft sand below the dunes, without another word.

On the drive home he had tried to apologize, but she had cut this down, too, with a shrug and an impatient shake of the head. "It happens. Don't let it get to you," was all she had said before carefully turning the talk away from them. And he, not knowing how to ask what he wanted to know, and wishing no more distance to come between them then, let her go on and tried to hide his hurt.

The Boat had gone to sea again the day after, but when it returned Jonathan called her. "Ya been seasick yet?" she asked, giggling down the line. And he had grinned at the wall calendar above the family telephone, because there was pleasure as well as teasing in her voice. "Only when th'others weren't lookin'," he replied. She had laughed at that, with more fondness than he knew. He was the only male she had known to put himself down. Next day, she said, sure, she'd bike ride with him round the Cape.

But when they reached the bar on East Main, Carlo was there, sitting on a stool and chatting up the hostess. He saw them in the mirror as they came in and turned with his most familiar grin, the one that suggested he was in on the secret, too.

"Hey there," he called. "What you kids gonna have?"

There was no shaking his insistence that they share the counter with him, as well as a beer and a bite. Nor would he let them go when Jonathan began to make moving-off noises an hour later. Who the hell'd want to go bike riding, said Carlo, when he had his pickup parked out back, just brushing and combing its pistons and ready to go? He had a weakness for putting things like that in front of women, usually with a wink to heighten innuendo.

Jonathan was about to say no again, but Carlo got in first with a calculated afterthought. "Could go to the Common," he said. "There's a great crop of blueberries up there right now."

It was a shrewd move. Ellen turned to Jonathan with entreaty on her face. "Oh, I'd love some blueberries," she said; and, seeing reluctance as well as his desire to please her, she gave one more small shove. "Go on. If we get enough I'll make you a pie."

So they put the bikes in the back of the pickup and climbed in beside Carlo, who drove with one hand to show how easy life was. If the two kids hadn't turned up at the bar he would have spent the whole afternoon in there, trying to make way with the hostess and wondering all the time how to appear more offhand than he really felt. You had to play it cool with the chicks, otherwise they started to get big ideas about themselves and soon they'd have a guy running round so he didn't know his ass from his elbow. A perfect play, thought Carlo, to push off for an hour or two and leave the dame wondering whether he was coming back. "Ya ever seen what a Chevy can do when the goin' gets rough?" he shouted as they swerved round the rotary on the outskirts of the Town.

They were heading for the upland in the center of the Cape where once, before the Revolution and for a little while after, there had been another township of sorts. People had subsisted there on small farms until independence from the British had made the community down by the harbor quite safe from attack. The smallholders of the Common had then forsaken their frugal pastures and joined the fishing folk to take a richer harvest from the sea. It was a hundred years since the last tenant had been carted off to the poorhouse, leaving what was left of the township to collapse into the ground, its cellars to be choked with vegetation and its walls to be tumbled one by one as the brush returned across the empty hillocks and saplings grew into trees and stealthily regained their own. For a while after the Common's end, man had continued to use the upland to improve himself; to the north of the ruined walls were the quarries he had worked for stone. But even these were now abandoned, stagnating pockmarks surrounded by tangled growth. So thick was this now across the middle of the Cape that, although the upland rose a couple of hundred feet above the sea, there were few places where you could actually watch the Atlantic's sweep beyond. It was a primeval wilderness again, as it had been before man's intrusion, before he had turned his back on it to fatten himself with other spoils.

"Hold on to your innocence then," roared Carlo, as he charged the Chevy off the road and up the track that climbed to the Common. It was deeply rutted in the middle, where winter snow water had gouged a drain, and the pickup listed sharply this way and that as Carlo ripped it around one tight corner after another. He enjoyed the helpless lurching of his passengers while he rode the thing under his control, with an elbow on the door and his free hand gripping the edge of the cab roof. To really make your way in this world, you had to get where you called the shots. This was why his people had come from Sicily all those years ago and why, when they sometimes went back for a vacation, all they could talk about afterwards was how goddamn lazy the people were in the Old Country, showing none of the spirit Carlo felt as he smashed his way up the hill, off the track and over the bumpy scrub beyond. He didn't stop until the wheels started to spin on a patch of marsh and Ellen, beginning to feel pale with the rough riding, looked at him tartly and said, "Blueberries now? Perhaps?"

They left the pickup there. Jonathan and Ellen wandered off down a path, and he forced his way through the growth at one side when he saw a bush laden with fruit. He was irritated that the day he had planned was interrupted by Carlo, and he let Ellen go on up the path some way before calling her back to where he was. He snatched at the berries silently when she came and she, sensing his mood, tried to soothe it by popping the first fruit she picked into his mouth.

"That's for the nicest guy around," she said, "who doesn't need a Chevy to get me off my butt."

He relaxed a bit at that and they began talking in the amiable way that had linked them from the start. "Did old Half-Cut ever tell your class about the guy who came up here and fought the bull?" he asked. It was a gory tale of ages ago, recounted annually at the high school by a teacher obsessed with the spooky legends of the Common.

Ellen nodded and pulled a face. "Yeah, he did, too. And Sally Hollis fainted 'cos she'd just started her period that morning and the bloody bit really got to her."

Jonathan smiled. "That so? Well, I damn near wet my pants 'cos Half-Cut had just got to the bit about the horn goin' into the fella's guts — you remember how he did it? lookin' sick like his own were going to fall out — when *bam* the window smashed in and I collected a softball on my lap. And guess who was lookin' horrorstruck out in the yard?"

"Jonathan, do you remember that? Was it you who got hit by the ball? God, I never heard the end of that. But I didn't know it was you. You were only a kid then."

"Beginning to feel like the bull, though." He grinned at her, slyly. But she looked away, so that he wouldn't see her face. That last year at high school was when she had gone wild and hungry, before the pain had come to clench her tight and close off all but a trace of appetite. She had started to think the pain would never dull.

A wild whooping from nearby announced Carlo's desire for attention. As they moved into a clearing in the direction of his sound, he was climbing to the top of a boulder, which rose fifteen feet or more above the ground. On its flatter face the word INITIATIVE had been carved with a mason's chisel, the lettering then tarred so that the outlines would stay visible after years of weathering.

"Ya gotta have initiative folks," chanted Carlo from the top, posturing with upraised arms like a harpooner about to strike, "else ya'll get cut up for blubber, just like the whale." He beamed down at them, self-conscious in his pose. "How'm I doin' kids? Where's with the camera?" He clambered down, grunting with the effort. "Dozens of these goddamn things around, d'ya know that? Guy who did it all was a real nut."

Jonathan and Ellen both recalled that, too, as another bit of Half-Cut's lore. There were many such boulders on the Common, the most recent legacy of its ghostly past. They were the work of a leading citizen in the twenties, who preached the virtues of survival to fellow businessmen in the Town ("Unfortunate are those who get on the wheel when it is at the top and get off when it is at the bottom, while fortunate are those who get on when the wheel is at the bottom and get off when it is at the top") and did pretty well for himself by practicing what he preached. So concerned was he to transmit his morality through the surrounding district that he caused his workmen to carve texts in these tablets of stone, until the Common was much more liberally decorated with injunctions than the average nineteenth-century household. Jonathan went rambling off through the undergrowth to see if he could find some more, and within minutes had discovered INTEGRITY, INDUSTRY, IDEAS, and LOYALTY, as well as a rock inscribed front and back. On one side the masons had carved STUDY; on the other, BE ON TIME.

Ellen was giggling with him over that one when Carlo called from the other side of some scrub. "Guess my Pappy must've been here, too," he said, pointing to a stone almost overgrown by brush; HELP MOTHER, it advised. "And that ain't easy, the way the old lady's built," said Carlo with a smirk.

But Jonathan was not listening. A sound up above had turned his head and he was watching a great wedge of birds cruising across the sky. Black necks outstretched, bellies sagging with weight, ponderous wings beating a passage with an appearance of ease, the Canada geese had returned to the Cape from their cool summer in the north. If you listened very carefully, you could hear the creaking of the quills as the wings flexed upward and down in a ripple of power toward their tips. They were banking now, in an arc away from the lowering of the sun, looking for the place where they would settle for the night, perhaps for the seasons that must pass until spring came again. In the next few days they would be followed by

other migrants from Labrador and soon all the marsh-
lands along this coast, all the mud flats exposed by its tides,
would be restless with the clustering of geese. Their
flat-footed pacing of the shore would complete the turning
movement of the fall, and their speculative flights would
dramatize the winter skies. And when the snows began to
melt, when the days lost their sharp edge, when people
began to hail the prospect of great warmth, the geese
would reassemble in their squadrons and take off for the
north. Jonathan shaded his eyes, as the wedge of birds
dipped down behind a hill. He wondered how they'd be
making out, by the time the geese had gone home. Him
and Ellen. And all of them on the Boat.

It had not been a good time aboard the Boat. A series of
misfortunes had followed one after the other with such
awful regularity that the men worked in silence more
often than they knew, their minds turning over troubles
that seemed private to themselves. Only Big Boy grumbled
loudly, day in and day out, that if things didn't improve
he'd be looking for another site. And only the Skipper
bore the setbacks with his usual phlegmatic calm. As it
happened, he was not aboard when the first of the troubles
struck; and, perversely, the confusions of that day sprang
from a celebration of their most successful trip for
months.

They had been on Georges for nearly two weeks, staying
longer than normal because the fishing was so good.
Almost every trap they hauled had three or four lobster in
it and uncommonly few were prohibitively undersized.
After a week of working the Boat slowly along the
continental shelf, the Skipper decided to take a gamble on
the outcome of the next voyage and ordered the men to
bait the remaining traps on this trip with only one bag of
gurry instead of the usual two. Then he took the Boat back

to where their first haul had been made, eight days before, and started to trawl the same ground again. Sure enough, those first traps were already full of lobster once more; and so were all the others they hauled for a second time. So they continued along the shelf again, hauling in trawls full of fish and setting them down on the seabed short-rationed with bait, until the gurry finally ran out. Then they turned for home, worn out with their work but excited by what it had earned. The Skipper reckoned they had pulled twenty-five thousand pounds of lobster off the sea floor in that one trip, and, even allowing for the fact that the division of spoils went six to four in favor of the company, each one of his men had made himself a packet. His own pleasure was swiftly dimmed before they reached land. As they came steaming up Cape Cod, the radio crackled out a message: his father had been taken ill; it was serious; he should hurry back. When they docked at the canal beside its lobster mart, the Skipper told Big Boy to take charge and get the Boat home after the fish had been sold. Then he climbed into a waiting car and drove off to Providence.

Big Boy was an experienced seaman who had conned the Boat across the bay more times than he could have counted, in good weather and bad, in clear light and fog, day and night. Though the Skipper was always at the helm when they entered and left harbor, Big Boy could have brought them in and out just as well: provided he was his normal self. But with a check for over thirty thousand dollars in his hand after the lobster had been landed and carefully weighed at the mart, even though only a fraction of it would go into his own account, he felt twice as large as life and five times as handsome. It sure was tough luck on the Skipper, getting that bad news, but there was no sense in everyone else being miserable, not on a day like this. Big Boy reckoned the guys deserved a break after two weeks at sea and he, as temporary commander of the Boat, would provide it: out of his own pocket. Having signed his receipt for the check, he slipped out the side door of the mart and hurried down the road to the liquor store. When he climbed back aboard the Boat, he had a half gallon of bourbon in his arms. As soon as he reached the galley, he found the other three reclining on the padded benches around the table. Each had a glass with a good measure in it, and on the table, freshly broached, was another half gallon of bourbon. Yank had seen to that, while Big Boy was totting up his figures inside the mart. So the Boat was untied from the canal dock that forenoon and set on course for home under an exuberant command, with an agreeably disposed crew and with a gallon of Jack Daniel's on board.

As Big Boy was to point out defensively some hours later, the water coming out of the taps on the Boat tasted like kerosene even if it were diluted with antifreeze. By the time they were halfway across the bay, with three hours remaining before they reached home, one empty bottle had been tossed over the side and the contents of the other were somewhere below the halfway mark. Big Boy and Yank, glasses in hand, were in the wheelhouse, swaying rather more than the motion of the vessel warranted, arguing fiercely about the need for the automatic pilot to be on. Yank was confident that they could steer themselves home without its aid, and kept lurching for the switch that would turn it off. Big Boy, sensing the reduced limits of his own navigational skills, kept pushing him off with the reminder, a couple of times, that he was the fuckin' skipper now. Meanwhile, down on the working deck, Carlo was prancing to and fro, arms outstretched, trying to balance Day-Glo marker balloons on his upturned nose, like a performing seal. And Jonathan, still naked after a shower, was hanging over the starboard rail from one hand, dipping a foot into the sea when the Boat rolled enough that side, hooting crazily every time a jet of salt water shot up his leg and smacked him in the crotch.

The day was not yet lost, and might never have been if the Tall Ships had not been anchored that weekend in Boston Harbor. But after the great transatlantic race was over, a number of the vessels taking part had come up the coast from Newport, so that the citizens of Massachusetts could gape at a historic gathering of sailing ships, the like of which would probably not be seen again in any one place on earth. Among the sightseeing craft that day was a sister ship of the Boat. She had conveniently been in port between her own fishing trips and the owners had cleaned her up, packed her with victuals, invited friends of the family aboard, and set off from the Town for a day trip to the Tall Ships and back. By the time Big Boy and his crew were trying to focus their attention on the breakwater, it was early evening and the day-trippers had just docked safely at the head of the inner harbor. Their party was by no means over yet, though. The owners had planned a barbecue before everyone went home, and grilles and charcoal were now being mustered on the hatch cover to start it off. Canvas chairs were scattered around the deck. People were lounging in them, or against the rails. They were flushed with sea breeze and sun over the darkness of their summer skin. Men kidded each other loudly and stood prosperous on check-trousered legs. Women babbled inconsequentialities among themselves and, their faces perpetually fixed in smiles, outshone each other with their teeth. A handful of children scrambled up and down the ladders, squealing with delight. It was a convivial occasion, toward the end of a truly wonderful day, and there wasn't a body on board who would have wished to be anywhere else. One of the owners, properly pleased with himself, was being told so by his insurance broker's wife, a tanned, stringy woman whose toenails resembled a row of cherries and whose spectacles glittered with diamanté. "It really was a brainwave of yours," she said, jangling the bracelets on her wrist. "You do realize, don't you, that you've just given every one of us the thrill of a lifetime?"

It was at this point that the Boat came steaming into sight past the opening of the Neck. Big Boy, at the helm, stood four-square in the full authority of his command. He'd brought his craft up the harbor right handsomely and well, at full speed ahead, the way no one had ever dared do it before. When that goddamn dragger had got across his bows inside the breakwater, he had blasted it out of his way with three quick bursts on the horn and, finding this an effective deterrent, had proceeded upstream at the rush, loosing off one volley of hoots after another. By the time he came abreast of the Manufactory, the waters had cleared miraculously before him and he felt as well as he ever had in his life. The blood of the old schoonermen raced through his veins and he was all set to tell his triumphant tale the moment he hit the first bar ashore. His crew had been gathered around him in the wheelhouse, shouting encouragement as he wrestled with the helm. Now he deployed them for the final maneuver of the voyage. "We're goin' to bring this sonofabitch alongside smartly now," he roared, "so get to your stations."

The owner, hearing the Boat's horn somewhere behind him, detached himself from the broker's wife and stepped to the rail to take a look. Another of his guests, vivid in tartan suit and bow tie, strolled up to him and watched the Boat's coming. "She's another of yours, isn't she?" he asked. "That's right," said the owner, "and they've just had a great trip." But he was frowning now. The hooting he had dismissed as justifiable high spirits at the end of a successful voyage. But the Boat should never be coming up the inner harbor at that rate of knots. And there was something damned odd about that guy in the bows, who should have been getting the rope straightened out for berthing but was instead unlashing the harpoon from its fixture at the rail. The owner began to stroke the inside of his lower lip. He wondered what the hell was going on out there. Thirty seconds later, with the Boat still steadily on course for the yacht basin and the roadway beyond, still with a great bow wave sloshing away on either side, the owner's hands were on his hips and he was braced for something catastrophic. Then the Boat turned ninety degrees and came straight toward the deckful of day-trippers, whose chatter had suddenly stopped.

It was Carlo who spotted them first. He had been seized with the idea of plunging the harpoon into the planking of the dock, like Columbus planting his flagstaff on American soil. But, seeing that bunch of dudes coming up dead ahead, he decided to modify this plan at once. He merely leaned over the bows and brandished the harpoon, as at an imaginary whale, with a powerful shout of "Thar she blo-o-o-ows!" The Boat was still seventy-five yards away from the Tall Ships party but the man in the tartan suit, convinced he was about to be impaled, went white above the bow tie, gurgled "Oh, my God!" and stood rooted to the spot. Others began to scatter as the wide, flared bows of the Boat came surging in. The insurance broker was already hustling his wife toward a gangway leading to the dock. The owner had jumped onto the rail of his own fo'c'sle, to make himself more visible, and was gesturing wildly with his arm and roaring "For Chrissake, go ASTERN!"

Big Boy's difficulty was that he could see nothing of the panic ahead because Carlo was blocking his view; and he was, in any case, concentrating hard on his angle of approach, waiting for the split second when he would reverse his engine, throw the helm over again, and come alongside the piles of the dock so smoothly they wouldn't know they'd arrived. He was not really aware that anything was amiss until Yank, standing outside the starboard door of the wheelhouse with one of the midship lines, let out an awestruck gasp of "Jeesus Christ!" as their ninety-degree turn brought the day-trippers within his kaleidoscoping vision. He backed and lurched through the door, shouting peril to Big Boy as he came, reaching for wheel, clutch, and throttle in one frantic dive. "Hey, what's goin' on, old buddy?" complained Big Boy, just before Yank's weight sent him sprawling to the floor.

The owner was himself about to abandon ship when the Boat came to a standstill a few feet from where he was perched. Behind him, his guests were gaping wide-eyed from wherever they had taken cover. Half a dozen were standing on the deck in attitudes of shock. A couple of heads peered cautiously round the fo'c'sle doorway, now that the confusion had subsided. The man in the tartan suit rose slowly from behind the hatch, whose protection he had finally sought, wiping ketchup from his sleeve. The children looked on uncertainly, hoping all this had been just another part of the day's fun and games.

Regarding them benignly across the water was Carlo, supporting himself on the shaft of the harpoon. On the main deck was Jonathan, whirling the stern rope round his head like a lasso and not at all sure, just then, what he ought to do next. From the wheelhouse window stared the puzzled eyes of Big Boy, who was trying to remember where he'd put the check. In the doorway stood Yank, with an upraised glass and an already cheerful expression beginning to expand. He waved the glass amiably in the direction of his audience below. "Here's to you and here's to us," he called.

"All right boys," said the owner, in a voice to chill the dead. "Bring her alongside and tie her up." Which they did, with exaggerated movements and meticulous attention to detail, so that everyone could see their care.

Then the three on deck made haste to the wheelhouse, before the owner could reach it first. In the ominous silence before he strode into their midst, Big Boy turned to Yank with a very sober look in his eyes and nodded toward the day-trippers outside. "D'ya think we should wait till they've finished?" he asked anxiously. "Before we go ashore, I mean."

Five days later the Boat was back at sea, a chastened crew still counting their good luck. They had, in the first searing moments of the owner's wrath, expected each of them to be fired on the spot. But, as Yank allowed to Big Boy, he had been pretty good about it in the end, simply ordering them to settle the damage to his guests out of their paychecks for the voyage. The final tally came to four dry-cleaning bills, eight floral sprays, ten quarts of bourbon, three baseball mitts for Little Leaguers, and four dresses for small girls; together with a doctor's account passed on by a lady who claimed treatment for shock but who, in fact, smuggled her chronic postnasal drip into the same consultation. Apart from that there was merely the threat — repeated by the Skipper on his own behalf when he returned from his father's sickbed — that if a drop of liquor should again cross the rails of the Boat, the guy responsible would be run ashore for good so fast that his feet wouldn't touch the deck. It could have been much, much worse, and even Carlo went quiet when he thought how close he had come to harpooning the most eye-catching mortician this side of the Tobin Memorial Bridge.

On the third day out, the Boat was working its way across the top of Lydonia Canyon in a swell running heavily enough to keep the men careful of overbalancing as they struggled to bring the traps over the side. Halfway through the morning, the ever-watchful Big Boy jerked his head toward the northern horizon and called out to the others. "We've got company," he said. The others turned and, as the Boat rose upon the swell's next surge, they saw the mast and wheelhouse of another boat fishing in the distance. "Looks like that bastard out of New Bedford," muttered Yank. "And he's got his fuckin' traps set ahead of ours."

This was an occasional hazard of their trade, the result of fierce competition to plunder the richest grounds for commerce in a prosperous marketplace. There were but a handful of boats like theirs, built for taking lobster from the offshore seas, each large enough (if the fishing was good and the vessel went home full of live shellfish in the water tank below deck) to keep even New York's greed satisfied for a day or two. So few were these boats that they rarely coincided on the grounds, though at any time two or three might be working well outside each other's vision along the continental shelf. The hazard therefore was not that they got in each other's way, which could happen to net fishermen pursuing the same shoals of herring or mackerel across the bank. But the deep-sea lobstermen sometimes set their own trawls of traps across or alongside those of another vessel which had passed that way a few days before. That meant real trouble. It was easy enough to get your own trawl line in a tangle when it was a long way from anyone else's, particularly close to the shallower edges of the bank, where the currents ran strong and could tease a mile and a half of submarine rope into a fantasy of knots and loops that took precious time to straighten out when it was hauled to the surface after a week or ten days. Much more exasperating was the discovery that you had your line mixed up with someone else's down there on the sea floor. This had happened once since Jonathan joined the Boat, and for an hour and a half they had wallowed in the same spot, trying to sort out the serpentine confusion of yellow nylon that hung in great hanks from the block and tackle dangling over the side. In the end, having decided which line belonged to whose trawl, they had seen no alternative to cutting the other man's in order to free their own. But the Skipper, surveying the operation from the jog station above the deck, where he controlled the hauling of the winch, watched tensely while they accomplished this and tied the two severed ends together again before allowing the stranger's line to slip back into the sea. Jonathan had been impressed by their care for someone else's livelihood, even when he was a competitor.

They had almost come to the end of a trawl when they sighted the New Bedford boat. Having baited the emptied traps, they set them again along the same line. It was good fishing just there, with every chance of another fine trawl when the traps were raised on their next voyage. As they steamed on toward the next marker, over to the north, the Skipper noticed that their rival was also moving away. He blew out his lips with irritation and hoped they weren't going to be stuck with the guy for the rest of the trip. If they were to set so close together for days on end, it would probably mean trouble next time out. He could reduce this likelihood by changing his own planned course, by setting his traps elsewhere once they had been hauled. But he wasn't anxious to abandon this patch of sea. There was plenty of lobster in it right now.

As they came up to the marker, Big Boy stood by the starboard rail with the grappling hook on a line. He caught the trawl beneath the marker with his first cast and Yank came to his side as the marker was hauled toward the Boat. Together they manhandled the tall pole, its balloons, and its concrete weight out of the sea, while Carlo leaped onto the rail and stretched up with the trawl line to run it over the pulley above. He had to do this with one hand, clinging to the derrick arm with his other to stop himself from going over the side when the swell tipped the Boat. He passed the line to Jonathan below him and Jonathan walked it over to the drum of the winch, a great grooved hub projecting from the fo'c'sle break. That was where the power lay, to heave up a mile or more of sodden rope with fifty heavy wire traps from seventy-odd fathoms down.

The Skipper leaned out of the jog station so that he would be able to see each trap as it broke surface. He slipped the controls of the winch onto power, poised to take the enormous strain to come. He waited while Big Boy and Yank carried the marker toward the stern. It weighed heavily on their arms, so that the tendons stood out between the muscles, and their bodies leaned away. They were halfway down the deck when the Boat rolled again, and their feet broke into a pattering sideways dance as they strove to counterbalance the lurch. They paused, as the Boat itself paused at the bottom of the roll, then carried on to the stern and laid the marker down there, ready for the resetting of the trawl. Then the Skipper pushed the winch into gear and the great grooved hub revolved. It rattled like a cartwheel when it began to turn. The rope tensed under the strain of power at one end, dragging weight at the other. It creaked quietly, like a wet dishcloth wrung tight. But this sound was menacing with the threat of what would happen if the rope snapped. Men had lost limbs in the terrible whiplash of parted cable along a fishing boat's deck. Some had been beheaded. Others had been ripped overboard.

One by one, the lobster traps came up from the depths. Big Boy was working the rail and it was he who had to reach out over the Boat's side to swing each trap in from the trawl line as it rose, dripping, to the pulley above his head. He rested an end of the trap on the inside edge of the rail, and jammed it there against his belly so that it shouldn't slide outboard again, while he unclasped the iron gadgets securing it to the trawl line. The rectangular trap was as wide as his arm span and his cheeks were blown out with the effort of lifting it off the rail, half-turning as he did so, and dumping it onto the metal table that separated him from Yank. The two of them unfastened the hooks that kept the trap's lid in place and, flinging this open, they thrust their arms in to get at the lobster. There were three compartments to each trap and lobster were caught by entering a string funnel in the middle section at the prospect of bait dangling in the compartments on either side. As the funnel was much wider at the entrance than at the end giving access to the bait, and as the end was arranged to hang in space, there was no escape for any creature once it had crawled in. The lobsters were hauled out by the two men, facing each other across the opened trap, and tossed over to Jonathan, who stood by the banding table amidships. While he was fixing strong rubber bands to keep closed each lobster's claws, Big Boy was turning to the next trap coming out of the sea. Yank, having baited the empty trap and shut it, took it in his arms and staggered across the deck to stack it on the port side, ready for setting in a new trawl when the old one was hauled. Carlo was by the drum of the winch, making sure the rope did not snag on anything or slip off the revolving hub. He left this task at short intervals to run each gadget and its halter down the deck, trailing the trawl line behind him to link it to each newly baited trap in turn. The heavy work was at the rail and in the stacking of the baited traps, which was why the men changed positions with each succeeding trawl. But all of it needed the rhythm of craftsmen with deft manual skills. If one of the crew lagged, the whole trawl was slowed up. And that delay was measured in dollars by every man aboard.

They had hauled in ten traps and were making good time, and Jonathan already had in front of him one basket full of banded lobsters, waiting to go below into the tank when the trawl was done. Only the Skipper, at his watching post above the working deck, had noticed an oddness in the behavior of the Boat so far. Normally, when fishing in a flat calm, it leaned over to starboard a few degrees, pulled there by the dead weight of gear below the surface. This inclination was hard to measure in a rolling swell, but the Skipper sensed that this time it wasn't happening at all. He watched impassively, as the traps rose one by one and the men below him worked intently as a team.

The eleventh trap was swung in, Big Boy released it from the line, and the Skipper powered the winch again. Suddenly, the gadget flew over the pulley with a clang and on to the drum, where Carlo had to duck to avoid being struck in the face: and out of the sea came the end of yellow rope.

The Skipper swore quietly to himself and switched the power off. Big Boy turned from the new trap on the bench to see what had happened. The rope's end dangled a few feet from his head. "Bastard!" he shouted. He reached for the end, cursing whatever hazard on the sea floor had parted the trawl. But, as he took the rope in his hand, he saw it was not the seabed's fault. He stared up at the Skipper with fire in his eyes. "The fuckin' thing's been cut," he called.

They got the grappling hook again and bent it onto the hundred-fathom line from the forepeak, and cast it over the side. For half an hour they rolled in that spot above the severed trawl, groping patiently for something they could not see. They found nothing, so the Skipper decided to waste no more time and make for the other marker buoy. They could haul in the rest of the trawl from that end and splice the parted rope when they had all the fish safely aboard. But when they got there, they discovered the full extent of their loss. Only three traps came out of the sea this time before the trawl line ended in the crisp severance of nylon by knife.

The Skipper went red with anger when he saw what had been done and banged his palm against the jog station wall; but this was nothing to the fury down on the deck. "Those cocksuckers," roared Big Boy, "they've taken the whole fuckin' middle section out!"

Yank inhaled a glob of catarrh and spat it powerfully over the side. He looked up at the Skipper and there was challenge in the air. "Why don't we just get after those bastards and sort it out right now?"

"That's right, Skip," yelled Big Boy, gesturing to the horizon with his arm. "Let's get alongside of 'em and see who's really good with a knife."

Jonathan, standing mutely with hands on hips, felt a queer, anxious thrill when Big Boy said that. He'd never seen a knife fight; he wondered if he could somehow keep out of the way. "It'll be one on one," said Carlo with a cocky grin, "and right is might!"

The Skipper stared grimly at the end of the sabotaged trawl. There was no doubt at all that someone had sabotaged it. Maybe they'd hauled up the middle section themselves, in which case they'd be thieves as well; maybe they'd just made the two cuts to warn the Boat off their own patch on subsequent trips.

The others had instantly made up their minds about this, and about who was to blame. "We goin' to let our fish get landed in New Bedford?" said Big Boy. He turned to Yank. "How many traps we hauled that end?" They counted them together and Big Boy looked up to the jog station again. " 'leven that end and three this. That's fourteen traps we got out of — what was it — fifty traps this trawl? That's thirty-six fuckin' traps those mother-fuckers stole. Man I didn't come out here just for the fresh air. Let's go get those lobsters!" He meant it, and he was throwing the full weight of his age and experience behind his grievance.

Except for Jonathan, the Skipper was the youngest man aboard; college boy, with all the right pieces of paper but not enough sea-time; might be he could be pushed. The Boat rolled heavily and the men on deck shifted their feet quickly, bending their knees into the slope of the deck. The Skipper shook his head, but looked no one in the eye. "Get ready with the hook again," he said; then turned to the wheelhouse and started the engine up.

"Chicken," Big Boy muttered to Yank, who was ponder-ing mutiny and other black things. Jonathan strode over to the grappling line and hauled it to the rail, anxious to distract the others from talk of revenge.

They were still quibbling fiercely among themselves, while the Boat turned in a wide arc and approached the set of the trawl at a right angle. The Skipper's head appeared round the wheelhouse doorway and he shouted them to cast out the hook, and they fell to their places in a reflex of obedience. Big Boy climbed up to the jog station to control the winch, and checked with the Skipper just what he wanted done. The young captain at the wheel moved the throttle to slow, while Big Boy let the full length of grappling line out so that the hook would drag along the sea floor. Carlo went into the galley, to grab a quick bite. Yank sat on the metal table and morosely glared in the direction where he thought the New Bedford boat had gone. Jonathan lit a cigarette and sat on the rail, and watched the changing angle of the grappling line on the swelling surface of the sea.

For an hour the Boat crossed and recrossed the direction of the trawl, the four tines of the grappling hook trailing far below. Twice they thought it might have caught the trawl, and stopped, and began to haul. Both times it had caught nothing but some rocky knob down there. The anger on deck became a sullen discontent. The Skipper was testier than anyone by the time he had decided it was a hopeless quest. By then, no one was trying to push him into a pursuit of the New Bedford boat. They did not see it again during the rest of the trip. But their sense of injury remained and each man knew very well what it had cost. They rolled the figures back and forth as they ate each night, as they waited briefly for the setting of a new trawl or the hauling of an old one. Thirty-six traps at twenty-eight bucks apiece. Most of a trawl line which cost thirty-five hundred dollars new. And Christ knew how many lobsters; there could be twenty-five pounds to each trap when the fishing was good; as it had been there. That was one hell of a lot of bread they'd lost.

When they got back to the Town, it was for three of the crew the first topic of every new conversation they had in the bars of Main and East Main during a weekend ashore. The Skipper got it off his chest when he reported to the owner in the company office, then drove off to Providence for home comforts and golf. Jonathan told Ellen about the discovery of their loss and about the time they had wasted grappling for the trawl; but he left out the New Bedford boat and did not speak of Yank's call for pursuit. He wanted more time to think about that.

Then began the worse misfortunes of all, though the first sign of this did not appear until they had docked after their next trip and started to land their catch. The weather

had been fair and the fishing had been smooth. They h₂
known more plentiful times but, as they steamed towaɪ
the Cape Cod canal, the Skipper was well content wit
what they had taken, considering the season of the year
For the sea was beginning to cool and the lobsters were on
the move to the deep refuges they sought each fall, where
they could lie torpid and secure from the shallower
turmoil that issued from the winter storms above. At least
that was the speculation of the fishermen and scientists
alike, who between them knew much but understood not
so well. The Skipper recalled a lecture in his first college
year; how startled he had been at a biologist's news that a
lobster could walk ninety miles in three weeks along the
alpine bottom of the sea. He now knew for a fact that
fishing was less predictable when the cool had begun.
They had taken five thousand pounds, which was not bad
at all for a week just now; after patiently passing the fall
their catches would rise once again.

As they turned round Race Point, the Skipper checked
the temperature of the water in the tank below deck.
Securely banded so that they could not attack each other,
penned in wire-mesh compartments to reduce the bruis-
ing they received when the Boat pitched and rolled, the
lobsters were eased with painstaking care into the brief
time on shore that heralded their end. They had come
from the seabed at 45 degrees or thereabouts and they
were bound for display in water much warmer than that,
in seafood establishments wherein the gourmandizing eye
liked to pick and choose its prey live before gobbling it up.
So the lobsters were elevated to this temperature zone by
stages on the passage home, in the interests of quality. The
Skipper was most meticulous in watching the thermometer
reading of his tank. It was part of his profession.

As soon as they had tied up at the dock, Jonathan and
Carlo took the banding table off the hatch and removed

e hatch cover. Yank climbed down into the tank below,
ausing at the foot of the ladder to push lobsters away with
is seaboot and give himself enough clearance on the tank
oor to stand with the water above his knees. The Skipper
had gone into the lobster mart, to keep tally of the landing
with the manager. Big Boy and the other two mustered the
baskets and, peering down at Yank over the rim of the
hatch, lowered the first one to him on the end of a roped
hook. Yank bent toward the biggest lobster within reach,
floating on the surface. He picked it up, and his body's
swing checked as he did so. He stayed crouched, frowned,
and waved the lobster sideways in his hand. Its legs
dangled uselessly and its two arms sagged with the weight
of large claws, without the tension that even in torpor
indicates life. Yank slowly put it in the basket and looked
around him in the tank. Always some lobster were visible
on the surface, lying on the backs of those submerged
below. But always, too, there was movement in the mass of
bodies. Now, with the Boat still, with the water having
ceased to slosh and swirl, Yank could see nothing that
moved down there beside him in the tank. He picked up
another creature. It hung limply from his hand just like
the first. He dropped it and came upright. He looked up at
Big Boy, one of three heads framed against the sky.
"Come and look at this," he called out. His buddy
descended and together they groped among the carcasses
drifting in the tank. In ten minutes they found three
lobsters that were feebly flexing their limbs. But most of
the catch in that tank was quite obviously dead. When the
Skipper was called, the mart manager came with him and
he, taking one look around, shook his head in dismay.
"Jeez," he said. "Never did see nothin' like this before." He
sniffed the air loudly, and wrinkled up his nose. "You
know," he said to the Skipper, "maybe this place needs a
scrub-up and a repaint job." It was true, and the Skipper

knew it. The steel walls of the tank were stippled with rust, and what had been white when the Boat was first sent to sea had turned creamy brown with the use of four years.

For all that they were scavengers on the seabed, lobsters were delicate creatures whose environment must be balanced within the finest margins for them to survive in good health. They were especially vulnerable between high summer and the end of fall, for that was the season of the moult, when the flesh had grown too far to be contained within the shell. Not every year, but at intervals throughout its life, the lobster cast an old shell in an agony of struggle to be free. Doubling itself up when the moment came, the body squirmed and twisted until the carapace split along the back as cleanly as if it had been cut with a knife. Through this fissure the creature within wriggled out, withdrawing all its extremities — claws, antennae, legs, tail and eyes on stalks — from their separate protective cases. When the agony was done, an empty shell lay discarded in the sea; a perfect replica of a lobster; and a like creature, but more vivid than before and soft with new life, was able to crawl away and, with luck, to grow on. Many were taken by cod and by other lobsters (who are cannibals), while some succumbed merely because their bodies were so excessively sensitive until the new shell had hardened that it could be death merely to be touched by a fisherman's hand.

The Skipper couldn't see any new moults in the shambles of his tank, but they'd been taking a lot of soft shells for several trips on the run. It could just be, he thought glumly, that the tank water was too impure for such weaklings to survive. He climbed up the ladder, feeling wearier than he could remember. It was one of those things, what had just happened, and no one was to blame. But what a goddamn waste, to have been at sea for eight days and to end up like this. There was no question of selling what they had; the mart manager had made that plain without even saying a word, though he was warm with talk of lousy, rotten luck when he saw the unspoken point was clearly taken. But he was already making calculations in his head about how to spread more thinly his supplies in the market of New York. He only hoped that another boat due in later that day hadn't fouled things up, too. Then he said so long to the Skipper and returned to his mart, where two assistants had been waiting to grade a landing that would not now be theirs. "Whole catch fucked up," said their boss. "Poor bastards." He was whistling to himself by the time he had opened his register of accounts.

No one said much to anyone aboard the Boat during the trip home across the bay. When the deck had been cleaned up, Big Boy and Yank settled down to a game of crib in the galley; Carlo and Jonathan took to their bunks. The Skipper called up the owner on the radio to tell him the bad news and, when they docked, the two of them agreed that before the next trip the tank must be cleaned and repainted.

For a couple of days the crew was set about this task and, when it was done, all gleaming and white, Big Boy declared that maybe they should move in there and leave the bunk room to the lobsters.

Then they went to sea again. They trawled the canyons across Georges for five days, but the lobster had moved and more than half the traps they hauled contained nothing but the usual invasion of crabs and the occasional cusp or eel. They set course for land with seventeen hundred pounds aboard, and no one was going to get excited about that, on a vessel that was built to carry thirty thousand pounds if its tank was full. "One whole catch lost," said Big Boy bitterly, "then the fishin's as slow as molasses goin' uphill."

But it was much worse than that. When they reached the dock and opened the hatch they found the lobsters in the same condition as before: whatever was killing them, it had not been lurking in the surfaces of the tank. The Skipper had a long conversation with the owner on the telephone, while his crew sat around the deck and the lobster mart, denouncing both owner and captain for their failure to detect whatever was threatening their livelihoods.

"These guys are supposed to know what they're doin'," said Big Boy, "and we work for 'em 'cos we *think* they know what they're supposed to be doin'." He grolched loudly, and spat out his phlegm in the direction of a gull that was eyeing him coldly from the top of a pile in the wharf. He stared back at it, pleased with the neatness of what he had just said.

"Guy don't have to do too much 'cept think ahead to problems when he's sitting up in the wheelhouse all trip," said Carlo, indicating the figure at the telephone inside. Yank rose and, hitching up his trousers, finished off Carlo's thought. "Maybe we should have him down on deck and get somebody else to run the Boat." His reflex sniping at the Italian was abandoned in the resentment of their common cause.

"Reckon I could get this old bucket from one trawl to another," said Jonathan, wishing to identify with the other three. But he was, in truth, uncertain where his loyalties lay. He didn't quite see how anyone could have predicted this second catastrophe. He wondered vaguely whatever was going to happen next.

The Skipper came striding out of the office, his face red and a glitter in his eye. "Let's get movin'," not pausing in his stride, "Old Man's getting a biologist down to see what's wrong." By the time the Boat got home, the owner's car was drawn up at the dock and a young man was sitting beside the driver in the front. They got out as the Boat nosed into her berth and the owner took the line that Carlo heaved across from the bows and made it fast to a cleat on the wharf. The young man stood watching, hands on hips, bright interest on his face. Big Boy stared down from amidships while two thoughts slipped in tandem through his head: some guys have it easy; and this one looks like just another college kid — all wind and piss.

"This is Jim Morris, Fisheries Services," said the owner when the Skipper climbed ashore, "and he thinks that if it isn't your water's too cold, it's probably gas disease. Let's go see if he's right."

The Skipper shrugged and led the way back aboard. The owner had already come up with the cold water theory on the phone and the Skipper was irritated at the implication of negligence on his part. He knew damn well the importance of the water change, particularly when there were lots of soft shells in the catch, which could be shocked to death if the temperature in the tank wasn't carefully controlled. The gas disease theory was no better, from his point of view. It would have arisen from an air leak in the tank water pump and supersaturation of nitrogen in the water, which would be lethal within hours. But he'd thought of that one on the first bad trip and had checked out the pump on the run home across the bay. There'd been nothing wrong with it then, but they'd still lost five thousand pounds of lobster.

The young marine biologist was not at all discountenanced to find his theory of gas disease invalid. The three men examined the water pump together and Jim Morris smiled up at the Skipper when they'd done. "You're absolutely right," he said, "clean bill of health there."

The owner blew out his cheeks with frustration. "Okay. So where do we go from here?" he asked.

"Well," said the biologist, "there's not much more I can

do in the way of on-the-spot surveillance now. I think we've got to go for laboratory testing on some of that meat in there, and I'll take some water samples from the tank and all and we'll see what we come up with in due course."

The Skipper eyed him cautiously. "How long would that be?" he inquired.

Morris rubbed his cheek thoughtfully. "Today's Friday. Should have some news for you Wednesday at the latest. You got any ice round here? — just a little, to pack round a couple of lobsters on the road south." They took ice cubes from the galley and fished some carcasses from the tank and when Morris had put them in a thermal box and collected two jerrycans of water, he shook hands with the Skipper and said, "Don't worry. We'll work it out between us."

As the owner's car disappeared through the gate of the fish pier, a car driven by Big Boy, with Yank beside him, came roaring past. Big Boy climbed over the rail with a purposeful look on his face. "All is not lost, my friends," he said, "all is not lost. We've done a deal with Barney and he'll take the tails from anything that's still live and kickin' at fifty cents a pound."

It wasn't much of a deal, as Big Boy knew, for few of the lobsters in the tank were left alive by now. But it was something to relieve the sense of helplessness, a small redemption of a week's otherwise wasted work. So Carlo drove off in his pickup to collect fresh ice and wooden boxes from the stores down on Fisherman's Wharf, while the others hauled baskets full of lobster from the tank. When he returned, the five men of the Boat stood on its deck and dismembered the fish that showed any signs of life, snapping off the tails just behind the carapace and putting their noses close to the wound to sniff for freshness. Jonathan, picking up a three-day-old carcass by mistake, realized that you didn't have to put your nose too close to catch a whiff of decay; the smell that met him as he raised the mutilated body to his face made him drop it at once, shuddering with disgust. The acceptable tails were put into the boxes, surrounded by ice, and when they had finished they had filled five containers. At the price they'd been offered, this would almost cover the food bill for the trip; no more than that.

What should have produced some sort of wage lay heaped up on deck, a slimy mess of torn shell and dribbling guts which now attracted a plangent swirling of gulls overhead. When the men moved away, to load the five boxes into Carlo's truck, the gulls dived one by one feet down, wings flaring high, necks bent so that beaks could snatch and gulp in midair. One bird, a herring gull as large as a small terrier and bolder than the rest, seized by the exposed tissues a huge lobster claw whose shell was partly broken away. It walked with it to an empty corner of the deck and began to beat the remaining shell against the rail, to loosen the flesh inside. When the flesh came away it was still in one piece and the gull tried to swallow it whole, but it was too wide to pass the gullet. The gull dropped the flesh on the deck and prodded it fiercely with yellow beak, but only inflicted wounds. Once more it tried to ingest the thing whole, its head lowered like the head of a menacing dog, but jerking back in spasms with the effort of trying to swallow. Very slowly the flesh entered the distended mouth of the gull, whose neck began to bulge with its entry; but then the flesh stuck and the bird regurgitated it upon the deck and prodded it again. Again it took the whole claw meat in its mouth and suddenly, with a new effort, a hidden surge of muscle power, it got the thing down, swiftly, with a ripple along its neck to mark the food's passing. The bird blinked, looked surprised, and stood there motionless at last.

Yank, turning from the opposite rail, stooped to pick up

a torn off tail and, with a savage cry of "Greedy cock-sucker," hurled it at the gull. Before the tail came anywhere near, the bird took off over the stern, dropping a little like an aircraft leaving a carrier, then slowly climbing safely across to the other side of the inner harbor. The Skipper regarded the carnage on his deck and shook his head resignedly. "Well, the sooner we get it finished," he said to the others, "the sooner we'll have done." He went up to the wheelhouse to start the engine and back the Boat out of her berth and then to do what they had done after the previous trip. They steamed down the harbor and out beyond the breakwater and, when they were a mile or two off the eastern shore of the Cape, they hove to and shoveled the remains of their week's fishing over the side to feed the crabs. "You'd think they'd be getting sick of fuckin' lobster by now," said Big Boy as he pushed the last remnants through the gap in the rail by the starboard table. He straightened up and threw his shovel down on the deck. "I know I am, that's for sure."

He went on a blinder that night with Yank, on money the company advanced against future wages, and the pair of them were barely able to stand by the time they climbed back aboard at two in the morning. "I'll tell you what, old buddy," said Big Boy to his friend, as they sat opposite each other on the edge of their bunks, shoulders drooping and jaws slack under the anesthetic weight of booze, "tell you what — if we don't strike it proper next trip, I'm gointa put my name on the board in St. Peter's Club. That'll always get yer a new site. D'ye know that. Never fails. I got friends down there. That's what I'm gonna do. 'n when I've made a pile I'm gonna get me a boat meself and show these motherfuckers how to fish fer lobster."

Yank stared across the gap between them, frowning hard to concentrate on what was left of the night. "How the hell can you put your name in at the club? Club's for the Guineas."

Big Boy grinned and slapped his friend heavily on the thigh, so that Yank all but tumbled to the deck. "Tha's right, old buddy," said Big Boy. "Didn't know I was a Guinea, didya?" He made an effort and swung his legs into his bunk and lay there heavily for a moment, his eyes beginning to close. "All these years," he mumbled thickly, "I've been a member of the fuckin' Mafia and never told no one."

Yank kicked off the cowboy boots he affected when ashore and rolled over the bunk edge on to his mattress. "Better that goddamn biologist comes up with the answer," he said to the bulkhead, "else we'll have the cocksucker for bait next trip."

The biologist came up with the answer a few days later, and it was something that no one aboard the Boat had ever thought of. The laboratory tests showed that the lobsters had died of acute copper poisoning. Morris explained to the owner on the phone that the normal copper content of the sea was three parts per billion of water. Increase that content to fifty-six parts and you had a lethal dose for shellfish. The carcasses and the water samples from the tank had revealed something over three hundred parts of copper. "In short, sir, you could have poisoned a sea elephant in that tank of yours; lobsters never had a chance from the moment they came aboard." The fault, he thought, was almost certainly to be found in the refrigeration unit which controlled the temperature of the water in the tank. "If you take the reefer apart, I think you may find that the plastic coating of the copper tubing has become worn away; and that would certainly be enough to pollute your water to the level I've indicated."

It was as Jim Morris had guessed. When the crew

trooped down into the engine room behind the Skipper and removed the covers from the reefer, the culprit was immediately revealed. The serpentine tubing which was the effective core of the temperature control system for the fish tank should have been green with a plastic coat, but in places this had vanished to expose the bare copper beneath. There was nothing for it but to take the whole unit to pieces and to get the pipes recoated. The first part of the operation was no more than half a day's work: but the pipes had to be trucked down to Boston and all the owner's pleading that his men were losing wages — hadn't, indeed, earned a cent for the best part of a month — could not propel the works there into a sense of urgency. It was five more days before the pipes came back and by then the men were withdrawn into themselves with their discontent.

Yank pushed off to Boston for the waiting time and sounded out his old boss in the meat trade about a possible return to butchery. Receiving little encouragement, he looked up a man who had served with him in Vietnam, and spent the next three nights acting as a stand-in bouncer at a strip joint in the Combat Zone, sleeping with a different stripper each day, they finding his inarticulate muscularity much more of a turn-on than what normally came their way from the lecherous terraces of Brookline and the robust patronage of the Harvard football squad. It was as well there was distance between him and Carlo that week, for the Italian's way of keeping head above water was to be more provocatively sharp-tongued than ever to all and sundry; as a result of which he took a beating one night at his usual drinking place on East Main, this half-closing one eye and swelling that side of his face. Big Boy, bereft of Yank, wandered lonely around the Town, making every single Bud last an hour or more as he occupied one bar stool after another and contemplated the long succession of serials, cash quizzes, pre-season football games and commercials (*Laverne and Shirley, To Tell The Truth*, Raiders versus Patriots, Fenway Franks, and all the rest) that, did he but know it, had been spawned by the television companies for the perpetual blandishment of just such as he.

Jonathan was alone, too, for Ellen had taken a week off her work in the plant shop to visit friends and relations in New York and did not return until the day after the Boat went to sea again. He missed her so much that one afternoon he sat down and tried to write a poem about her, though he'd never committed a free thought to a piece of paper before, not since his third year at high school, when a football victory had inspired him to eight lines of doggerel that had made the magazine. But now, when he tried to say what he felt about Ellen in verse, he couldn't make any of it rhyme and thought it a useless thing without that. After a couple of hours he gave up and, screwing the scribbled notepaper into a ball, he dragged on a windcheater and got his bike from the garage.

He pedaled toward the harbor against a stiff breeze from the south, the surest sign so far that the weather was at a turn of the year. It had blown up the night before and stripped half the trees in the Town of their muted fall foliage. The day was bright, but this wind had been missing for months. It cut through the windcheater, the sweater beneath, and the shirt under that, so that Jonathan could feel its coldness against his skin as he rode. When he came down to the harbor the waters were rumpled into small waves and at the Pier 7 yacht basin was another sign of the season's approaching end. For the first time since April, Jonathan could hear the hollow jangling sound of wire halliards slapping against the steel masts of the pleasure craft, the lamaserie note that would ring down all the days till winter was done. He shivered as he paused by the yacht basin and looked across its pontoons to where the Boat was berthed.

Carlo's pickup was parked there on the wharf and men were hauling things off it across the tailboard. When Jonathan arrived, everyone but Yank was there and he was somewhere on the road from Boston. The owner had turned-to with his men, to get the new reefer pipes aboard and fitted without further delay. He was a short and gruff man, who had come to this business to make money, and the disasters of the past month had put him deeply in the red. But he had also sailed deep-sea himself and knew well enough that the most demoralizing thing of all was to be idle with a skill that hard times could not employ. For the rest of that day, and well into the next, he set to with the others in the engine room to make the repair that would send them back to work.

They finished on the eve of Columbus Day and cast off at two in the morning, no one wishing to spend another twenty-four hours ashore even for a national holiday. But the fish factories of the Town had closed, which meant that they would have to seek their bait elsewhere. As soon as they had cleared the breakwater, the Skipper set course for the canal where, just beyond the lobster mart, there was a store which supplied the inshoremen who set traps around the adjacent arc of Cape Cod Bay. He turned the watch over to Big Boy for the night passage down the coast, where sprinklings of white lights gave away the townships, a great yellow glare betrayed Boston, and red dots warned aircraft from time to time of dangerous projections into the sky. Too many of those red lights ashore these days, thought Big Boy, content to be sitting once again in the wheelhouse chair. Too many and too close together at times. A man could be fooled into thinking there was shipping in there, all steaming in your own direction, port-side on: and the searchlight that swiveled round the runways at Logan could be taken for the Minots light, if you didn't keep track of where you were at. He checked off the buoys in the bay as they came up, one by one: white, green or red flashings on the blackness of the sea. The Boat rolled a bit, though she was steaming fairly close to the land, but Big Boy could not hear the rising wind outside for the noise put out by the nocturnal disc jockeys on the radio by his head.

It was broad daylight when the pale green cubes of the canal power station climbed into view above the coast. While the Skipper went ashore to negotiate for bait at the store, the rest of them fried up breakfast and spoke lightheartedly of the prospect ahead. It was an hour before their captain returned and he was shaking his head in exasperation when he entered the galley. The store wouldn't sell, claiming it had only enough bait for local needs. But after a lot of work on the telephone he'd managed to do a deal with a place in New Bedford, provided they could be there by noon. They cast off again and moved down the wide canal that separated the mainland from Cape Cod. An hour later they were plowing between the two lines of buoys that issued from the canal's end into Buzzard's Bay, then making their turn to the southwest to bring them to the old whaling port that was the Town's greatest rival in the annals of the sea. The last whaler had sailed from New Bedford some time before the last schooner put out from the Town and since then its deep-sea fishing had been spent on Georges, too, or closer inshore with a fleet of scallopers. Its history may have been as proud as that of the Town, but in one respect it could never compete, for it lay on low ground with no natural protection from the open sea. So dangerously exposed was the harbor there that a hurricane barrier had been flung across its mouth, a massive construction that

he sat down, and the bitter note in his voice made the other four look straight up. "Well t'ain't so. We've just had a bastard of a forecast for tomorrow night."

Big Boy swallowed half a potato with a gulp and looked hard across the table. "Not a fuckin' hurricane, for Chrissake?" he demanded. It was a possibility still, even in mid-October, for the season had been known to stretch from August until the end of this month.

"They don't know yet," said the Skipper, prodding a sausage with his fork. "They're calling it tropical depression Holly at the moment and she's roaring up from Dominica right now. May get worse; may not. May come our way, may go out into the Atlantic first. They don't know that either. What they do know is that waves have built up from twelve to fifteen feet in the past hour. And they don't look as though they're going down yet awhiles."

"Jesus Christ," said Yank, "that's all we need." Even if the weather became no worse than that, it would make their kind of fishing impossible. A vessel that lists under a dragging weight on the beam in a calm is in danger of being rolled over by the pull of such a weight in seas fifteen feet high.

"Better we make sure that stove can't come off the deck." It was Carlo, claiming his share of the talk. He turned to Jonathan at his side. "You hear about *Judith Lee Rose* a couple of years back? You know *Judith Lee Rose*, the big dragger ties up 'cross the other side of the fish pier? Couple of years back she got caught out here in bad storm. Rolled her right over, right over so she was upside down and came up other side. Stove in the galley came loose, red hot and roarin' with flames. When she righted again they looked up at the ceiling. There was stove maker's name, from the top of the stove, branded right there on the ceiling." It was not true, though Carlo believed it to be true. It was a legend among the fishermen of the Town from the nineteenth century when (as historians have recorded) such a thing did happen twice, to the schooner *Onward* and the schooner *Helen G. Wells*, in storms that blew up in these waters thirty years apart.

Jonathan listened and kept silent, then glanced at their electric stove, which was riveted to the deck. He had long since stopped believing half that Carlo said. But he felt he might not be kidding this time. Jonathan had seen a photograph of a boat like theirs, taken during bad weather at sea. It seemed about to slide sideways down a great hill of water; and you could see the sky under a third of its keel.

"Anyways," said the Skipper, "we'll turn-to first light and work right through till we have to stop. If we have to stop. Weather boys have been known to get it wrong. "

When they came out on deck at six in the morning, conditions had changed from those at dusk the night before. The sun was climbing toward banks of cloud, but there were plenty of open spaces in the sky. There was a wide running swell, which made the Boat roll and hid the first marker buoy from continuous sight until it was a hundred yards away to starboard. More frequently than on the night before, however, a wave slapped the hull hard enough to shower the deck with spray and wet a man unpleasantly if he caught its full force. This was no more than a small shift in the elements: but it was enough for the deckhands to put their oilskins on before emerging for work. They clumped out into the daylight with the stiff movements common to all who wear protective clothes. The oilskins swished as they prepared for the first haul: swish of slicker jacket upon the top of the overall; swish of overall legs upon the rubber seaboots. Only hands and heads could get wet and, if the flying spray got worse, only hands and face when the slicker hood was pulled up. For the moment, each man was content to cover his head with a woolen watch cap and leave it at that. You could see what you were doing better with the oilskin hood down.

As usual, Jonathan took the first trawl at the banding table. It was the lingering reminder that he was the least experienced man aboard, the one place where negligence could not imperil another member of the crew, where unsureness could not seriously slow the rhythm of everybody's work. If you lagged at the banding table, someone else could help you catch up in the interval between hauling a trawl and setting it afresh. But if you didn't get the bands on properly you could most certainly harm everybody's pay check at the end of the voyage. Slip those rubber bands too near the base of the lobster's claw and prey might still be seized in spite of the restraint; leave the band too close to the tip of the claw and the lobster would probably work it off. In either case, a cannibal would be loose in the fish tank on the journey to land and every voyage left a small telltale flotsam of severed limbs and crushed shells. Banding small lobsters was child's play, because of both the size and the comparative regularity of the claw's shape. But some of the bigger brutes had very wide and misshapen claws, when it would be a hell of a job to prize a rubber band into the one position where it would stay put and keep the claw closed. There were occasions when the banding tool would not stretch the band wide enough to go over the claw and two men would struggle to pull it into place with finger strength alone, while the other claw groped for their hands, to grasp and crush these tormentors.

Jonathan had never been able to work out why it was that, while some lobsters came up from the depths inert and apparently stunned by the change from one pressure to another, others were fighting mad from the moment a trap broke surface. The men working the rail usually had a job to disentangle these from the traps, so ferociously did

not believe she knew any of those. Fishermen were coarse and wild. Jonathan was a nice boy who, so far as she knew, had never done anything to shame his folks.

Ellen would probably have gone down to the harbor or the beach anyway, for she craved their fresh air after a week in New York. But she had Jonathan on her mind, now she knew he was at sea, when she borrowed the car and drove along East Main. She was still not sure what she wanted of him, but an identity was shaping and the knowledge that he was out there in weather that must be very rough made her want to be close to a degree that surprised her. She noticed the gulls crouched along rooflines as she drove past the turning to the Neck, not one in flight anywhere that she could see. The gateway to the Point was deserted, now that the summer folk had all gone and the residents felt no need of their policeman, and she swept through to the private road that would bring her to the coast guard station and the breakwater. As she came through the last clump of trees, they were bent with the force of the wind, springing back in jerks between one gust and the next. Ellen felt the thrill of deep urge at the struggle that was there and her nose dilated at the impulse. Only the lighthouse and its buildings stood beyond in the open, and the untrammeled wind rushed upon the car and rocked it. Then she saw the sea beyond the breakwater and gasped.

She had known this place since childhood. Her parents had handled her along those granite cubes almost as soon as she could walk. Bike rides before puberty had often ended here, while she and some friend had searched the little beach for shells. Her first carnal experience had occurred on a night of moonshine, when she had lain with another fifteen-year-old at the end of the breakwater and they had stroked each other into rapture: it was not until she had gone deeper into the deliciousness of sex, years later, that she had recalled the winking of the red navigation light above them, and by then it wryly amused her.

She had been out here on hot summer days and on wet and windy days before spring came; she had even been here once in winter, when the sea had crashed against the granite and leaped vertical in foam. But she had never been here before on a day like this. It was not the smashing of the sea against the breakwater that made her gasp, though that was powerful enough. The water was hitting those stones with white explosion and it was seething madly round the iron supports of the navigation light. It was coming in such awful quantity that the breakwater was not always deflecting it up into the sky; at intervals, the sea gathered itself so massively together that it rolled right over the top, so that fifty yards or more of the stone was obliterated beneath a mere undulation in the waters. But if you looked beyond this trifling thing in its path, the sea seemed much more terrible still. It was driving into the land like a range of rolling foothills. Ellen got out of the car and forced her way against the wind until she was standing on a spit of sand in the lee where the breakwater joined the shore and where no water poured. The top of the breakwater was higher than her head and yet she could see that the ocean beyond looked higher still. It seemed as if the planes of the universe had gone amok, as if part of the world was slithering down to obliterate everything of the rest. It was the liquid part of the world that had gone mad, a leisurely liquid movement that suggested life of such magnitude, of such confident control, that no other form of life could possibly resist. It was sheer mass, weight, force — ultimate, crushing power. There was no white water out there, beyond the shore. Just this gray sinuous endlessness of the ocean moving in.

"Oh, Jonathan." She was barely conscious that she had spoken, never heard the sounds she made. It was an expression of awe as much as anything. She was trying to measure the Boat, in her mind, against what she saw. And she was afraid for its insignificance.

She turned away and ran back to the car, with a sudden ache of loneliness that came from the sea and not from herself. Even the coast guard station seemed a deserted thing, a bleached bone on the land that would be lost in grayness when the moment came. A flag stood stiff from the halliards on a mast, and Ellen wished she knew what it meant. She guessed it was a warning, but it felt like a cry for help. She drove off and, at the gateway to the Point, took the long road back to the Town that wound round the rocky edges of their corner of the Cape. Another car had pulled in at an exposed section of the road and its occupants were looking out to sea.

Hastily, she swerved in behind them, half-expecting to see something bad. But the people ahead were simply watching what she already knew. The inshore was shallow here, where beyond the breakwater it had been deep and so, though the power was the same, the sea's effect was different. Huge breakers were piling into the land, rearing perhaps fifteen feet before toppling with a crash that catapulted white surf into the air and all manner of filth as well — gobbets of weed, lumps of mud, handfuls of gravel, sticks, and other refuse from the sea. A mist seemed to hang over the coast, as far north as you could see, from this perpetual explosion of the storm. And out there, to the east, was much more of the ocean to come. From her height on the road above the rocks, Ellen could now see an infinity of white waves rolling to land on the sinuous gray mass of power. She screwed up her eyes, searching that mass for some sign of other life. But nothing had gone to sea that day. Not even a fool would put out in this. The only men on that ocean's back were those who had been caught there unprepared.

As she drove on, Ellen tried to know what was frightening her so much: how much it was fear for Jonathan, caught in that boat two hundred miles away out there; how much it was fear for herself if she recognized a fear for him; how much it was simply a response to the terrors of the world which put her spirit helplessly at bay. She felt weary from a struggle that had gone on now for years, in which she had battled elements within and without herself, always giving in too soon or holding out too long, but never yet gauging herself or anyone else so that peace would follow in their course.

The worst lost battle had been the last, the losing of the child — much worse that than the losing of the man, for that, she soon knew, had been no loss at all; worse, too, than the damage to her parents' self-esteem, for that had been a thing she had never understood. But with the child she could have made a peace; and it had gone. She gulped, then frowned hard, to banish the self-pity. For the first time since childhood, she wished she had a good girl friend; someone who'd lend a shoulder without making a demand.

She went into the Stop & Shop parking lot, to get the supper things. As she joined the line at the check-out, an elderly woman in black was stooping over her shopping cart, looking for her purse. When the woman straightened up, Ellen saw that it was Carlo's mother and smiled when the woman turned.

"Hello, Mrs. Rosario," she said, "I sure brought some bad weather home from New York with me."

Rita Rosario didn't smile back; her mouth had rarely been known to do more than twitch with any emotion since her man had died. But her eyes twinkled and she was warm to this girl that she barely knew. "Why hello, Ellen," she said. "You've been to New York? They tell me that's a terrible wicked place. Set off to go myself once, but a wheel rolled right off the old Chevy when we were going through Cooperstown and by the time the mechanic had it fixed and straightened out, m'husband had decided we'd do better staying there instead. So we did. Five whole days. I reckoned later that he'd weakened that wheel apurpose so it'd come off just where it did. He was a great Red Sox fan, you know. And he'd always wanted to see that Hall of Fame. But it's a pretty place, Cooperstown. Lakeside views and hills and things. You should go sometimes. Get that Jonathan to take you."

Ellen shrugged. "He's a football nut, you know. I'm not sure he'd go for the Hall of Fame. Mrs. Rosario, can I talk with you please?" It came out in a rush that she couldn't have stopped even if she'd known it was coming.

Rita Rosario looked at her sharply. There was something in the girl's voice that she had heard in her own once, long ago, when her man had first gone to sea. "Why of course you can, Ellen," she said. "You in a car?" The girl nodded. "Then we'll just put these things where they go and you can follow behind me back to the house."

It was the first time Ellen had ever entered an Italian home, and she was suddenly ashamed of that, for it was a taboo of her people's making, not of theirs. It was not very different from her own, except that the colors were stronger and there was a picture of the Last Supper hanging over the fireplace. Below it, on the mantel, a row of glass animals separated two photographs in silver frames, one of Carlo taken not very long ago, another of an older man who was clearly his father. She remembered Jonathan telling her how Carlo's father had died. He had been in the wheelhouse of his seine, where they kept a shotgun to scare off the seagulls that descended in clouds to plunder the seine net as it was being drawn in. The boat had rolled and the gun had gone off, blowing a hole in Mr. Rosario's leg. His mate had fixed a tourniquet above the wound, but the injured man had screamed so much at the pain that they had loosened this to give him relief, and he had slowly bled to death, with the boat still five hours from land. Ellen couldn't recall how many years before; but this small, wide woman with fleshy arms had been clad in black ever since.

She had not withdrawn from the world at her husband's death, as some women in her place had done. Her name was often in the newspaper, for she was a leader of the Fishermen's Wives, forever lobbying City Hall, the harbor authorities, and even Beacon Hill in Boston to obtain better pickings for the fishing people of the Town; pickings generally going to those who built property round the harbor, processed fish that was landed in the harbor, or merely sold commodities of one kind or another to those who sailed from the harbor and gave it life. And when Rita Rosario was not in combat at the head of Fishermen's Wives, she was usually in the middle of the Italian community's life, stitching children's garments for Fiesta, cooking seafood specialities for the St. Joseph's Day party, or simply doing what was asked of her by the priests and sisters of the Italian church. She was a very full-blooded lady, inside that tight pale face.

"Guess those boys'll be feelin' pretty sorry for theirselves right now." Mrs. Rosario spoke briskly as she moved about the kitchen with the makings of the coffee. She had played this role many times before, but never to a Yankee girl, always to one of her own. She wouldn't be able to talk about blessed St. Peter to this one, and the girl didn't qualify for the Fishermen's Wives. "Does that Jonathan of yours get sick at all?" — without stopping for an answer — "Carlo don't, but that's a matter of luck 'cos his father used to be sick as a pup. But when Carlo started the fishin' he was worse than seasick; he used to mess himself up something terrible 'cos it'd sometimes catch him when they was haulin' in and he couldn't break off to go to the john. Terrible ashamed of himself, he was. Said it was all due to change of water. 'It's that water we carry aboard, Mama,' he used to say. But me and his daddy, we knew different. There's the cream if you want it, dear."

"Jonathan just turns it into a joke if I ask him whether he's been sick. I don't really know. I don't think he wants me to know. He's very proud of being able to do that job."

"They don't wanta know about things like that, Ellen. Even when you're that close they tell you almost anythin', they don't wanta know. It's like bein' frightened; they don't wanta know about that either. They think that's a woman's thing."

"Did you . . . do you . . . get frightened still?" Ellen watched Rita Rosario's face carefully. She wanted the truth from this powerful, comforting woman.

Mrs. Rosario shrugged. "I worry still, wouldn't be natural not to in weather like this. There's my son in that boat. Of course I worry. But don't get real scared till bad news come. You'll wear yourself down that way. But of course you gotta worry. It's part of you. And that's a thing people don't understand unless they been with fishin'."

"I don't think my parents understand. They like Jonathan and they know it can be dangerous. But I don't think they try to think what it must be really like." Ellen frowned at the accusation, which was also of herself. She hadn't thought about it very much either until this day.

"They should have a man come home from the sea. They'd understand. Mind you, the men don't understand too well either, sometimes. I remember once, Peter was late coming back after bad weather. His boat came in with some others and when they'd done with landin' he just

went down to the club with the crew. Never rang me nor
nothin'. I just happened to see those two Novello boys
drivin' past and I knew they'd been out in another boat on
Georges that week. Well, I started to walk up and down
this kitchen and I got in such a state I didn't dare ring
Novellos' to find out if they knew anything about Peter's
boat. Carlo was sick that day, I remember, I couldn't go
out either. Hour later Peter walks in, never says nothin'.
Walks right over to that chair and starts takin' his boots
off. Then he opens his mouth: 'You got any coffee on?' he
says. I didn't know whether to hug him or hit him."

Mrs. Rosario paused and drew in breath, slowly, deeply.
Her head was nodding gently to herself, as a lot of
memories went by. Ellen watched and said nothing. The
widow consciously straightened her back and shrugged
her shoulders again.

"But we take care of each other, you know," Mrs.
Rosario said. "Fishin' people, I mean. I remember when
Peter lost his first boat. Hit Parson's Reef out there in a
fog. I got woke that mornin' with the phone ringin'. Six
o'clock in the mornin' and the phone rings. I picked it up
and the caller put it down. So I got out of bed and I looked
out the window and there it was, all that fog. A half hour
later phone rings again. I picked it up and a woman at the
other end said 'Hello' before I had time to answer. When I
answered she put it down. I got real panicky then, 'cos I
knew what those phone calls were. They was women from
the other crewmen who knew the boat had gone. They was
checkin' up to see if Peter had come home safe and they
didn't want to risk frightenin' me case he hadn't. I didn't
know the boat had gone then, but I knew when they rang
somethin' was wrong. But it was all right. They all got off
safe. And the insurance was good about it."

Ellen looked past the widow, at wrought-iron gondolas
sailing across the kitchen wall. "There's nothing you can

do, really, except wait, is there? I mean, there's nobody you can find out about anything from?"

"No, there ain't much you can do. You can say your prayers, if you've a mind to. Helps some, don't help others. Best thing is to keep doin' things to take your mind off it. Even so, you get awful fidgety when you're alone." Mrs. Rosario drew another breath, decisively this time. She got up and walked over to a chest of drawers near the fireplace. When she turned round she was dangling from her hand a collection of beads strung together on a yellow thread; each was twice as large as a pea, shiny and brown. She saw the girl stir, quickly on guard, and shook her head at Ellen with a mocking twitch at the corner of her mouth.

"No honey, 'tain't a rosary. I'm not aiming for to bring you to the Church. A person's religion is their own affair and an awful lot of folk go to church who don't have too much religion."

She held the beads up to the light, and Ellen's eyes changed from wary to surprised as the brown spheres were transformed into a lighter shade that glowed. "Pretty ain't they?" said Rita Rosario. "Supposed to be amber. Came from the Old Country. You know, some folks there wander around with these things in their hands all the time, and they ain't all a-thinkin' of the Mysteries when they're doin' it. They reckon it helps 'em to stop frettin' about things." She dropped the worry beads into Ellen's lap. "You have 'em and see if they help. No . . ." — she held up a hand to stifle the girl's protest — "I ain't got no use for 'em. Rosary keeps me occupied when I need. And Carlo don't look like gettin' hisself a regular girl yet awhile. So you take 'em for if there's another day like this."

Ellen rose, her eyes gleaming, a lump in her throat. "Mrs. Rosario, thank you, you've been terribly kind. I think I'd better go now. Mother will be waiting for the supper things. Thank you. If I . . ."

"You drop by any time, Ellen. You come here any time. You'll be welcome. I guess you're fishin' folk now."

The girl blushed, then leaned forward awkwardly and embraced the older woman. Rita Rosario's body did not yield to this clasp: she allowed it to happen, but smiled at the girl when Ellen straightened back. And, at the door, she blew her nose loudly as she waved her visitor away. As Ellen walked down to the car, a gust of wind took her hair across her face and billowed out her skirt. Thick, dark clouds were scudding across the sky. But she no longer felt the oppressive fear of being alone.

When Jonathan awoke next morning, he was being rolled across his bunk and came up against the sideboard hard enough to make him gasp at the impact, though his body had moved no more than a foot. In the fuddle of his awakening he felt as though he was falling through space, and would, in fact, have shot straight out into the aisle between the bunks if it had not been for the board, which rose just above the level of his sleeping head. He clutched at the board and levered himself up so that he could see over the top, his full length pressed against it with the force of gravity. His bewildered eyes took in two things when he looked down: Yank's sleeping form in the bottom bunk across, twisted into an S, with the feet jammed against his own sideboard and his shoulders against the cabin wall; and the drawers that were normally shut into the undersides of the bottom bunks, now wide open and meeting in the middle of the aisle, without space between. Jonathan took this in at a glance, felt his stomach turn as he began to fall through space again, the opposite way this time, and was rolled violently back the way he had come, to slam hard against the bulkhead which separated him from the sea. Something seethed viciously by his head. He struggled up again to look out of the porthole. He saw nothing but water, bubbling past the thick glass, and could not understand how this could be. He blinked at it, astonished, trying to work it out. Then the bunk began to turn through space again and slowly the porthole rose above the surface of the sea, so that the glass now streamed with pouring water, opaquely hinting at brighter light beyond. As Jonathan began to roll away from it, he stuck out left leg and right elbow and held himself in the middle of his bunk, so that it seemed to revolve around him.

And suddenly he felt sweat break through his skin, nausea in the pit of his guts. It dawned on him what the Boat had just done. It had rolled over so far, twice, that the portholes had been submerged, first to starboard, then to port. Those portholes were but three feet or so from the level of the fo'c'sle, nearly six feet higher than the working deck aft. It meant that the Boat had come very close to lying on her side.

Panic-stricken, Jonathan lay there braced against the sides of his bunk, waiting for catastrophe to strike. His eyes were focused on the light fixture above his head, a stable thing in a disintegrating world. He knew he would stay like this while it happened, for he knew of nothing else to do. He felt horribly alone, abandoned in a tomb. Jesus Christ, he thought, please. . . .

The Boat began to roll again to port and Jonathan held his breath, ready for that roll to go on without end, until he was pitched into the ceiling and the electric cooker broke away from its rivets and everyone and everything aboard was flung into a nightmare heap that the sea would swamp as it rushed in through the stove-in glass. . . . But this time the Boat did not roll quite so far as before; as she steadied, Jonathan's head turned to the porthole and he saw white-flecked waves sweeping past, just below the level of his eyes. His breath rushed out and his sweat went cold, the nausea still had him in the guts. He lay there for a long time, not wishing, not daring to move voluntarily, while his body was jerked sideways with the rolls, while his feet and then his head seesawed alternately above each other in response to the pitching of the hull.

He tried to follow the pattern of the Boat's motions, but they were crazy and without regular shape. And all the time the sound of massive power bludgeoning at this hollow thing of steel. The world boomed and clanged and rumbled; and outside, just beyond that thin steel sheath, the vastness of the ocean incessantly seethed.

No one else in the bunk room showed any signs of life for an hour or more, though it had been eight o'clock when Jonathan awoke. But eventually he heard a curse below him as Big Boy struggled to his feet amid the jumble of clothing and drawers filling the deck between the bunks. The fisherman carefully climbed out of this mess, hauling himself along to the doorway, where he paused as the Boat pitched forward, and leaned against one upright, his arm braced against the other, all his energy concentrated on the effort of standing in one place. He waited till the bows began to rise again, then disappeared in the direction of the wheelhouse stairs.

A little later Jonathan heard the Skipper come below and go into the cabin next door, for his first sleep in almost thirty hours. Big Boy then came down, his fatness vibrating beneath the tightness of undershirt and longjohns, and reached for more clothes from his disordered drawer. He caught Jonathan's eye as he lurched through the door. "Fuckin' seas out there like the world's comin' after ya," he croaked. "We ain't goin' nowheres today, that's for fuckin' sure."

"What are we going to do?" asked Jonathan.

Big Boy did not hear the anxiety in his voice, or understand the drift of what he asked. "Two hours on watch," he replied. "Rest of the time where you are right now, old buddy. Only place to be in a motherfucker like this." For the first time since Jonathan had known him, Big Boy sounded tense. He clawed his way out of the bunk room again. Jonathan heard the door of the refrigerator open, a crash as something hit the deck, a curse, the slam of the refrigerator door. It was to be another familiar sound inside their clamorous drum over the next two days. Jonathan badly wanted something to drink, for his mouth was tacky and sour. But he did not dare move from where he was, for fear that he would be sick. He lay there, spending his strength on staying put in his bunk, legs pressed against one side, shoulder against the other, his trunk jerking this way and that as the Boat revolved upon the seas. And he watched the mad careering of water and sky through his small window on a furious world.

He took over Big Boy's watch toward midday, and both hung on to the helmsman's chair while the older man explained what to do. "Only one thing," he shouted in Jonathan's ear. "If anything gets carried away, if one o' these windows cracks or stoves in, you reach for that alarm button and press it fast. And keep goin' down the engine room to check for leaks there. And the forepeak. Don't forget to watch that bilge, mind. If it gets over the beam, turn on the pump and tell me." He nodded, waited for the deck to level off, and made a dash for the stairs.

Jonathan hauled himself into the chair and almost at once was flung out over one of the arms as the Boat rolled deeply to port. He crashed into the wheelhouse side and slumped there, winded, until the next roll tumbled him back toward the chair. When he climbed back into it, he jammed his legs against the dashboard and held on to the chair's arms, rising to his feet for the worst movements of the Boat and taking the strain at his knees.

Jonathan had no idea how high the seas were that came pouring onto them from the west. One moment the Boat was at the crest of the steep, short swell and, from the wheelhouse, it was then like looking down into a disintegrating glacier, full of unfathomable holes and heaving hollows. The next moment, the vessel had plunged down to this glacier floor and was surrounded by hills of water, which hemmed it in and threatened to engulf, their ridges and their peaks being high above the wheelhouse top. All the time, from each ridge and peak, with a separate existence of their own, waves were creaming off in a fury of smashed water that the wind drove horizontally through the air. Spray hissed violently around the Boat, slashing at the wheelhouse windows and hosing down the decks. The windscreen wipers could not keep pace, so that the view ahead was distorted by the sheeting of water down the plated glass. It seemed to Jonathan that they were as helpless out here as a cork in the rapids of a stream. Their engines were off, they lay broadside on to the seas, and one hundred fifty tons of steel, which towered over the fish pier dock at high tide at home, could do nothing but submit to whatever was already writ in the origins of the storm two nights before. The broadside rolling was bad, sometimes tipping the Boat forty-five degrees from the vertical so that Jonathan felt himself sliding out of the chair, in spite of his feet on the deck and although his knuckles were white from gripping the padded arms. But the rolling was not the worst thing of all. Much worse was the way the Boat shuddered with a sideways jerk, when she had failed to ride one swell before its successor struck at a different point. Sometimes she was jarred, like a car that had hit a curb. And sometimes she whirled around dizzily on a confluence of waters, shaking herself one way and then another. This was the worst thing of all, for then the young man sensed how easily the ocean was toying with its prey. Biding its time.

He climbed out of the chair after a while, tired of the

strain and the buffeting from side to side. But he held on
to it, like a child learning to walk, not daring to let go while
he turned round to look astern. That was where the
greatest danger lay, across the low, wide, open-ended
deck, built so that lobster traps could pour off into the sea:
and where the sea could itself rush aboard with crushing
weight and power if the Boat's back was turned and the
moment was terribly right. It only needed a maverick
swell, one that had cut loose from the regular running of
the pack, to hit them in the bows and swing the Boat
stern-to; the pack would do the rest. The Atlantic would
come aboard across that open stern, a wall of water would
collapse upon the wheelhouse and, long before Jonathan
could reach for the alarm, the Boat would be pressed
down to the bottom of the sea. He gulped as he remembered the *Zubenelgenubi,* a deep-sea lobsterman like them
that had vanished last winter on her maiden voyage, with
only an oil slick over eighty fathoms on Georges Bank to
suggest where she had gone. Some fishermen in the Town
believed she had been run down by a Russian or other
foreign boat and bitterly stuck labels on their cars in mock
Cyrillic script — *Beware Crashboats* — to chide authority,
which they thought diplomatically blind. But others said it
was simply a running sea from astern that had pooped the
lobster boat and taken four men with her. Jonathan
watched the swells surging in upon the starboard beam.
Every so often a wave, toppling down the smooth hill of
the swell, swept over the rail where yesterday he had stood
pulling lobsters from the traps, and poured across the
deck to the other side. When this happened, he thought he
could feel the Boat sink back upon her heels, wallowing
there for a moment before springing up again with the lift
of some force from below.

Jonathan had not been sick by the time Yank took over
the watch, but he felt faint from lack of food he knew he

dare not touch. As he lowered himself carefully down the
ladder to the galley, one rung at a time, he wished only to
reach his bunk and there to be anesthetized from all
knowledge of the raging sea. When he got to the bunk
room, Carlo was curled like a fetus, evidently fast asleep.
Big Boy was wedged between pillows and rolled blankets,
reading a magazine by the buttery light of his bunk-head
lamp. He was deep in an article entitled "Protect Yourself
and Your Lover against Those Debilitating Anxiety At-
tacks," and he was scratching his balls as Jonathan clambered past. Even glancing at that page made the young
man feel more queasy; he didn't know how anyone could
possibly read with the world swirling in every direction
around the type.

He had hoped to fall asleep at once but instead lay there
weakly, trying to hold his body so that it would not bang
against the sides of his bunk. Occasionally he dozed, but
then the Boat would slide sideways into one of its deepest
rolls and Jonathan would wake and look at the porthole
and go tense as it plunged beneath the surface. He held a
deep breath when this happened and only released it
when his head rose again above the waves. He was in a
doze when Carlo got out of his bunk and went to make a
sandwich. Sound of refrigerator door opening; crash as a
carton of eggs shot out and burst on the deck. Jonathan
awoke. Then a headaching descent into sleep.

Some movement of the Boat pulled him into semi-
consciousness again and, almost at once, a tremendous
crash startled him into life. Big Boy and Yank were
struggling out of their bunks, their heads turned toward
the door, their eyes straining to see something beyond, the
sound of splintering wood and smashing things out there.
Jonathan was only half out of his bunk by the time the
others were through the door. He banged his head against
the sideboard as he trod through the debris in the aisle

and stood dazed a moment by the shackled-open door. The cupboard containing all their dry supplies had torn itself away from the starboard bulkhead of the galley and lay in pieces across the deck, in a confusion of paperbacks, aerosol sprays, medicines, paper cups, towels, tinned foods, and odds and ends of junk. Jonathan felt his heart slow down again; it had leaped, as his body had leaped, and it had seemed to lodge at bursting point in the dry recesses of his throat. It took the three of them over an hour to clear up the mess. One hand for holding onto a stability while the other hand mopped or picked or pushed. Feet stuttering like a tapdancers' to stay balanced whenever you came upright. Mad exhilaration when the deck suddenly dropped beneath you, and you went bounding across the galley as though it were a trampoline. But mostly just holding onto something, and being swung away from it, till you were clinging at arm's length with bruised ribs where something hard had stopped an inevitable fall.

The weather didn't get worse. It stayed the same. And in the middle of the night the forecasters changed their opinion about the movement of the storm. After roaring up the Atlantic seaboard for days, it had now come to a standstill two hundred miles offshore, its center just over the horizon from the Boat. So far as the meteorologists could tell, it would stay there for some time; they held out no hope of an improvement for two or three days at least.

Big Boy was on watch when this bulletin was announced. He had just turned down the radio again when the Boat lurched to starboard. It was steeply tilted when a swell, following its predecessor closer than usual, shed a huge wave smack on the fo'c'sle. Big Boy flung an arm across his face in startled reflex as he saw the bows disappear and sea rush toward the wheelhouse glass. It arrived with a monstrous thud and the Boat shuddered at the impact.

After the thud a sound of pouring water all around, almost deafening, yet Big Boy was curiously aware of the quiet bubble and trickle of the water as it seeped through the sealed edges of the wheelhouse doors. As the sea dropped back, its level descended the windscreen, so that Big Boy seemed to be looking into the draining of an aquarium tank. The Boat rose pointed then, its bows thrust high in the air. Looking through the cleared glass, Big Boy saw that something was different now. The harpoon had gone, together with the tub of line; and the starboard rail had been wrenched and buckled along the top. He heard a footstep on the ladder and a voice behind him said, "We just lost somethin'?" The Skipper came into the wheelhouse, balancing himself on the balls of his feet. Big Boy pointed to the misshapen metal in the bows. The Skipper nodded grimly. "Yeah. Heard it go. Thought it might have taken a plate." They watched another wave hit, a little lower this time. Each man was standing at either side of the chair, holding onto the dashboard top. As the Boat leaned sideways again, both Big Boy and the Skipper moved their left legs out along the lowering deck, bent their right knees to take the rising thrust of the starboard side: they did this in perfect unity, like two ballet dancers practicing at the barre.

Big Boy told his captain of the weather report, and the younger man swore under his breath. "Two days minimum before it shifts? Ya. Ya. Ya-ya-ya-ya-ya-ya-ya." He stroked the stubble on his chin. "Ain't much point stickin' around in this. Be another day on top of that before it settled enough to fish. See what they say in the forenoon. If it ain't goin' to get better before Saturday, we'd best get the hell out."

It was much the same by 11 A.M., when the meteorologists were venturing to predict an even longer standstill in the storm. It might be as much as four days, in their view,

before any improvement could be expected in the area of
the Boat. The Skipper was in the wheelhouse alone when
the report was broadcast and, switching the radio off when
it was done, he went straight down to the bunk room.
"Okay, let's get that bait salted down," he called to the
others. "Then let's go home, for Chrissake."

The five of them got into oilskins and boots and thick
thermal gloves, and manhandled two sacks of salt from the
forepeak to the sea-door by the bottom of the wheelhouse
stairs. When the Boat rose for'ard, Carlo banged off the
clamps of the massive steel door and swung out with it
onto the deck, holding it open while the others stumbled
over the coaming with the sacks, then swung it shut again
instantly and clamped it from the outside. The Boat was
secure again, though its crew was now totally exposed.
They paused there, hanging on to winch, door, hatch top,
and each other, while the vessel pitched back and rolled
over to port, and the wind howled coldly about them,
tearing at their hoods and plucking at their cheeks. The
deck steadied for a moment and they dashed like a rabble
for the starboard rail, where they had lashed down the oil
drums of unused bait at the end of their long working day.
There was enough gurry left for a week's fishing and, by
pouring salt into each drum, they might preserve it for
another trip. Tarpaulin had been tied tightly atop each
drum and the long, heavy weights that held the two ends
of a trawl line on the seabed had been secured to the tarps:
but the canvas was flapping wildly on three of the drums
and four weights had disappeared.

The men worked hurriedly, to have done with it,
ducking their heads to take the spray on their hooded
necks, handling two drums at a time, one man flinging
handfuls of salt onto the bait while his partner held him
with one arm and clung to a lashing or a stanchion at the
rail with his other. The Skipper moved alone, tying down

the tarpaulins and the weights when each drum was filled. Thrice someone lost his footing and went flat upon the deck. Once the wind drove under a tarpaulin that was slattering like a slackened sail, billowed it up and took Yank, who was holding an end rope, a foot or more into the air.

Jonathan, who was shoveling salt with Carlo's bearhug round his waist, finished a drum and looked up, ready for the next one. As his head turned toward the bows he froze and his jaw dropped open. He was about to say "Christ!" but the word would not form. The wheelhouse was high above his head; and there, high above the wheelhouse and just beyond it, was an overhanging precipice of gray water, with ribs and gullies and gleaming slopes flecked with white; and another precipice, just as huge, crowding in to port. Jonathan could not have moved a muscle even if he had known in what way to move it. He was transfixed as he waited for those two mountains to fall upon the Boat. Instead, suddenly, the vessel rose like a rocket to the mountaintop ahead, swayed there drunkenly, and slid down the other side while water poured over the five men in long thin sheets and the deck gyrated through a score of angles between the horizontal and the vertical. Only Carlo was still standing when the Boat had calmed down again. Big Boy was rising from the scuppers with an ashen face and blood on his chin, Yank full-length beside him, holding his back in pain. Jonathan was slumped over the drum he had just finished, retching for air which had been driven out of him by the blow across his stomach. The Skipper was beyond the drums, three-quarters of the way to the stern, on badly bruised knees and clinging frantically to a loose rope from the rail which alone had stopped his somersault straight off the end of the Boat. Slowly, and very unsteadily, they picked themselves up. Without a word, they finished what they were doing.

Within the hour, they were clamped inside the shelter of the Boat. The Skipper started his engines and brought the nose of his vessel round from the south, where it had pointed for a night, a day, another night and half another day. In all that time, lying there broadside on to the pounding sea, its heading had veered by no more than twenty degrees. The Boat bucked desperately as its head now came round into the storm, as it finished its turn and moved at last to the northwest. Down below, where the four deckhands were collapsed in their bunks, the hollow steel thing still echoed with clangs and rumbles and booms; but now there was also the chattering vibration from the diesels. Once under way, the awful rolling from side to side was lessened. Not by much; but by enough to reduce the drowning of the porthole glass to few and far between. It was the pitching that became bad now, so that a man lying full length was looking up at his feet one minute, down at them the next. But that was not as hard a thing to take as the rolling, it did not sap a man of energy, for he did not need to lie in the perpetual tension of trying to stop himself banging into the sides of his bunk.

For twenty-nine hours the Boat pitched her way toward the land, through the somber tumult of the sea. Clouds streamed low in the sky, but there were blue gaps and occasional shafts of pallid sunlight. Once or twice a fulmar wheeled through the air near this alien, struggling thing, and on Jonathan's forenoon watch next day, a whale's mighty back broke surface a hundred yards away. Best leave the sea to the whales, he thought; it don't worry them at all. He wanted to be home now, in the safety of the land. He was more anxious than he had been when they were laid-to, fearful lest something should happen to snatch away his safety when it was almost within reach. He watched the big seas more carefully, eyed the alarm button more often, kept glancing over his shoulder to see if they were pursued by malignant force astern. But the weather never changed; the seas neither rose nor fell. They simply battered at the Boat, pushed it and shoved it about, lifted it up and sucked it down as before: then let it pass to the comfort of the shore.

Jonathan had been home half an hour or so when the telephone rang. He had been sitting in a daze since coming in, unable to adjust to the stillness of the room. He swayed as he got up and went to the receiver in the hall. "Jonathan? Are you all right?"

It was a moment before he focused Ellen's voice. "Oh, hi! Yeah." He paused and steadied himself against the reeling wall. "Yeah, I'm okay."

Silence down the line, which Ellen needed to break. "I have to go into town. Can I drop by for a minute?"

Jonathan tried to think, mumbling to himself; he'd done a lot of that these past few days, up there in the wheelhouse, trembling before the sea. "Yeah, sure come round. Only me here. Mom's out someplace."

On the doorstep she found herself looking at someone changed. Jonathan's eagerness, his nervy boyishness were gone. This was a quiet person with tired eyes, who seemed in no hurry with himself; for one split second, she thought he was going to hold out his hand to shake hers. He stood there, looking at her, smiled faintly, then opened the door wider and inclined his head a fraction. "Come in," he said, "it's good to see ya."

He led the way into the front room and went straight to the deepest chair, barely indicating that she should take the chair opposite, on the other side of the fireplace. Before, he had always steered her toward the settee and sat closer than she sometimes wished. "Just got in," he said, his eyes on the artificial coals.

"I know. I saw Carlo drop you off." She was sitting on
the edge of her chair, uneasy, wondering what to say. That
had never been a problem for her with Jonathan before.
She broke another silence. "Was it bad? The trip?"

"Pretty bad. We got one day's fishin'. And they were
banged up so rotten in the tank, half of 'em were useless
when we got to the mart." He looked her in the eye for the
first time. "Do you know how much we made? Fifty-six
bucks. Every man made fifty-six bucks." He turned to the
fire again. He was shaking his head, as though he didn't
understand something profound. His face was rough with
a week's beard, and the sourness of his body was drawn
into the room by the warmth of the fire. It must have been
too bad even to have a shower, thought Ellen. There was a
small cabinet in the washplace next to the sea-door, she
knew; Jonathan had shown it to her the day he took her
aboard the Boat.

"That's awful, Jonathan. All that work for fifty-six
bucks." She wanted to touch him, to take the hurt of it
away. But she sat still on the edge of her chair. "The next
trip's bound to be better. The weather's not as bad today."

He grunted. He was plucking at an eyebrow, looking
past Ellen through the window, seeing spray hiss down in
sheets of icy shrapnel.

"Mrs. Rosario said you mustn't expect the worst to
happen. You've had such terrible luck lately, it can't go on
like this. It's bound to improve now."

"What would she know about it? She's never been out
there."

Ellen was startled by the cutting edge of anger in his
voice. She was about to say that Rita Rosario knew an awful
lot about the sea, but stopped. Jonathan had started to
tremble and his throat was moving as though he was trying
to swallow something stuck. His head had turned side-

ways, away from her. He could feel the nausea again, and the burning of the broken skin where he had been flung across the bait drum.

"Jonathan?" He heard her voice low, little more than a whisper. He felt her gentleness, though he did not see the tears that had come to her eyes. He was watching a mountain of sea about to fall onto the deck and his heart was bursting to free itself from a life that might end in an instant. He shuddered and a hand went to his face, trying to hold it still, trying to hide it from her. His whole body had turned sideways and his legs were pressed together. He was neither the eager youth nor the withdrawn adult now. Ellen heard a sound that a man had never made in her presence before, a gulping sob and a hiccuping of cries. Jonathan's shoulders began to shake and his hand was clamped over his mouth to stifle his noise.

She came out of her chair urgently and she crossed the space between them awkwardly on her knees. As she reached for his head, he held himself tightly, trying not to give way, but she pulled him fiercely to her and, for a moment, she felt his resolution go. "Baby, baby," she murmured, "please don't cry. I won't let you go again." She was with him, and not with him, in some distant past besides. But he would not let her take him now. His face jerked up, wet and ugly with shame. He pushed her off and clambered to his feet, coughing out hoarse words that were scarcely intelligible. Then he was away from her and out of the room, and she heard the outside door open and bang shut. His steps beating down the path beyond. She knelt there, at a loss, as once before. But this time she was not empty.

WINTER

BEFORE THE WINTER seals New England under ice and snow, there is a last surge of people up and down the land. The winter sportsmen thereafter break the seal alone, in resorts considerably arranged to incite their extravagant skills in slalom, jump, and apres-ski. But for a week or two between the dying fall and the winter's time, Everyman takes to the inland hills and forests with a gun for the perennial rite of shooting it out with the beasts. This brave moment is itself preceded by inordinate business at the emporium of L. L. Bean, whose singular boast it is to be open for 24 hours on 365 days in the year. There, in an enormous wooden shack on a byroad in Maine, Everyman can equip himself with hunting boots, bowie knives, Havahart Animal Traps, and other incidentals of carnage (not excluding Royal Coachmen, Black Ghosts, Gray Hackles and the rest of the fly-fishing range). L. L. Bean will supply almost anything from a canoe to a snowshoe, by way of maple syrup and a wood-burning stove. There is thus, at this season, a final rush of traffic up to the emporium in Maine, led by husky fellows seeking tartan shirts, mackinaws, and other rugged accoutrements as they make their preparations for the field. Then the beloved land hears the crack of gunshot, feels the puddles of blood, and the traffic of hunters rushes south again. A station wagon bowls triumphantly home to Concord with a buck lashed upon the roof, its horns curved toward the sky, its eyeballs dulled with a coating of dust, its tongue hanging down over the road, its last evacuation dry-staining its legs, a red-rimmed hole at the base of its neck. The driver and his pals belong to an army of 140,000 who have been let loose for sixteen days to produce (among more deadly things) a license revenue of twenty million dollars. In beautiful Vermont of all places on earth, in Vermont alone in one weekend, 4,500 deer have been shot in their tracks. And New England has three other hunting states besides Vermont.

Some carcasses found their way to the Town that year; others would have done so if more townsfolk had been able to exercise their instinct and their will. Carlo, for one, had a gun which he prized but which was mostly dis-charged in harmless skeet shooting on the edge of the Common whenever he was at home. He was invited to join two hunters on the deadliest weekend of all, but missed this particular display of his manhood because the Boat, having spent part of it during another rough trip, came back from Georges two days later than planned. Big Boy was even more put out by the delay, having hopefully acquired tickets for a belly-dancing show in an otherwise unspectacular little town some miles inland from the coast. If you went fishing, social life often fell apart like that. And, at this season above all others, the fishing boats of the Town put out whenever they could, knowing that when winter settled in there would be far too many days of being bound to the land. But no one had expected such a winter as the one that fell that year.

Its onset was first marked, as it was every year, down in the harbor. A lot of the pleasure craft had been removed at the beginning of the fall but many of the bigger boats remained and protective measures were now taken for these at the yacht basins. Huge launches, the waterborne Cadillacs of the playpeople, were craned out of the water and placed on cradles ashore. Wooden frames were then constructed over their decks, as beams and battens are in the roofing of a house. Over these were stretched plastic sheets, followed by heavy tarpaulins which, tightened and tethered somewhere in the region of the keels, covered every inch of the immaculate hulls. When the work was done, the launches lay high and dry, like whales stranded in formation on a beach. Only a few smaller fry were left to make what shift they might upon the exposed surface of the harbor. It was the beginning of December and, next day, the temperature dropped like a stone.

Overnight there were 28 degrees of frost; 50 degrees if you counted the wind-chill factor, which mattered as much as simple cold to anything out in the open air. In the conversations of the Town for three months and more to come, this phrase would be employed to describe a savage product of the wind, which dropped the temperature of anything in its path another two degrees for every mile per hour it blew. In winter the Town was perpetually chilled by wind, which swept up the harbor from the sea and rammed intense cold into every corner of the land. It was this which, as some people said, made your toes freeze up to your haircut. It made the eyes run, then left the tears crusty at the corners of the eyes. None of the words usually employed to describe intense cold in a nominally temperate zone were quite adequate to deal with it. This cold had the ultimately numbing power that obliterates all sensation and even the ability to think.

There were lines of cars at the gas stations the day the cold came, all demanding a special antifreeze mixture for their fuel systems, to stop ice forming in the pipes and tanks. Henceforth, every car trailed a long jet of steam, whether stationary or moving fast, as hot air from the exhausts was instantly vaporized by contact with the cold outside. A new sound was to be heard every day, when cars were started up after the night: as the driver slipped it into gear there was crunching and fracturing underneath, which was the sound of icicles being displaced from all the slowly moving parts. This was echoed by the sound of people climbing wooden steps to their hillside homes around the harbor, a creaking and cracking as their weight went on each step, though they were not yet treading on ice itself; that was to come a little later, after the first snow had fallen. It was frost and nothing more, at the start of December, that had suddenly made winter as keen as a butcher's knife. It was frost, intense cold alone, that one morning started the great freeze-up of the harbor. This began between the pontoons of the Pier 7 yacht basin, no more than a thin layer of ice in small, irregular segments with creases separating each, so that it resembled the pattern of a snakeskin. Daily, from now on, the line of ice advanced down the inner harbor and thickened as it went. Presently, at low tides, the piles of the wharves there were rimmed with ice at their high-water marks; almost all were tree trunks, sometimes still knobbed where their branches had been, their rotted dark shapes now picked out in white. Presently, too, the ice between the pontoons and for a little distance beyond acquired a rippled surface, as if waves had been frozen in the act. One morning, the yacht basin's own launch began to maneuver back and forth, to break up the ice around the frozen berths and to preserve some sort of passage into open water toward the Neck. It did this not by going headlong with its bows, but by running gently astern. When the pressure brought it to a stop the engine was gunned to produce a convulsion under the stern, this shattering the surface into mush and tiny floes. Yet, by nightfall, the frost had taken the ice edge another twenty yards down the harbor. In the narrow places between the pontoons, the opaque ripples of the morning had been transformed into a crystallized white, in spite of the day's watery sun.

Then sixteen inches of snow fell in one night and the Town came to a standstill for the whole of one day. The people in the hillside homes woke to find straight chutes of snow descending from their verandas to the street, where before had been long flights of wooden steps. Below these, where cars had been parked, were white mounds, as if giant moles had been burrowing across a snowfield in the dark. That forenoon was abrasive with the scrape of shovels on ground as the population started to dig itself out. City Hall mustered trucks with bulldozer blades up front and the angular clearing of the streets began, though not for the welfare of pedestrians, whose sidewalks were now piled even higher with snow. Otherwise, nothing much moved very far from home. No longer did the gulls wheel in squadrons over the harbor, nor did they line the rooftops anymore. They squatted on the ice, where it met the water, and they huddled in flocks to preserve some mutual warmth. But the wind coming up from the sea made that hard for anything alive. It also created the illusion that half the Town was on fire, gusting powdered snow from the rooftops to eddy like smoke in the air.

This was but the beginning. The townsfolk had barely cleared their streets and excavated their cars and resumed their patterns of life before another great snowfall came.

Whereupon they had to start all over again. And would proceed in this half-beleaguered fashion until February was past and March was nearly through and North America in general was trying to make up its mind whether it had just endured the most awful winter in creation, or merely the worst one since the white man came. One snowfall followed another but nothing thawed in between so that, before long, all traces of the earth disappeared and all the roads vanished beneath a rising layer of hard compacted white. The Stop & Shop and the other supermarkets sold bags of rock salt by the ton. There was a clamor for sticks with a brush at one end, a scraper at the other, with which to clear car windows at the start of each day; and at times in between, as often as not.

The rhythm of life changed as winter's seal began to set. On days of blizzard, when neighbors lost sight of each other's homes, the Town became still and dark with thought; or simply sat tight beside the television and heard the tale of other people's woes. But there were clear days, which were most beautiful as the sun began to set, bringing out the pastel shades of clapboard walls and transforming snow heaps into gentle mauves and pinks. On such days people drove slowly along the frozen roads to the icy quarries on the Cape and to the ponds a little way inland. There, in multitudes from many towns, skaters skimmed and swayed, in a bobble of scarves and woolen hats; eternal New England by Currier and Ives.

Few people walked anywhere and no one cycled now. The postman, doing his round at the top of the harbor, descended from his jeep, pulled tight his fur-flapped gray hat, and went from one house to another at a slow shuffle, never allowing his legs to go too wide apart; he moved like a trembly old man, afraid of the harsh world he inhabited. He was almost the only intruder to venture past the portals of the Point, once the snowfalls began. The "No Trespassing" signs there became redundant the moment icicles began to obscure them, as soon as the drifts buried half their poles. The inhabitants no longer needed a home-made law and wealth to insulate them from the mob, for the winter performed this service free of charge.

Fishing boats now returned to the Town with ice gleaming thick around the stays of their masts and slithering down from upturned dories on the wheelhouse tops; and some came home with ice hanging out of the scuppers in wide and rounded gushes petrified by the cold. They had slush on their decks and their crews did not leave the warmth of cabins and wheelhouse until the very last moment before berthing. The mooring ropes were dragged out of cabins, too, and each man's breath produced small fog banks over his head as he strove to wind hemp around a frozen cleat. The boats were finding it less and less easy to get to their berths as the ice formed down the harbor. First it traveled slowly from the waste-land and the yacht basin, in two sheets separated by the fish pier. When these had met beyond the pier and formed a single line of advance, they were joined by a third tract which issued from the left, coming from the landlocked cove behind the Neck.

By January this ice was so thickly formed in a great arc — barring the way to the inner harbor and cove alike — that the coast guard summoned an icebreaker to smash a passage through.

It was a small, black, butty vessel, graceless as a bulldog, but mightily effective for its size. It had a curious curve at the chine of the bows, so that these rode up onto the ice and crushed it under the weight of the boat itself. In this fashion the breaker barged its way up the inner harbor's arms, circling slowly then backing with great turmoil, so that floes created by the first impact tilted lazily and slipped out of sight, to rise gently a few feet away, less ominous than before. But, within a day or two, the ice up there was as hard and fast as before the breaker came. It was, moreover, accelerating downstream. Where it had increased by twenty yards a day, it now secured another fifty. Before the winter was through, it extended almost to the breakwater, two and a half miles away from the top of the Town.

By then, all the coves were icebound, and only the breaker's daily labors maintained an open channel from the wharves down to the sea. Visibly, the breaker was using more power to crush the developing thickness of the ice, rushing at it so fiercely that she pitched as if in rough water when she rode up onto its edge. Once she came to a deliberate standstill in the middle of the field. A large dog had passed over from the fish pier, inquisitive nose to the ice, vainly trying to scent something in the aseptic air. As the breaker stopped almost in its path, a man came out of the wheelhouse and shied something at the dog, to drive it back to the safety of the shore. The animal did not change pace much, but trotted right under the waiting bows and wandered onto land again amid the piles flanking East Main. That afternoon, six hours after the breaker had left, boys were playing ice hockey where the new channel had been. Apart from the main breakout down to the sea, water was to be seen only by Fisherman's Wharf, where most of the boats still working docked. Small rafts of ice floated there and seagulls perched on these, watching men trying to chip ice from stays and shrouds. Many of these boats lay jammed together in the cold, the creaking of their timbers counterpointed by the low, dull, echoing boom of the ice, as the current below made the hulls shift uneasily in the ice's grip. Fenders made from old Firestone tires drooped over bulwarks and were frozen fast below the waterline. Immovable.

More and more boats were coming back from sea and

staying put at the wharves, where they were soon locked into the ice. Fewer and fewer were struggling out to face the high risk of becoming top-heavy with ice in a stormy sea; and the certainty that, even in relative calms, their crews would have to stop work on deck from time to time because of the appalling oceanic cold. A number of larger draggers went up to Nova Scotia in pursuit of cod and haddock. They found fish in plenty, but could not take them for four days out of seven because the conditions up there were so bad. So they came home again, and sold what they had caught for forty cents a pound, which more comfortable landsmen promptly resold for two dollars. This was an ancient grudge among fishermen: that they who faced the hazards and the unpleasantness inseparable from catching deep-sea fish, should be rewarded less than those who sat safely ashore and made profit from the sea, risking nothing but a piece of real estate and the opportunity for gain. It was so ancient a grudge that it was rarely voiced anymore, except in rough weather at sea and in the company of other fishing folk ashore. The custom of the marketplace was so sanctified by age that the landed world would have scoffed at any public plea for an alternative founded in equity. So the fishermen muttered among themselves, but otherwise held their peace.

There were other grudges of more recent origin, however, and on these the fishermen did not hold their tongues. The meeting in City Hall that winter showed the temper of the times. It demonstrated, too, the truth of what Rita Rosario had said to Ellen Fremantle on that tempestuous day in the fall, that the fishing community of the Town was a community apart from the rest. For only they turned up to demonstrate their belonging to the deepest tradition of the Town, which always had been the catching of fish. There was not one citizen who did not boast of this when strangers were about, who did not pronounce himself a guardian of this heritage from the past, who could not tell tales about the old schoonermen and their daring craft. But when the great meeting was held in City Hall, only fishing people were there and people who labored in the fish processing plants ashore. No shopkeepers came, though in their time they had all, one way or another, made a dollar or two out of fish. No commuters were there, though in the office blocks of Boston they liked to think themselves more roguish and more salty than anyone else in sight. None of the artists, none of the poetasters, emerged from the haven of the Neck, though they above all others claimed spiritual kinship with those who fished the sea. Nor did anyone come forth from the sea-girt fastness of the Point.

The great grievance aired that night affected conservation along the entire American Atlantic coast. The fishermen of the Town, however, preferred to see it almost wholly in terms of the foreign boats fishing their traditional grounds. This was, indeed, a problem of great political weight as well as of ecology and economic wealth. Since 1961, when a hundred Russian fishing vessels began to work on Georges Bank, great armadas had crossed the ocean from Europe to tap the wealth of this Atlantic coast. Others had very nearly circumnavigated the globe to get there. For three seasons the Russians had Georges to themselves, watched with great suspicion by the American boats, who at first believed there must be some military threat in this hammer and sickled fleet. There was nothing anyone could do about it, though; at two hundred miles offshore, Georges was well outside the territorial limits of the United States. In 1964, the Russians were joined by Poles and, annually thereafter, more foreigners rolled up from the east. Rumanians were followed by East Germans; Japanese and West Germans came together in 1967; Bulgarians were subsequently pursued by French. By the

1970s, all these nations were fishing what had once been only Yankee waters, together with vessels from South Korea, Cuba, Greece, Spain, and the Republic of Ireland. Their numbers varied from year to year. There were nine hundred fifty of them in 1971, just under eight hundred by 1975, though they never appeared in such quantities at any one time. The most recent surveys made by a vigilant Coast Guard reckoned that at the peak periods of the year — in winter and spring — between two hundred and two hundred fifty alien boats might be working Georges and the adjacent grounds along the continental shelf.

The American fishermen were indisputably at a disadvantage. No boat sailing out of the Town took more than a dozen men as crew; and no larger fishing vessels sailed out of any Atlantic port. Some of the foreigners were gigantic by comparison. That very summer, the West German stern trawler *Mainz* had berthed in the inner harbor to take on fuel and supplies, and dwarfed everything else in sight. Few of the local vessels reached 100 feet from stem to stern, but the German was 285 feet long, so large that she needed a crew of eighty to work her. The foreigners were not often fishing boats in the sense used by the Americans. They caught fish, to be sure, but they also gutted it, filletted it, and deep froze it on board. Sometimes they cooked it and packaged it as well. They were nothing less than small factories and the *Mainz* was built to handle nine hundred tons of fish every day. They sailed from their country of origin and cruised the American grounds for weeks at a time, their holds being emptied when full by cargo vessels at sea, which sailed home with the periodic takings of the fleet, leaving the fleet to fish on. These foreigners were working with an efficiency that Henry Ford would have admired, and in doing so they were leaving Americans some considerable way behind.

They were not simply catching fish to be sold on slabs

after landing from the sea, there to be evaluated eye to eye by the housewives of Europe in a thousand different towns. Nor was this dredging of American waters done merely to provide vast quantities of herring soused and pickled in infinite ways peculiar to the Baltic taste, though that was certainly part of its intent. A great deal of the foreign fishing was not aimed at digestion at all; at least, not directly. Millions of fish caught in these waters would end up as fertilizer and be spread in crumbs over the barren soils of the Ukraine and the poverty-stricken holdings around Wroclaw.

The fashionable environmentalists might see this as the most prodigal misuse of the American sea, but it was not what made the American fishermen most angry. What rankled with them, above all things, was that a proportion of the fish caught by these strangers found its way down American throats. Every week saw the arrival in the Town of a foreign freighter loaded with frozen fish, an occasion that one of the banks on Main Street hailed by hanging out the relevant national flag. Icelanders were the most regular arrivals, bearing fish from their own waters. A vessel often came down from Newfoundland, and the same went for her. But, increasingly, the *Dairyo Maru* or some other boat from Japan offloaded frozen fish at the deep-water berth just by the Neck. "*Sta minga?*" grumbled the locals, as the palleted cargo was swung ashore: and fervently believed that every fish in that hold had been taken on Georges and not in a Japanese sea. Wherever they had come from, one thing was sure. Those fish were not caught by American boats but they were turned into fish sticks in an American plant and would then go all over the U.S.A. in American trucks.

They were a potent force in the life of the Town, those trucks. They were huge, articulated juggernauts, built to carry heavy loads across a continent if need be; as some of them did. Not all of them shouted out their origins as violently as those belonging to Gangloff and Downham of Logansport, Indiana, whose sign was painted in giant italics along the long length of the refrigerated container trailing behind the cab. Other owners were content with neater legends on the cab door, to proclaim the distances they traveled between the New England coast and home. From St. Paul (Minn.) they came and from Amarillo (Tex.); from Sidney (Ohio) and from Bloomer (Wis.); from Rapid City (S. Dak.) and from Sioux City (Iowa); from Russelville (Ark.) and from Denver (Col.); from Eustis (Fla.) and from Montebello (Cal.). They pounded up and down Route 128 every day of the year, menacing all other vehicles with their sheer bulk and speed, occasionally shedding thick slices of tire on the highway and not always noticing their loss. The teamsters who drove them were among the most belligerent of men, who followed only one rule of the road when they were high behind the wheel: to eat up the miles and to tolerate no delay. They had bunks backing the driving seat, for some journeys could take a week. They had air-conditioning, because this continent could be hot. They had CB radios, for a guy had to stay in touch. They were that part of American history that is forever toughly on the move. Their trucks had been constructed to look every inch this part. The cab tops were festooned with a fantasy of colored lights, a silver klaxon or two, an aerial flexing like a whip. Exhaust pipes stood upright to the sky, drums of oil were held by steel hoops in place above the wheels and enormous fuel tanks were slung just above the road. The registration plates of half a dozen states might decorate their fronts — California, Nevada, Wyoming, Mississippi, New York, and Georgia in one deck of colorful cards because, man, there were an awful lot of state lines that you usually had to cross. When they came to the Town, these trucks clogged its narrow streets. Sometimes they lined both sides of the waterfront road as they waited for the fish factories to disgorge. The wasteland above the harbor was rarely without a few and the motors that kept the cargo space cold whirred incessantly there by day and by night. It was these trucks that made the wasteland such a grit-blown place at most times of the year, for the deep treads on their tires gouged wide ruts out of the ground. But now, in winter, the wasteland was an icecap with spindrift of snow, and the ruts were frozen so hard that even the juggernauts were made to bounce over them and lurch. Yet still they came and went, to take the fish the foreigners had caught in such bulk that American seamen could not compete.

A lot of patriotic Americans made good money out of the foreign fish. Others justified themselves by invoking patriotism in a blatant way. In the lobby of the Town House Restaurant an artful notice hung, just before the warm welcome and the bill of fare. It was a diagrammatic representation of many foreign boats familiar these days to the fishermen of Georges Bank: a Russian factory ship, a German trawler, and so on, with details of their capacities, their complements, their power. Above these drawings was a slogan, devised to catch the diner's eye. "The price of fish is going out of sight because these people are fishing out of sight." No one responsible for this propaganda had tried to explain how such a thing might be. Nor did anyone in the Town ever question the assumption it contained. The diners swallowed their pride and forked out for the lobster thermidor (the lobsters had been brought in that day by one of the inshore boats) and grumbled that Uncle Sam should be so weak with the foreigners when he was tough enough in collecting tax.

Government, above all, was the object of the fishermen's rage when they converged upon City Hall through the silent, icy streets. Already this year they had clashed with officials of the Marine Fisheries Service, who had wished to explain how the 200-mile limit would work when it was enforced next spring. But that Monday meeting in the St. Peter's Club had been an unfortunate choice of time and place. Most boats from the Town were out at sea, getting in their last trip before Fiesta. A handful of men had turned up and they stayed only long enough to hear officialdom's preliminary remarks, before denouncing it for ignorance of the working ways of the sea. Then they marched out, leaving the officials stranded comically on the fishermen's own ground.

The winter meeting now was more carefully arranged, in a civic place, in weather so bad that almost every vessel belonging to the Town was bound to the land. On a low stage, the officials sat to pronounce upon the politics of the sea, together with a marine biologist who would feed them his considered facts. A state senator was also there, at whose behest it was not quite clear. They did not look at ease, any of them, as they cleared their throats and prepared to address themselves to the audience in the hall. The meeting at St. Peter's Club had clearly been someone's aberration. City Hall had brought the fishermen out in droves, row after row of them, laughing and joking among themselves, but with eyes that flicked suspiciously over the personnel on stage and were very ready to deride. The Fishermen's Wives had turned out, too, in some strength. Rita Rosario was at the end of one row, black and four-square, unsmiling and upright, whispering strategies in another woman's ear. Just before the meeting began, there came the noise of many feet from the lobby outside; and in tramped more women, clad in white under their winter coats and scarves. These were workers from a fish factory, taking time out from the night shift, for they also had a stake in the politics of the sea: most of them belonged to fishing families, too. As the chairman coughed once more and fiddled with the mike, he knew that this was going to be a difficult meeting. Not one person out there had a face that looked as if it were accustomed to working in committee.

He began laboriously, with a history of the legislation that would make a new deal in the Atlantic fisheries by March 1, and did not fail to mention the work of Sam Favazza in bringing Congress up to scratch. Favazza was a local man who had led the fishermen's lobby for years. He was dying of cancer, as everyone knew, and there was a stir of sympathy down the hall as his name and his work were praised. Everyone recalled the emotional scenes at Favazza's retirement during the week of Fiesta, when he was presented with the pen the President had used to sign the bill that would keep foreign fishing boats two hundred miles from the American shore. The chairman scored a point there, and it kept his audience quiet while he maneuvered into a position that he knew would find no favor in that hall. "The purpose of the law," he said, looking sternly along the sceptical rows, "the purpose of the law, the primary purpose, is conservation." Everyone, he said, had a part to play in that; including American fishermen. That was why quotas had been fixed, to limit the amounts of fish that could be caught by anyone, locals as well as foreigners, so that other fish would be left to breed in peace. This was ABC stuff to those on the stage, but it was like a red rag to the bull-necked men in front of them.

A fisherman rose to his feet and stabbed his finger at the chair. "Look mister," he said, "we keep bein' told that it's us that's been overfishin', but how come you people up there never explain certain things that never happened before the foreigners came?" A roar of approval behind his back and on either side, and his finger waved more pointedly than before. The chairman removed his glasses and sighed. He was about to say that there'd be time for comment from the floor later on, but the fisherman cut him down. "No, mister, you listern to me right now." A mighty roar round the hall at that, the sort that applauds base hits at the bottom of the ninth when a game is tied. "How come you never explain that years ago, before the foreigners came, Memorial Day was the day whiting would strike the bay and you could seine for mackerel right here in the harbor. That all finished when the foreigners came . . ." He flung an arm wide to summon all who sailed the seas with him. ". . . and there isn't a man down here who won't tell you that's the goddamn truth of it." He sat down heavily, to more mighty applause. The women from the factory were cackling with glee. Some were stamping their feet on the floor. The fisherman was barely aware of that for, deep down, he was glad to be out of the firing line. He glared at the stage to see the effect of his first salvo.

The chairman held up his hands and said they'd get nowhere unless they worked to some sort of order. As the hubbub died, he started a careful explanation of how fish moved in mysterious ways, an almighty phenomenon of which the herring was especially part. The seasonal disappearance of whiting from the bay, of mackerel from the harbor, were irrelevant to this evening's work, and he knew that the man who had made the point knew this very well. So far as the chairman could tell, from the faces he was able to identify in that hall, there wasn't a single inshore fisherman present. There wasn't a deep-sea lobsterman, either, because their interests didn't clash with the foreigners, who had long since been banned from shellfishing. He respected fishermen for their virtues of courage and industry, but sometimes he despaired of them, too. They were men of limited vision, he thought, who could see nothing but their own immediate interest, who fought fiercely among themselves when one seemed to threaten another's prosperity, and only made common cause in the face of disaster. Then they could be magnificent, shaming all others with their devotion and their guts, their utter refusal to quit until all hope was long since gone. He'd heard tell that coal miners in West Virginia were the same. But he doubted whether anyone alive was as boneheadedly individualistic as these New England fishing people.

The herring was the biggest issue in sight because the foreigners were after it in quantity, too: it was the foreign threat that had brought these people out in force, as virtually no other subject could have done. Government had divided the American sea into sectors, to ease fishery control of the dwindling stocks, and two of these were the subject of dispute. From Georges Bank south to New Jersey was Area 5Z, in which the American boats were allowed to catch 12,000 tons of fish a year. The adjacent Area 5Y covered the Gulf of Maine, and here the permitted catch was only half as much. The dispute over these areas was twofold. In the first place, foreign boats were granted certain access rights to Area 5Z which they were denied in Area 5Y, the latter being much closer to the coast; and the American seamen were aggrieved that their own larger quota was established in more distant waters, which could be more profitably plundered by foreigners sailing bigger craft than theirs. They were also at odds with government in their conviction that the herring found in the two areas belonged to the same enormous body, which moved from 5Y to 5Z in its migration down the Atlantic coast. The biologists begged to differ, and on their assumption the different quotas were based. They reckoned there were two distinct bodies of herring moving round the ocean, and that the one found in the Gulf of Maine was much smaller than the other, in much greater danger of being wiped out.

The biologist on the stage began patiently to explain these professional theories about the movement of fish, but he was shouted down. "There's no fence around the herring in 5Y," someone called from the floor; and another voice added that the Russians and the Germans were just waiting for the shoals to cross into the area they could fish. The chairman came to his henchman's aid, tried to call the meeting to order again, but another fisherman was now on his feet. "Once we had a bird and butterfly man telling us about fisheries. During the war we had an orange expert inspecting fish . . ." The rest of his anathema against all experts was lost in the noise of cheering him on. Half the fishermen in City Hall were now roaring their own versions of his tirade in the general direction of the stage, the others grinning slyly at the hapless scientist's plight; poor guy didn't have a chance, not on a night like this. The women from the factory had not seen such sport before and were beside themselves with delight, poking each other in the ribs with a shaking of heads at that Joe-Caracciola-well-isn't-he-just-somethin'-else. Rita Rosario, no stranger to this battle-front, allowed herself a twinkle and a softening around the mouth. She guessed the men wouldn't need her weight this time. They had those officials well and truly on the run.

The biologist took a deep breath and decided to let them all blow themselves out. He'd never been in at the deep end before, but he'd been given a few tips from colleagues who had. Play it cool, Johnny, they'd said. Those people won't, but you've got to. They're okay, but they're awful sore, and they'll let it all off at you because they think we're giving the foreigners all the breaks. They don't want to face facts, half of 'em wouldn't know a fact from a superstition if it took 'em by the hand, but you can't tell 'em that straight. You've gotta use your sense of innuendo. And for God's sake, whatever you do, don't lose your cool. They'll bury you.

The biologist was recalling this counsel, word for word, as a priest will recollect his office at the prospect of sin. As an indication of his cool he was leaning back and contemplating the balcony of City Hall, way above the heads of his audience. A sudden drop in the level of noise made him look down again, then glance nervously at the others ranged beside him on the stage. A man had gotten up from his seat halfway down the hall and was advancing on the stage with the tread of someone who might not know when or how to stop. His shoulders were hunched forward under a blue reefer jacket and his eyes were very sharp beneath the peak of his seamen's cap. He looked like an old salt of the most old-fashioned kind; as indeed this Charlie was, having fished the deep seas for more than thirty years, the last dozen of them as skipper of his own seine boat. He was recognized by everyone in the body of the hall, and the uproar had died a little because no one knew what to expect. Charlie was a bit like that — doing his own number; never a man to fit into anyone else's plan. Was he going to punch that biologist on the nose? You never knew with Charlie.

The biologist allowed his eyes to fall from that determined, oncoming face, and decided that the worst was not about to happen. The man's right hand was bunched into a fist, to be sure, but it was trailing a long screed of paper, and no one had ever hit anybody with that. The screed wafted behind Charlie as he came up on the stage and stopped in front of the biologist. He laid it down on the table, propped himself against the table edge with one arm and jabbed a forefinger at the paper with his other. He loomed over the scientist and his eyes threatened violence, but his voice was so quiet that the microphone did not pick it up clearly and all round the hall people said "shshsh" before they strained to hear what he had to say.

"You see those marks," he was saying, "you know what they mean?" It was a rhetorical question, and it was answered with an impatient nod. Charlie had no need to ask a marine biologist if he recognized the reading of a fathometer, a zigzagging line that told what lay between the keel of a boat and the bottom of the sea. Charlie himself marveled, when he was alone in his wheelhouse for hours, looking for fish, at the way science had made things much easier for his people in his own lifetime. He never could figure how the hell the old schoonermen had found fish, with only instinct and a leadline to help them pick up the shoals in their wayward swimming of the sea. God knows it was hard enough even now to find the right patch of ocean in the middle of all that emptiness. But at least, with a fathometer aboard, when you struck fish you knew it for sure; there was no danger of sailing right over them, and ignorantly past. You didn't even have to watch the reading all the time. The fathometer's sharp sound, like a chisel gouging wood, scratched out the hours of loneliness on watch; and deepened when something was there below the boat. That was when the zigzag on the rolling screed of paper thickened into cramped verticals. If a huge body of fish was cruising down below, these verticals were drawn so close that there was no space between. The screed Charlie had laid on the table now was nearly four feet long; and half of it was black with the telltale marks of a mighty shoal, a submarine horde of epic proportions.

"Those marks tell you something, huh?" said Charlie, as the biologist bent over them, fascinated. "Let me tell you something about those marks. We read 'em on Jeffrey's Ledge a few weeks ago. That's in the area where you say there's only fifty-six thousand tons of herring. I say there's at least a hundred thousand tons up there. So what'dya say to that?" He paused and the biologist cleared his throat before starting to reply.

"These are very impressive . . ."

Charlie cut in on him before he could get the rest of the sentence out. "You're goddamn right they're impressive." His voice was rising; not by much, but by enough for him to be heard by the straining ears in the hall. "And I say they're impressive enough to back up my estimates of herring in 5Y. What are ya going to show us to back up your estimates? Nothing? As usual? Where the hell do you people get your figures from? It don't seem to me they come from where I get my figures, and my figures don't come from no laboratory, see. They come from out there, where the fish is." Charlie was breathing heavily, looking along the table at the collection of officials, one by one. The biologist had passed the fathometer reading along and others were scrutinizing it now. Charlie sensed that he had them uncertain of their ground at last. "So what are you going to tell me now? You'd better tell me somethin' different from what you've been saying all this time. First you tell me to go buy myself a boat to go fishin' for herring, because herring's what we need. So I mortgage my house, so I can buy my boat. And when I'm up to here in debt you tell me to quit fishing for herring, to convert that boat to fish for somethin' else. Well, I'll tell you somethin'. I'm not even going to try unless you can give me good reasons why I should." He stopped. He could not think of anything else to say. He was watching the officials shaking heads at each other, mouths quirking in surprise. He was intent on seeing signs of doubt. He did not hear the wave of clapping from the hall behind him.

As this died down, as the audience waited for Charlie's next thrust, murmuring in their anticipation, the state

senator at the end of the platform passed the fathometer
reading back to his neighbor and removed the spectacles
he had put on while he looked at it. "I have to say . . ." and
his voice was not confidential ". . . I have to say that I'll
believe the men out there fishing every day before I'll
believe a government biologist." He carefully did not catch
the biologist's eye, paid no attention to the biologist's
response, but sat watching the front row of fishermen clap
what they had heard, and the rows behind take up this
cue, until the hall was full of applause for this ally in the
enemy's ranks. The senator tapped his dentures delicately
with the tip of his spectacle frame and decided that the
evening had probably been worthwhile after all. It needed
to be in weather like this. Some of his colleagues on
Beacon Hill had thought him a fool to venture forth just to
hear fishermen let off steam on an issue that had long ago
been settled beyond their reach. Fishermen did not figure
highly in the calculations of American politicians, for there
were not enough of them to make much difference to the
vote. The senator, however, had come to office in the first
place by the narrowest of margins and ever since, had
been obsessed with the awful thought that he, too, might
one day be rejected by a failure to cultivate support
wherever and whenever he could. So he had faced this
wintry night with some sense of purpose, even though he
recognized that the two-hundred-mile limit and everything it involved was beyond his intervention and most
certainly not to be altered by any clamor from these people
who, right now, thought they had just spotted Messiah in
City Hall. The Commonwealth of Massachusetts itself
could not do a damn thing to change the statute, with all its
corporate power. Not even Washington was the ultimate
arbiter of these fishermen's fate. That had been slowly and
tortuously settled over a couple of decades by international politicians and public servants perambulating round

the world in an episodic conference on the Law of the Sea. These people were peanuts, and they knew it: only they didn't know that they'd already been roasted.

The biologist, having hastily conferred with his chairman, cleared his throat and tried not to look victimized. The reading they had just been shown, he said, was indeed an extremely impressive one, as he had already conceded. He didn't wish to hold out hopes of something that might not eventuate, but certainly, on the basis of this reading, there was perhaps a case to be made for a careful and structured reappraisal of the herring stocks in Area 5Y. . . .

He got no further. "Attaway, Charlie," shouted someone from the middle rows; and Charlie, looking uncomfortable at this publicity, at last detached himself from the biologist's table, turned and strode back to his seat. People were standing now and clapping him back, others were simply cheering him home. The women from the fish factory rose to their feet and began to file out of the hall, swathing their scarves firmly round their heads again, and a wave of icy air swept in as doors were opened onto the street outside. The senator pointedly put his spectacles into their wallet, got up, and made his way down to a face he distantly recognized in the third row, his right hand coming up to the shake as he approached. All at once, the meeting began to break up, though no one had declared it closed. The officials were shuffling their papers together, looking at watches, relaxing at last. The clapping and cheering died, conversation bubbled up, and only a few people sat still and quiet. Rita Rosario hauled herself to her feet, shaking her head in disbelief. She was wondering why she ever bothered to spend herself so much on behalf of men and women who threw away their advantages so easily. Just one smart-ass politician, that's all it had taken, to get those fisheries people off the hook Charlie had landed them on. There wasn't a man in that hall with the brains to see how they'd all been railroaded, like they'd been railroaded so many times before. They were great tough talkers, but they were as innocent as kids of the tougher world beyond the Town. She moved out of the hall, into the searing night, thinking bleakly of that world beyond which paid no more than lip service to her own.

Next day the deep sea was on everybody's lips and fishermen obliquely reached the international news. Within twenty-four hours the whole of America was speaking of the *Argo Merchant*, of how this oil tanker had gone aground off the New England coast and of how it was beginning to break up in rough seas, pouring its cargo into waters near the great Atlantic fishing grounds. Pollution having become a dirty word in the vocabulary of every well-meaning citizen, the name *Argo Merchant* thus achieved an overnight currency from end to end of the continent.

Its grounding on the Nantucket Shoals was not the only marine disaster along the Atlantic seaboard that winter. On the last day of the old year the captain of another tanker, a Panamanian vessel which a crew of Chinese was sailing from England to Providence, made a distress signal in high seas off Nova Scotia. The ship was never heard from again and thirty-eight men vanished with it, leaving only a patch of oil and two stenciled life jackets to tell where they had gone. The old year had scarcely rounded the corner into the new year before another vessel went down, this time within sight of the Cape. A coastal tanker was sailing in ballast through twenty-five foot seas just seven miles from the Town when she broke in two: one of the crew said later that bows and stern had simply snapped apart like a twig. He was one of five lucky men, rescued by the coast guard which answered the coaster's Mayday call. But a shipmate, one of those stranded on the sinking stern, never saw the land again. The helicopter lowered a metal basket to him and this swung like a pendulum above the heaving stern. As the deck tilted and began to go under, the man made a dive for the basket but missed and was swallowed by the sea. His body was not found although, weeks later, half of that sunken vessel was discovered within a few hundred yards of the breakwater below the Town. The currents were like that round the Cape, swirling strong enough to drag hundreds of tons of metal miles along the sea floor.

Nobody died in the wrecking of the *Argo Merchant*, yet her loss was regarded as a much greater catastrophe by a world which scarcely noticed the sinking that drowned thirty-eight Chinese, and only briefly mourned the American who was lost when the coaster went down. The world itself seemed threatened by the *Argo Merchant*, therefore it paid attention to the columns of newspaper report and the hours of television coverage that extended from the middle of December, when the accident happened, until well into the new year, when the threat was dissipated by natural good fortune. The tanker — owned in New York, registered in Liberia, captained by a Greek, crewed by an international brigade — was steaming from Venezuela towards Salem with 7½ million gallons of crude oil in her holds. Coming north up the American coast, she should have turned inland after passing the Nantucket lightship and steamed to harbor along the Boston shipping lane. She never reached either the lightship or the shipping lane. She missed her way in bad weather and ran aground on the shallows of the Middle Rip, which only fishing boats could have expected to negotiate safely. Her crew was soon taken off by the Coast Guard but a greater alarm had already sounded along the New England coast, that was swiftly to echo across the States and reverberate in the general direction of Europe.

When *Argo Merchant* struck the shoals, the oil in her
tanks at once flowed into the sea through the leaks sprung
in her hull. At first, it glugged slowly into the ocean while
the tanker remained in one piece. But the seas were
terrible that week and gradually battered the vessel apart.
For several days the unbroken length of *Argo Merchant* lay
like a breakwater across the Middle Rip, while the swells
crashed ponderously into her weather side and tumults of
foam surged across her decks to stream down from the lee
rails in a torrent of white waterfall. Then more steel plates
gave way, bulkheads began to collapse and, one night, the
Atlantic wrenched *Argo Merchant* in two. The oil no longer
flowed sluggishly then; it poured out in a glutinous mass
and blackened the waters all around. The television
reporters pointed out the predicament the American coast
was now in. The aerial photographs made the dying boat
look a very lonely thing, a tormented hulk surrounded by
a vast emptiness of sea. There was no land for twenty-
seven miles, until the beaches of Nantucket climbed out of
the water. Yet it needed but a change in the direction on
that winter storm for the oil, within days, to pour toward
the island, to clog its sands ankle deep in black glue, before
passing on to foul the shores of the mainland as well. From
the moment of grounding, the gale had blown steadily
from the southwest and, so long as that held, the shores
would be safe. But winds are variable and wayward
beyond the predictions of man and, in the knowledge of
this, a panic spread across the land. All those miles of
beaches might be ruined, and whatever would happen
then to the tourist trade next summer? Bad enough to
have the oil streaming away to the northeast, to the
fisheries of Georges Bank. But those beaches, those
beaches.

The alarm felt for the sea itself and what it contained
was never as loud as the fear uttered for the land: but the

greater peril did not go unheeded by the people of the land. They were told that, even if nothing worse befell, a catastrophe had already occurred. The shoals on which *Argo Merchant* lay were a breeding place of the gray seal, a creature which for many years had been nearly extinct. Within three days of the grounding, a layer of oil surrounded the wreck by anything up to fifteen miles; and it was spreading quickly. It was gradually covering waters in which the humpback whale lived, where all manner of fish swam. Not all of these were thought fit for human consumption and some were said to be as ugly as sin. But cod and haddock and hake were here, and the yellowtail flounder along the Great South Channel was already swimming in a poisoned sea. Daily, marine biologists flickered into view across the nation's television screens and explained precisely what was at stake, even if those precious beaches were unstained. Adult finfish were relatively safe. They would scent the danger before it overwhelmed them and would be able to swim to where the waters were clean. But shellfish would never get out of the way fast enough. Nor would the smallest swimmers in the sea. Worst of all, the spawn and the larvae that represented future generations of all marine life would lie where they had been laid, incapable of movement, while this great black miasma sank lower in the water, settled over them like tar and extinguished them in millions. Herring larvae were on the sea floor right now; within the next few months the haddock and the cod would spawn eggs which might soon be coated in the drifting of the oil. The biologists looked grim while they spoke of this doomsday. By and large the nation shook its head in front of its flickering screens and was mighty impressed when statistics were announced; then switched over to another channel when the concentration ran out. The fishermen

raging at what might happen out there in
saw their living at risk, felt themselves at one
ing larvae; and almost were, in their own
manner of speaking.

All the mighty effort of which America is uniquely
capable was now mustered to provide some protection for
the precious shores. Squads of men were formed with
equipment to spray beaches with solvent to disperse
encroaching oil. Pontoons were made, that might be
floated some distance into the sea, to form a barrier
against the black horror from the east. Earthmoving
machines were trundled down to vulnerable parts of the
New England coast, ready if need be to reconstruct the
land so that, even though it might be unrecognizable to its
familiars, it would at least be clean. While this preparation
for a local D-Day was going on, the Coast Guard took some
barges to the *Argo Merchant* during a pause in the storm,
with a thought to pump out the remaining oil; but the
weather went bad again and the barges were recalled. By
now the oil slick had created a path a hundred miles long
and it was very close to the edge of Georges Bank; a
helicopter pilot saw masses of black pancakes, each twenty
feet or so across, bobbing like an endless roller coaster
between Georges and Massachusetts. It was at this point
that people began to wonder whether the oil could not be
burned away by American ingenuity, so that it would
merely pollute the heavens with its smoke. A similar
accident, it was recalled, had happened once at the other
side of the Atlantic; and the British had removed the
threat of pollution within days by sending naval aircraft to
blow the tanker to bits and incinerate its cargo. But this
was America, and its lurking pack of lawyers had gathered
around the *Argo Merchant's* corpse, their presence threatening all other comers so terribly that government itself

was stammering with indecision. Bad enough to get
polluted; but, my God, who wanted to be in a lawsuit that
might cost several million bucks? So the oil drifted on and
the *Argo Merchant* settled more firmly on the shoals and
was dismembered even more by the sea; until the last of
her was eventually covered by the waves.

And then, mercifully for America, the direction of the
storm changed. It swung round to the northwest and blew
the sea's poisonous stain onto a new course. Slowly, over a
period of days and weeks, the oil drifted past the edge of
Georges and out toward the Gulf Stream. When the
television coverage finished, when the newspapers no
longer bothered to report, the slick was reckoned to be two
hundred and seventy miles long. If it threatened anybody
other than the unappetizing fishes of the deep Atlantic, it
would be the fishing grounds off Iceland. But these were a
long way away and, though no one wished the Icelanders
any harm, some people were reconfirmed in their belief
that God was truly on their side.

Locked in by the ice and deterred from trying to get out
by the winter seas which eventually sank the coastal tanker
just offshore, almost all the fishermen in the Town
followed the saga of the *Argo Merchant* on television, like
everybody else. Not one of them wished to be anywhere
but ashore in weather like this, even though home
comforts cost plenty and they earned nothing enjoying
them. Many fishermen spent their idle time in the gregari-
ous warmth of St. Peter's Club, playing their card games,
drinking their beer and their wine, complaining (endlessly
complaining) about the hard time they were having
ashore, going broke. The young men losing money this
winter were loudest of all in their complaints; but they
were only boisterous, without malice, when old men told

them to quit complaining, or get back to sea, or face the
fact that they had gone soft. There were always old men in
the club, at every season of the year, sages who would
never sail the seas again. They sat there for hours each
day, reminiscing, playing cards, drinking red wine; always
red wine, like their ancestors in Sicily. They reminded the
young ones, by their presence alone, of the heritage, the
blood, that set them apart from others in the Town. They
dispensed advice, even when it was not asked; loudly, so
that their wisdom should be heard by all. "That beautiful
wife of yours run away with that guy? You get her back
and you break her legs with baseball bat. That way she
don't run away no more." The advice was not always easy
to follow, but always the young men heard it with respect.
It was something of their heritage, one of the ways that set
them apart.

As Christmas approached the club became emptier and
men, cursing the tyranny of women, yielded to the
demand for help about the home. Main Street was
festooned with colored lights and the shopkeepers arranged for canned music to pursue customers along the
sidewalks from the drugstore at the top of the hill, right
down to the club at the bottom. It was thus possible to take
in an earful of "Jingle Bells" outside the delicatessen,
hearken to the herald angels near the jewelry store, and
hear Bing Crosby dreamin' of a white Christmas by the
time you reached the book shop. There was no need for
anyone to dream of it this year. The country was blanketed
in white, as picturesque as the most old-fashioned and
most sentimental of Christmas cards. But it was still
possible to move between the towns, as it would not be for
long stretches of the new year, when the bulldozers and
the sand-spreaders could not keep up with the succession
of blizzards that obliterated roads for days at a time. A

month later, Jonathan and Ellen would never have made it as far as the Merrimac.

He had been keeping her at a distance since the day of his return from the October storm. He had been guilty, on that occasion, of the one unforgivable act known to his kind, by showing his weakness to a woman. He was still haunted by this treachery to his manhood though he did not, as some would have, see Ellen as a culprit to be blamed for his disgrace. She was merely its witness, therefore a reminder of his shame. Punishment was not in his mind when he deliberately found things to do alone or with other men, that he and she might otherwise have done together. He was not yet ready to look her in the eye, that was all, and have to acknowledge what she knew. So when they met, he made sure that others were about or close at hand; and Ellen had let this be, telling herself that only thus would he return. She was almost surprised when he rang a few days before Christmas and asked her if she'd help him choose a present for his mother. "It'd mean going up to Newburyport, mind," he warned. "She's bin ravin' about a boutique that's opened there. She saw a shawl or somethin' in the window a couple of weeks back." Ellen thought carefully while she made small talk in return, suggested a day when she'd be free, and hoped that Jonathan had not caught the edge of tension she knew was in her voice.

They drove along the byway that wriggled north from the main route into Boston. The workmen had so far managed to keep it open but it was narrower now, winding its way past continuous banks of snow, piled high by the bulldozer blades and spattered with mud. Beyond the road, flatlands, marshes and rolling tree-clad slopes were immaculate with snow; and the wooden fences were almost buried beneath the drifts. Jonathan drove slowly, for the path cleared by the bulldozers was already coated with a layer of ice that would not disappear now until spring was advanced. A couple of times the car skidded gently, coming round bends after leaving the main highway, but Ellen sat quietly and let Jonathan drive undisturbed. She was content to be there in the warmth with him, where she could enjoy the frozen stillness of the land around. As they drove over the causeway leading into Essex, she could see figures sitting on upturned boxes in the middle of the creek, fishing through holes in the ice. All were padded thickly against the cold, and hooded like Eskimos. Some were protected from any prevailing wind by small sentry boxes which would remain there until the ice began to break up at the end of February or early March. Then small floes would drift away downstream, along the creek's winding course, until they reached the sea. Just like the old schooners, thought Ellen.

This was where most of them had been built, in this small township on the edge of a creek that didn't look wide enough or deep enough for the launching of anything bigger than Huckleberry Finn's raft. But there had been fifteen yards here at one time, scattered at intervals on the banks of that creek. Not big yards, only a handful of men working each: laying keels, bolting in ribs, fashioning transoms, planking decks, finally caulking seams with tar and cotton waste; craftsmen with great pride in the use of adze and ax, saw and mallet, anvil and forge, chisel and plane; who did what they did well, not only because other men's lives depended on it, but because they had been taught that there was virtue in this by the preacher in the box-pewed church that overlooked their yards. Thus were great schooners made, their prows slowly rearing above the causeway over the marsh and the creek until each hull was done. Then anxiously they were launched down the slips into the meager stream and towed out to sea, round the Cape and up to the Town, where other yards rigged them with masts and spars and cordage, blocks and deadeyes and tackle, till they were ready for their trade: and where other men were waiting to sail them into the Atlantic and onto Georges Bank for the catching of fish. Now nothing was here by the causeway, but eating places for the summer folk and one boatyard for the playboys; and, at one end, an antique shop for the nostalgic. All of them tightly shut to keep out the winter.

A December sun made the ice glisten on the deceptively rural creek. At high tide there was twelve feet or more of water under those holes where people now sat hunched over their fishing lines. Gulls balanced on the piles driven into the banks of the creek, hopeful for any scraps that might come their way. Eventually, their patience unequal to that of the Eskimo figures on the ice, they took off and flew elsewhere in their search for food: over the wooden church on the slope above the creek, over the neat houses that bordered the road after the church, over the snow-bound fields and the distant prickle of trees, where the creek had once carried the schooners carefully to their destinies in the sea.

Ellen was moved by this Yankee heritage as the car rolled through the little town. Jonathan had glanced at the ice fishermen and murmured his recognition; but he was too conscious of the present to think of the past. He was puzzled that Ellen had not said a word about that shameful day after the storm, for he expected all women to make what they could of opportunity, to put a man down with their sharp, demanding talk. He was still on his guard against this, for women also schemed a man into false security: every elder he had known had informed him that this was so, and every observation he had made for himself had seemed to confirm this belief. Cautiously he had begun to wonder whether this woman might possibly be different from the rest, might allow him to enter without swallowing him up. She was strong as well as sexy and this was her potent force, the desirable thing that repelled almost as much as it drew him on. He would have felt easier now if she had sat closer to him in the car, for that way he could have made any gesture he wished to reassert himself. But Ellen had left space between them and lay easily back with one elbow propped on the back of the seat. She had unbuttoned her coat when the car became warm and, the way she was leaning, her breasts swung gently sideways beneath her sweater as the Buick went round the snowbanked bends. Jonathan had shifted with excitement when he first noticed this; he had never known her to leave off her bra before. As he drove north, his want began to rise and caution became a childish thing: he wondered how Big Boy and Yank were making out, felt something of their practiced strength.

By the time they had done Jonathan's shopping, he was teasing Ellen again. And she had grabbed his arm in delight as they walked past the lot beside the church. "Just look at that," she said, hauling him to a stop. There, behind a high wire fence, was the manger to end all Christmas mangers. A life-size stable had been built, with a manger inside. Tailor's dummies clad in Oriental dress had been grouped around the manger, but all of them were much the worse for wear by now. In a transcending leap of the imagination, live animals had been introduced to add realism to the scene; a donkey, two sheep, two bullocks and three geese; and things had not gone well for the human figures after that. Mary and one wise man were totally stripped, Joseph was beheaded and a second wise man ended at the trunk, his torso lying shattered at his feet. The bullocks were blundering amiably in the midst of this rubble, the donkey and the sheep munching hay from the rack on the stable wall, the geese cackling harshly at the spectators over the fence. "Jesus Christ!" said Jonathan, seriously; so loud that Ellen reached for his mouth with her gloved hand, while other people giggled nervously and hurried their children away.

They had lunch at a place crackling with Christmas cheer, which Ellen swore was like her idea of an old English inn, all beams and bare brick and rainbows of light from Tiffany lamps, as well as historic maps of the Merrimac, old prints of its port to decorate the walls. And after finishing her bowl of chowder, she stretched her arms above her head and said, "Well, what shall we do now?" laughing as his eyes lingered a fraction too long at the rising of her breasts, and at his confusion in the knowledge that she knew. It was the laughter that made it right with them again. Jonathan paused, red-faced, on his brink between retreat and advance, and was propelled by a vision of naked breasts, two Bloody Marys and a gut feeling that something was owed him after all this time. He paused long enough to chew the last mouthful of celery that came with each drink, then leaned back himself, stretching his legs to touch hers. "Wanna guess?" he said, a mockery in his voice, a final option to back off. But she didn't. She came on more powerfully then than he could have hoped. She stubbed out her cigarette, watched her thumbnail press into the butt, said, "Parents won't be back from Boston till late"; then looked him in the eyes, felt rather than saw him draw breath.

They drove back across the countryside in the afternoon's failing light, so that it was only just possible to see the wreaths on the doorways of houses lining the snow-banked road. The Eskimo figures had tramped home up the hill by the time they went through Essex. After that, every house they passed seemed to have its wide window frames aglow, each one with a Christmas candle standing sentinel and lit. Jonathan had kissed her fiercely, clumsily, before starting the car; and she, teasing no more, had sucked hungrily at his tongue. Now, close to him on the seat, she had his right hand in her lap, running her nails lightly over the palm and the veins inside his wrist. Instinct had been pent up for more than a year and now it recognized no bounds, no admonitions, no compromises with anybody's rules, no safety for itself. The art which had been first practiced in secret, in front of mirrors in the almost-innocent years, which had been given too freely when she had encountered appetites that matched her own, was to be spent now in a prodigal lust that Ellen could no longer contain. She had no need to rouse Jonathan to a like desire; she knew that well enough. But in his excitement lay her own. His fingers spread wide at the sensation of her touch, and she felt her body arch at the small ecstasy of that. Later, much later, when he was trying to recall every moment of this day, Jonathan had but the vaguest recollection of that drive. Long before they reached home, he was in a daze of sensation and dreaming of more, aching hard through the bliss of her fingers playing across his hand. He knew that he, who had fumbled greedily with sex before, plunging naïvely in the backs of cars when he hoped no one was looking, could not hope to match this woman yet. He also knew that he didn't need to care.

It was quite dark when they reached Ellen's place. She paused by the light switch at the foot of the stairs, watched him for a moment as he stood uncertain inside the door. He could feel the hollowing thump of heart just under his ribs. She smiled very faintly, raised eyebrows above dark eyes, held out a hand, turned and led him by it up the stairs. The door of her room was open and as Jonathan entered he paused again, animal scenting another's lair. Bed with brass headposts, floral quilting, pale green pillows and sheets. Underclothes on beige carpet and wicker chair beside bed. Pine dressing table with cosmetics scattered around. A mirror, full-length, facing the foot of the bed. Poster from a Spanish bullfight taped onto one wall. Print of Winslow Homer's doryman rowing against a fog on another. Smell, only just, of cosmetic in the air. And Ellen, standing by the bed, unbuttoning her coat with those long, neatly pointed, knowledgeable fingers. Looking at him almost as if he wasn't there, as if she was here for some purely private act. Jonathan began to close the door behind him but she shook her head slowly. "No, leave it open." He crossed to her, wishing just to hold her now, wanting another pause before he knew he could go on. He reached to put his arms round her but her hands came up and gently held him off. Something in her eyes he had never seen before; an amusement, a quiet challenge, an unchallengeable sureness. She barely moved her head, but she was saying no; not yet. "Let me show you," she whispered. "Then you can show me." Then she stood away from him, in front of the wicker chair, and slowly, tantalizingly, took off her clothes, piece by piece.

January was well advanced before Jonathan went to sea again and by then he would have been glad if that notorious winter could have landlocked the Boat for months rather than weeks, so great was his obsession with Ellen. Their coupling had not only released a carnal mainspring that made his flesh leap at the prospect of hers; it had given him a new image of himself. His sexuality, which had previously been acknowledged under protest and accepted with anxiety, had suddenly been received with delight and without recrimination. He could not remember having been so much the subject of pleasure at any time in his life before. This woman had, moreover, presented herself to him as an accomplice and not as a potential captor. She had not spoken of another meeting when she let him out of her parents' house that evening: "See you, Jonathan," was all she had said, as she shut the door behind him, with a wide grin of conspiracy. It was he who had gone away nervous, lest the marvel should not happen again: and nervousness had vanished next afternoon, when he stamped into the warmth of the plant shop from the icy street, and the same grin had greeted him the moment Ellen looked up from behind the counter. Big Boy and the others would, of course, have told him that women were most artfully dangerous to a man when they appeared at their most casual. Sensing this, Jonathan now kept out of the bars where the fishermen gathered each forenoon to flirt heavily with the hostesses and to drink themselves out of their mounting gloom at the bitterness of the imprisoning winter. He rose late each day and excused his sloth as an investment in sleep against the times when he would again go short of it at sea. He spent much time in his room, watching the weather from his window, vaguely wondering whether he could find some other job that would keep him ashore for good. Almost every day he drifted down to the shop, an hour or more before it closed, and was astonished to find that Ellen was just the same. When Christmas was past they spent few evenings apart. Whenever possible, they went to places where they could keep their conspiracy to themselves, though this was not easy, for the Town was not big and its people were laagered against the weather; it was difficult to move about its closed world without being noticed. Twice in one week, Jonathan and Ellen sat through the same movie and the second time was not for the compelling attraction of *All the President's Men*, but to feel close and urgent and secret, undistracted from each other by either the psychedelic flickerings of Technicolor or the pervading and faintly rancid smell of warmly buttered popcorn. One evening, when the Buick was free, they ventured along the snowbound road beyond the Cut to an annex of the Town's intellectual life. Someone had established an art gallery in what had once been an old inn, and the cultured society that normally confined itself to activities around the Neck was patronizing a winter series of lectures there. It was Ellen's idea that they should go, though Jonathan approached this ground with caution. "Painting: Toward a Rediscovery of the Figure" didn't sound like his bag. He felt ill at ease among a solemn gathering that ran to so many beards and such long ropes of beads, and listened so intently while a gnomish young man spoke in terms that seemed to Jonathan as muffling as a fog bank. Some of the pictures that were projected on the small screen were pretty enough, and he recognized the name Cézanne. But these people, nodding quietly to themselves almost nonstop, Christ, they belonged to another world. They spoke a different language, empty of cusswords and much else.

At a gap between Poussin and Mondrian, a young woman dropped a question into the concentrated silence of the room. "Isn't something original," she asked, "when it has no meaning?"

The lecturer blinked behind his glasses, paused in his manipulation of two slides, and inclined his fuzzy face thoughtfully for a moment. "Well, I guess, like it's something like that," he replied, groping for his concept. "Perspectively!"

Jonathan glanced at Ellen's face and wondered uncomfortably what she made of all this. She was leaning forward in her seat, like a lot of them, the cigarette at her fingertips counterpointing the elbow on her knee. She looked as concentrated as anybody in the room and Jonathan was not happy with that thought. Maybe this was the catch that he had begun to believe would not happen; he knew she could teach him plenty, but he wouldn't be able to take it in public. He tensed when the applause came at the end of the lecture, when people began to rise and look round the room to see whom they knew. There was a coffee urn in one corner and conviviality was about to begin. But Ellen never looked in that direction. "Shall we go?" she asked, and was half turned toward the door before he replied. Outside, she rammed her arm through his as they crunched across the frozen ground. Her face was screwed up with irritation as well as cold when she looked up at him, framed in the fur of her hood. "Did you understand half of what was said in there?" she asked. He picked her up and whirled her in a reeling circle with the relief of that.

They bedded twice again before Jonathan went back to sea, as opportunity was presented in one or other of their homes, and both had made-up minds by then. It was he who uttered the word love, as he lay panting on Ellen's body at their second time. It was she who, at their third time, threw her last caution to the wind and suggested that they should move somewhere together when they could. She trembled at the idea, both at the excitement of it and at the hostility it would provoke.

Once before she had left home to live with a man and her parents still reminded her, when they chose to, of their shame at her shamelessness, which seemed to hurt them much more than the disaster it had become for Ellen. She knew that if something went amiss this time, she might not be allowed to find her way back to them. But her fears had been damped by the long restlessness of stifled desire and by a natural inclination to put herself at risk. Jonathan, for his part, was now heedless of anything that might stand between him and the ecstasy that Ellen's body gave, the confidence that her compliance had brought. So the thing was agreed between them. They would find an apartment and let all things follow from there.

Jonathan was pondering ways and means, glooming

over the slimness of his bank account, when he was summoned back to work. It was late on a morning sullen with the prospect of more snow when Big Boy rang up. "Care for a ride down to New Bedford, old buddy?" he asked. Jonathan glanced at the leaden sky through the fanlight at the bottom of the hall. "What, in this weather? You gotta be kiddin'," he said. It was hard to tell from Big Boy's voice whether he meant business or had simply devised some long-distance escapade to break the monotony of lonely weeks ashore, for Yank had holed up in Boston again and Big Boy never seemed to get anything together unless he was around. But he was in earnest about work. "Straight up, Jonathan," he said. "We gotta pick up the Boat tonight 'n we're goin' out to haul up the gear. It'll be the last trip, old buddy."

Jonathan wondered whether he had heard properly. "What d'ye mean, last trip?" Having decided to break loose with Ellen, unemployment was the one thing he didn't need.

"Last trip on Georges lookin' for goddamn lobster," said Big Boy. "We're cuttin' our losses and converting to pair-trawling after this. Tell ya about it on the way down. Me and Carlo'll be down at the bar roundabout noon. See ya."

Big Boy enlarged on the news when the three men were bundled close together in the cab of Carlo's Chevy, bowling down the highway south, where the three-lane route curved black and salted over the whitened land. The owners, he said, had been doing some bookkeeping lately and hadn't liked the look of all those figures in the red. The past year had been even worse for them than it had been for the crews of the three vessels they ran. It had cost them 110,000 dollars in lost gear alone, with the sabotaging of the Boat's trawl in the summer, and various bits and pieces that rough weather had taken overboard from all the craft. The fishing hadn't been good enough to make up these losses, and that wasn't counting the disastrous episode with the poisoned catches in the fall. If the winter hadn't been so savage, keeping the crews ashore, they just might have balanced the books by now, they might have been prepared to go on with the lobstering into spring. But there was no telling how long it might be before the weather let up. And the last straw, from the owners' point of view, had been the engine failure on the Boat's last trip before Christmas, which had caused her to be towed for repair to New Bedford.

"So ya see how it is," shouted Big Boy, as they swished along in the twilight. "We can't afford to lose any more money." He always spoke of company affairs as though they were his own, just as he invariably spoke of Yank as though they were an inseparable pair. "There's big money in pair-trawling, though. Those Maine boats were haulin' it in before the freeze. So we're goin' to convert, and Jamie's goin' to convert while the weather's this bad. 'n, come spring, we're a-goin' after the herrin' from now on."

Jonathan shifted position on the bouncing seat. "What's goin' to happen to the third boat, then?"

Big Boy yawned and scratched an ear. "Haven't decided yet. May go on lobstering a bit longer if the weather picks up. May sell her and pay off the crew." Jonathan thought, Thank Christ it's us that's being converted and not them; and dismissed the third crew from his mind.

It was pitch black when the Chevy reached the New Bedford wharf where the Boat had been berthed after her repairs. After the heat of the cab, the cold outside struck violently at the men as they climbed out onto the frozen planking of the deck, and they rushed for the shelter of the galley. Snow was caked hard upon the working deck and icicles dripped to a cluster of points below the hub of the winch. Even here, in the deepest recesses of the harbor, a wind was blowing strongly enough to fill the air with snow that still lay powdered on the ground after the last fall, and this swirled under the Boat's arc lights like a thin white fog.

Things were not much more comforting inside. Provisions had been dumped in cardboard boxes on the galley table and deck. The place looked grimy and bleak to Jonathan after his soft weeks ashore and, even though he had just been exposed to the bitterness outside, it was cold enough in the galley to discourage him from removing his sweater and woolen cap. Up in the wheelhouse, Yank and the Skipper were awaiting the three newcomers, stamping their feet and breathing vapor into the air. "What's up with the heating?" asked Big Boy as he came up the ladder.

The Skipper looked as sour as anyone had ever seen him. "Didn't go on till I came aboard an hour ago. Somebody forgot to connect up with the power from the shore when they'd finished the repairs. And there won't be any fresh water out of the tank this trip. It's all froze up, fellas. So we'll make this a fast trip if you don't mind. Then I can take that vacation in Florida." He kicked his boot against the base of the chair to get his circulation going. "Who's volunteerin' to cook tonight? I'm hungry."

Carlo produced the first unfrozen look of the evening. "Oh Jonathan's volunteerin'," he beamed with a hand on the young man's shoulder. "Ain't ya, Jonathan? 'Cos he's been havin' lots a lessons this past few weeks. An' if she's as great with a skillet as she is with the looks then, boy, Jonathan here's into that jazz with the cordon bleu." Yank muttered something under his breath and turned away to watch the spindrift of snow outside the wheelhouse window. Jonathan, irritated, shrugged off Carlo's hand and said, "Sure, I'll cook. Why not?" He was ready for some ribbing when the others knew about him and Ellen.

But he could do without Carlo's lead. He hadn't seen much of the Italian since the last trip and had forgotten Carlo's constant need to be smart.

Later, he wished he had been smart enough himself to duck Carlo's challenge and turn over the cooking to him. All four deckhands turned to for casting-off and this was an unusually laborious affair. The Boat was hemmed in at the dock by a couple of local scallopers. After untying their own lines from the cleats on the wharf, they had to secure the scallopers, the Boat nudging these into the space she had just left. The lines were frozen stiff where they had been tied, so that crowbars had to be used to prize open the loops. It was so cold on that dock that, even with thick thermal gloves over cotton inners, Jonathan could feel the sub-zero air bite into his fingers if he stopped pulling and levering for more than a few seconds. His other extremities went numb within minutes and stayed that way until he was back aboard and the Boat started her passage down New Bedford harbor, toward the hurricane barrier and the open sea. The icebreaker had done a great job down here, he thought, as he clambered over the decks of the scallopers to regain his own. There was a lot of slush floating around in the water, but the harbor wasn't frozen solid as it was now, back at the Town. Jonathan paused as the Boat got under way, before going through the sea-door into the wheelhouse. The deck gleamed with its coating of ice and, without realizing it, he was standing stiffly with feet apart and arms away from his sides, braced against the likelihood of a slip. It wasn't going to be funny out there once the deck started moving with the sea.

The others swaddled themselves in blankets in the closeness of their bunks, leaving Jonathan to cook in the galley, alone, as the Skipper headed his vessel slowly down the black and slushy waters of the harbor. Jonathan knew the moment they went through the hurricane barrier and out into the sea. He had the steaks starting to broil on the grill by then and was bending to shove in a tray of potatoes after them when the Boat suddenly bucked at the bows and Jonathan had to slam the stove door shut to stop the steaks from sliding out onto the deck. After that it was all hard work, keeping his balance while trying to juggle the cooking food, hot fat splashing up, pans jumping up and down, stomach beginning to turn at the warm greasy smell, forehead starting to sweat, though it still wasn't all that hot in there. Jonathan had forgotten these things. The steaks weren't done more than medium rare by the time he decided he'd had enough and called the others in to eat. Cutlery was sliding up and down the galley table by then, so they put wet paper underneath it all to give it some grip.

The meal wasn't appetizing, and no one had worked hard enough lately to put much of it away. Even the avid Big Boy sawed up only half his steak before tossing the rest into the bin. Jonathan himself took minutes to masticate a fibrous mouthful, was very glad when it was gone, and didn't try again. "Sorry, fellas," he mumbled as he lurched toward the bunk room. No one said anything. Each man was thinking hard about some better life ashore, where the table didn't drop and hit you on the knees, where you didn't have to worry whether your drink was going to pour down your throat or your neck. Above all, where you didn't have to face the next day out on that icy deck, manhandling heavy wire traps in God knows what kind of a sea.

When Jonathan stood his watch at three in the morning, the first thing he did after seeing Yank away was to peer at the thermometer clamped outside the wheelhouse window aft. It was sheltered from the wind but, even so, it showed twenty-two degrees below freezing. And some people were already at work out there. The Boat was well beyond

Nantucket by then and over to starboard a great glow lit
the sky above an horizon far removed from any land. It
looked like the warmth of a village, seen across empty hills
on just such a black night as this. But it was the telltale of
foreign boats, fishing in a massive fleet. They must be
bananas, thought Jonathan, real nut cases, to spend the
whole of this winter out there without ever seeing land.
Things must really be bad where those people came from,
to make them do a thing like that. If it hadn't been for
making some money so that he and Ellen could get set up,
if he hadn't known he'd be back again in a few days,
nothing would have brought him out here in this weather.
He clutched at the chair arms as a sea smacked them on
the port bow and the Boat staggered aside as she pitched.
There was no way a man could take months of this, if
someone wasn't holding a gun at his head.

They were a hundred fifty miles from land and over
Veitch Canyon when they reached their first trawl in the
daylight. Before the Skipper punched the warning bell on
sighting the buoy, the four deckhands had carefully
clothed themselves for action. Longjohns next to skin and
woolen shirts above those. Then a couple of sweaters. Two
pairs of heavy stockings pulled over their pants. Woolen
caps dragged down over their ears (Carlo had ear muffs as
well). Cotton inner gloves with thick rubber thermals on
top. All that under oilskins and seaboots. They stumped
through the sea-door like a line of penguins coming up a
beach. They moved very carefully, though the ice seemed
to have been washed off the deck by salt spray in the night;
which was just as well. Big Boy went over to the port rail
and examined the hose, which normally drank water
indefinitely from the sea. He threw it down again after one
glance. "Bastard's still frozen solid," he shouted. "Best
make sure we got them axes aboard. We're gonna need
'em when those traps pile up." That was what they had

come for this time, much more than any lobster they might take from the sea. There were two hundred fifty wire traps, worth thirty-odd bucks apiece, to be lifted from where they had lain for nearly a month and taken home. Jonathan wondered where they would stow them all. It had always seemed to him that there wasn't much deck space left when they were about to set a long trawl of eighty traps.

Standing motionless in the lee of the fo'c'sle before the buoy came alongside, the men could feel the cold beginning to chill their bodies, even though they were sheltered from the wind. They did not move to their working positions until the last possible moment and then it became supremely important to keep on the move. The wind was blowing strong enough to cut the tops from the waves and sling them horizontally through the air, though the Boat was not yet rolling as heavily as she had done during the storm in the fall: that desperate movement would come later, as the pile of traps rose top-heavy across the working deck.

The terrible thing about the wind from the beginning of that working day was that it penetrated every shred of every layer of clothing a man wore. Out of the wind, he felt the cold pressing bluntly upon him, sensed the warmth of his own body rubbing against cold surfaces of cloth. He could distinguish the temperatures of himself and his garments. If he stood still in the wind, such distinctions vanished almost at once. Even if he backed into the wind, so that his bare face was protected, it thrust the cold so brutally against him that he gasped at the shock; and could then feel nothing at all of either clothing or flesh. Whatever he did, this numbness spread throughout his body sooner or later — very quickly at the end of his limbs; a little more slowly along the thickness of his trunk. As for the face, it was at first an agony, so that the men bent their heads at uncomfortable angles to shelter the flesh as much as possible from the wind. Even so, the eyes streamed with water and the tears became small blobs of ice until, presently, the pricking of the ice was no longer felt. Nor was anything else upon the face. After a short while, the men communicated with nods and grunts alone. Their mouths could form nothing but a foolish-sounding slur.

As always, the worst place to be was at the rail, bringing the traps aboard and emptying them of fish. There you caught most of the flying spray, so that eyebrows and mustaches were quickly brittle with ice. The unpleasantness of *Argo Merchant's* trademark was something scarcely noticed in the freezing awfulness of being in that exposed place. The broken tanker's oil covered the gear the Boat now hauled. The buoys were coated with black muck, and so were the first few fathoms of every trawl line that came in. By and by, as each man took his turn at the rail or by the winch, his oilskins and his gloves were smeared with the stuff. The oil was no longer visible on the water, for the saving shift in prevailing wind had by now taken it out toward the Gulf Stream. But it had stained everything on or near the surface of the sea before it was carried away. Gulls flew by the Boat, with darkened bellies and legs, and they were the ones which had got off lightly.

The lobsters coming up in the traps, however, seemed to have escaped the poison. They were almost all inert when they rose from the depths. Very few showed any inclination to fight and Jonathan had never known them easier to band. They were smaller than usual, so that he had to put the measuring gauge to their shells more often than not. Perhaps, he thought, the big ones had managed to walk out of the area at the scent of danger when the *Argo Merchant's* cargo had started to leak the month before. The limpness of the creatures in the traps had nothing to do with the oil, for every shell Jonathan examined seemed perfectly clean. These lobsters were simply shocked by the cold that awaited them when they rose to the arctic surface of the sea from its merely chilly waters four-hundred-odd feet below. Within minutes, they had been dragged through a temperature range of perhaps fifty degrees. None of them was left banded in baskets until the end of a trawl, as normally happened. The man at the table carried them down below to the relative warmth of the tank, half a dozen at a time, to stop them from freezing to death on the deck.

It was the heavy work alone which stopped the men from freezing stiff. And, for once, the heavy work was not confined to the pair of hands at the rail. On this trip, in fact, they had it easier than usual because they were not concerned with baiting the emptied traps for a new set. As soon as the fish was retrieved from a trap, as soon as the trap was shaken clean of its refuse and unwanted intruders, it was carried down to the stern, where a stack of traps began to take shape across the whole width of the deck. It was possible to get ten traps side by side along the deck, jammed close between the port and starboard rails. Each of these rows was built four traps high and then lashed securely with a line running along the top from side to side of the Boat, and two men were kept at full stretch doing this: the railman's partner and the man at the table, when he wasn't banding the lobster and struggling down the hatch ladder to get them into the tank below. The fourth man on deck, who normally ran the gadgets for the setting of a new trawl as well as watching the line coming in over the winch, could forget about gadgets this trip, but instead had to coil up the trawl line as it came out of the sea and off the winch; and this was the most exhausting job of all.

For two days the Boat was out there, hauling her gear off the bottom for the last time, and every trawl she took up brought with it 1300 fathoms of icy wet rope that would not go into the sea again. It took a couple of hours or so to haul up each trawl and, all that time, the fourth man was bent double over his growing pile of rope, his arm moving round and round to lay the coils in place.

By the time Jonathan had finished his first stint there and changed places with one of the other hands, his shoulder ached with hot pain while his fingers were white and useless with cold; his frozen back felt as though it would never bend upright again, while his head seemed about to burst with the sluggish clogging of his blood. The second time he took his turn at the ropes, toward the end of the first day, he was so weary with the work, with stumbling against the rising pile of rope, above all so weary from the cold, that he could not move fast enough when the rope came off the winch. It was the sudden lurching of the Boat that caused a loop to slacken for an instant as the deck dipped sideways, a simultaneous pitch of the bows that jerked the loop straight off the hub. There was nothing special about this; it was always liable to happen; happened, indeed, half a dozen times in any working day. It simply required watchfulness by the man at the winch, and his quick reaction. He had to get the loop back onto the hub fast in that moment which always followed its displacement before the great weight of the underwater trawl took charge, pulling the rope and anything attached to it straight back over the side and into the sea: the buoyancy of an object in salt water upheld the heavy trawl for a second or so before it began to descend, and this was time enough for a man to act. But Jonathan never saw the rope come off the hub, was so concentrated on making his arm go round in defiance of his body's desire that he never even noticed the tumble of rope beneath the winch begin to fly through the air. He was fixed only on one thing; his body working faster so as to catch up the incoming trawl and get that tumbled rope into a manageable coil. Big Boy shrieked at him "Get your leg out of the line! Get your leg out of the line!" But Jonathan never heard the distorted babble of the words. He was bent double, fumbling slowly to keep the coils in place, his knees resting against the rising pile of rope, unaware that one coil near the bottom had looped round the outside of his right boot. He was sent flying sideways as Yank's weight hit him in the ribs — in spite of his own weariness, the ex-Marine had gotten across the deck space in three staggering strides. Big Boy, lunging behind Yank, snatched the coil from Jonathan's hands as he fell and got it over the hub a split second before it, too, would have flown out overboard. At the very least, the young man would have been smashed up against the winch.

Yank picked himself up off Jonathan's prone figure, and began to haul him to his feet without a word. Big Boy, now that the danger was passed and the rope was safely wound in place again, turned and cursed Jonathan obscenely with the violence of fear, in a torrent of rage that slopped incoherently out of his frozen mouth. Two icicles, dangling from the corners of his mustache, swung like small pendulums in time with his roars. Jonathan, open-mouthed with shock, slowly shook his head and bent double again over the coils.

As the stack of traps grew, so the rolling of the Boat imperceptibly increased. She lingered more at the bottom of each roll, too, before moving back the other way. The men carrying traps to add to the stack paused more frequently on their way when this happened, uncertain of their footing with their arms loaded on the slippery deck. The salt spray which, on the passage out, had thawed off the frozen snow the Boat had carried from the land, was itself beginning to freeze where it drenched the deck; the thermometer had started falling almost as soon as they reached the first buoy. Tumbles became more frequent as the day wore on. Carlo overbalanced with a trap in his arms, spun round in trying to save himself, let the trap go and saw it fly off through the air, bounce on the starboard rail and turn over into the sea. The others barely glanced in his direction as they doggedly struggled with their own tasks. Carlo got to his feet, clutching an arm, went back for another trap and shuffled wide-legged again to the stack. He was starting a top row, which meant that the trap he was carrying had to be placed higher than his head. He swayed a moment by the port rail, rested the trap on his knees, gathered more strength and, grunting with the effort, pitched the wire contraption up into place. The Boat's bows at that moment dug deep into the sea, the stern rose, and the three unlashed tiers in front of Carlo began to slide out toward him. He flung himself forward to hold them in place, arms outspread, frozen hands splayed, legs wide apart, toes pressed desperately down on the treacherous deck, head jammed sideways against a slipping trap. For half a minute he leaned there, straining to hold the stack in, crucified figure and Sisyphus both. Then the bows climbed out of their trough, the stern settled down, and the traps on the stack shunted back from their brink. Carlo dragged himself along the incomplete line, pushing and shoving the cages upright.

It was so bad on deck, from the moment they started work, that the Skipper brought the Boat to a standstill before hauling each new trawl, to give his men time to get inside the galley and restore a bit of warmth. It helped a little to pour hot coffee into mouths that were quite without sensation, as though they had been anesthetized by a dentist, so that the liquid trickled out of the corners and dribbled down the chin without the drinker being aware of it. For the most part the men slumped on the bench, blinking at each other, staring at the drink, uttering short obscene phrases at no one and nothing in particular.

They wiped away their icicles as these melted in the warmth. They thrust their bare hands under their armpits and hissed with the pain, rocking back and forth as the blood began to flow again. Only as circulation returned did they become aware of the raw red circles at the wrist, the patches of abrasion upon the jaw, where oilskin and sea were rubbing open wounds; they would all go home with saltwater boils this trip. Big Boy took to lying flat on the deck, his head pillowed on a deflated balloon, his hands clamped tight under his arms. But the important thing about taking refuge between trawls was not the brief rest, or the opportunity to thaw, or the shelter from the dreadful wind. It was the reminder that there was something endurable beyond the working on the deck, the promise that there was another world where everything was not reduced to blank exhaustion and stupefying cold. It was a taste of salvation after a kind of hell. The reminders and the promises, though, were far too short; almost a torture in themselves. Before the mind was anywhere near becoming clear, before flesh and bone had recovered from their pain, the warning bell sounded and the men staggered again to their feet, reached for a dry set of gloves, and plodded like zombies to the sea-door.

Each man had his own stratagem for measuring the painful progress of their work, the reassurance each needed that this would be coming to an end. For Big Boy it was simply the advance of the traps, row after row of them, up the deck from the stern. He had guessed, when they began, that by the time the last trap was aboard, they would be right up to the banding table and around one of its sides; and he was recalculating slowly, each time a new row began, to work out afresh whether his guess would hold good. For Yank it was a stolid concentration on the oil drums along the starboard rail. They should have been left behind in New Bedford, not being needed this time for bait, and they stretched from the metal table at the rail three-quarters of the way aft. On the afternoon of the first day, someone pitched the first drum overboard, to make way for the advancing row of traps; and Yank grunted with satisfaction as, one by one, the rest of that day and the day that followed, the others went over, too. He paid no attention when they had gone over the side. It was only Jonathan, if he happened to be turned that way, or if it was he who threw the thing over the rail, who paused to watch it bob out of sight astern, behind a swell in the ominous blackness of the sea. This became a staging point for him, too. Otherwise, like Carlo, he fixed his attention on the hatches midway down the deck behind the banding table. There was storage space down there, abaft the water tank, and there they were dumping the coiled ropes of the trawls when each had come aboard, so heavy with water, so massive in their own lengths, that it was as much as one man could do to lug them across the deck. When the rows of traps had crept up to the hatches, these had to be closed, even though the space below was not yet full. After that, the ropes were piled in the port scuppers, just below the fo'c'sle break; and that meant they were well over halfway through.

From his place in the jog station up above, the Skipper watched all these signs of their progress as he hunched miserably in the same position for two hours at a time and tried to imagine the warmth of the Florida sun. But, more and more, his eye was anxiously on the growing stack of traps and on the sharpening angle it formed with the sea as the Boat rolled more deeply under its high weight. Late on the first day, when they were almost finished for the night, he heard a new weather forecast and swore to himself with a sharp edge of tension. A full gale had started to blow offshore around Cape Cod, there were blizzard conditions up and down the coast and some way out to sea. And the temperature was dropping, up there, like a stone. He went over to the window where the thermometer hung. It was already down to 4 degrees where they were. Any time now, the Skipper thought, those traps'll start to freeze solid. The more we roll, the more they wet. The more they wet, the more they freeze. The more they freeze, the more we roll. Nightmare roundelay of the winter sea. Ships turned over on the last verse. He looked aft, through the wheelhouse window, trying to blow some warmth onto his fingers. Already, he could see the traps at the top toward the stern beginning to gleam with a coating of ice. So far it was a very thin coating on each strand of exposed wire. Presently, however, the coating would thicken and join up across the square inch of space that separated the wires of the cage. Once that happened, the ice on the traps would build up very fast indeed into a solid mass that would make the Boat too top-heavy to sail in anything but a calm. It looked now as if she would have to sail through gale force winds bearing snow before she reached the security of the shore.

Next morning strange birds began to take refuge on the Boat, a sure sign that there were violent winds blowing off the land, for none of them were normally seen so far out at sea. Three snow buntings were perched on the fo'c'sle rail when the men came on deck after dawn and stayed close for the rest of the day. From time to time they took off and circled the fishermen before coming to rest again on the rail or on the mounting bulk of the traps. Midway through the forenoon a purple finch fluttered onto the deck by Jonathan's feet as he groped stiffly among the lobsters on the banding table. It cocked its head to investigate the man and Jonathan tried to wink at it but somehow his face wouldn't work and so he stood there staring at it stupidly until Big Boy's voice cut harshly into his blankness. "C'mon, let's get movin'. Jesus Christ, we're not movin' fast enough." He was, as usual, performing prodigies himself and finding enough energy to sound off at the others as well. He had been watching the greater rolling of the Boat since coming on deck with deep unease and the worry was beginning to get to him. More and more, the men had to stand still and hang on to something as the Boat canted over and the deck rose steeply for long seconds at the bottom of a roll. They were finding it harder to stay on their feet and they were blundering into each other now, as their working space became more and more cramped.

By noon on that second day the man by the winch was perpetually laboring on a pile of rope, with nowhere else for it to go. The man at the table was hemmed in by a wall of traps on two sides, which at least gave him some protection from the wind. But the ice, by then, had solidified into a sheet on top of the traps at the stern and into stalactites hanging down from the sides. Twice they had to chop these away with an ax, before they got too heavy. Big Boy went out there first, along the flat top of the tail, clawing his way from one stanchion to another, where these stuck up from the rail to anchor the lashings across the traps. The other four men on the Boat watched helplessly as his bulky figure edged its way along the rail, as spray slashed across his back, as he wrapped an arm and a leg round the stanchion and struck heavily at the ice. There was nothing they could do to save him if he slipped and there had been no point in putting a line round him in case he fell into the sea. It was the lore of their trade, one of the risks that swelled them with pride, that to fall into such a sea meant instant heart failure from the icy shock. But the pride always came later, in the safety of the shore. While the risk was on, men waited and felt tight. When Big Boy came back to the three standing on deck, he shoved past them without a word and stumbled over to the rail where the traps were swung aboard. He stood there for a moment, his face to the wind and, though this meant pain and tears streaming from his eyes, he tried to gulp in some air. It was the nearest he'd been in a long, long time to vomiting when he wasn't drunk.

A little later, the Skipper called down from his vantage point above. "Best get some of that ice off the port side. Take it easy, though." He was shouting to no one in particular, but it was Yank who reached for the ax and clumped over to the lee rail. He moved astern more swiftly than Big Boy had done. He was lighter on his feet at all times and this sort of stunt was not so very much different from some of the jungle training he'd had in the Marines. He was elated as he swung out there from a stanchion, flailing at the ice with the ax. He was not content to chop the stalactites away; he'd shift all of that bastard ice off the back of the Boat, he alone, balanced out there upon the bucking of the rail, while the sea rushed past just below the heels of his boots. He very nearly did shift all the ice. He worked the ax blade under the sheet that had formed on top of the traps, worked it under in several places as far as he could reach, then carefully lifted and prized, completely absorbed in what he was doing and mindless of the exposure where he was. Suddenly, a large slab came away as the port rail rose high under Yank's feet; then slithered off over the stern as the bows were picked up by the swell. Only then did Yank start to make his way back along the rail, moving more slowly now because one arm and one leg had gone stiff.

He had clambered almost the length of the traps to where he could jump down onto the deck when the end of a lashing, streaming in the wind, wound round his boot and held him fast. He hadn't seen the end, hadn't felt it tether his leg. His eye was on the deck space, round the corner of the traps, where he would jump, and on Carlo, who was standing there, waiting for him to come back in.

Yank took the last step toward the deck but his leg wouldn't move and he overbalanced, slipped, fell, lost hold, grabbed at the rail as his body plunged — and hung there, body and one leg over the side, other leg and arms spread along the rail. The Boat rolled to port and a wave plucked at his dangling leg. Soon it would want more. He roared at Carlo to give him a hand; but Carlo, in the instant of Yank's fall, had turned away to make room for him on deck, never saw the stumble, never heard (through his ear muffs) the shout for help. Carlo was walking away when Big Boy — the ever-watchful and always dependable Big Boy — thrust him aside and lunged across the deck to the aid of his friend. He bent over the rail, clutched the hem of Yank's slicker, hooked an arm under the slippery oilskinned leg, and heaved as he had never heaved a weight before to bring the man back over the side. As Yank tumbled onto the deck, the still-tethered seaboot slipped off his leg. He lay there for a moment, frightened, winded, and bruised. Then, in a staggering, scrambling rush, he rose from the deck and hurled himself at Carlo. The Italian went down with a crash, Yank on top of him, hands clamped round the other's head, banging it up and down, their bodies locked, their legs threshing, two animals snapping and struggling for a death hold, slithering in ugly confusion upon the rolling deck. They were like that for less than a minute; but their savagery, pent up in months of nagging hostility, obliterated all consciousness of time and filled the small world of the Boat as though nothing else could ever be. The Skipper felt he had been bawling at them for an age before Jonathan and Big Boy managed to haul Yank off. Yank swayed there, still violent and straining forward, shouting abuse over Big Boy's shoulder, while Big Boy stood at his front and pushed him back. Jonathan pulled Carlo to his feet and held him until the Italian's screaming threats had run out.

But the two fighters only let it go when the Skipper's roars broke through their rage. They shrugged off the restraining hands then, angry with them too, and returned to their work, twitching still with the fever in their blood. Not one word would pass between them for the rest of the trip. They moved carefully, to keep a distance apart, while Jonathan and Big Boy eyed them surreptitiously until it was clear a truce had been called.

As darkness fell, the last trap came aboard and the Skipper turned his vessel for home. All day he had been pondering the strategy of their passage back and he announced it to the others over the evening meal, as the Boat rocked and plunged its way to the northwest. He wasn't going to take a chance on going round Cape Cod this time, he said. The blizzard was still blowing off there and it was too much of a risk with all the top weight they were carrying. Instead, they would steam for the lee of the land in the shortest possible time, which meant going west of Nantucket and up through Buzzards Bay to the southern end of the canal. "Only trouble with that," he said, "is that they reckon Buzzards is already freezin' over at the top end. If it's too bad in there we'll have to back off and try to get into New Bedford again till the weather clears."

He looked round the table, but there was no response from any of his men. They were eating their food slowly, the way men did when they were almost too weary for anything but sleep, prodding at it listlessly and chewing only enough to get it down. But something apart from exhaustion hung heavily over the galley that night, a brooding silence that came from men locked in dark thoughts. It helped the Skipper to a decision that was already half formed. For all his youth — of which he was well aware, most of all when he watched the sureness of Big Boy at work on the deck — he held the power of command. It was in his own sureness of this that he decided Carlo had best go.

Jonathan got the news when he turned over his watch that night. He had been up in the wheelhouse since eight o'clock and it had been an anxious time from the start. As the Boat pounded toward the sanctuary of the land it became clear to him how very much they were now at the mercy of the weather and the sea. He kept watch on what was happening under their arc lights astern even more than he scrutinized the blackness ahead for the first sign of another ship. In spite of radar a man's own sight was still a better bet so long as the skies stayed clear, for the sea was in such a turmoil now that a vessel's presence within two miles would never show up on the screen. As the golden beam of radar swept round the two inner circles it betrayed nothing but a seething mass of broken water, which obscured all else out there. Jonathan didn't need to glance at the screen to know that the seas were getting heavier. The bow was pitching deeper as his watch wore on and, more frequently, spray was flung back at the windscreen in torrents. Above the vibrating racket of the engines the wind was howling through the night, causing the flags on two marker buoys lashed upright against the fo'c'sle rail to stream and rattle like machine-gun fire. The rolling of the Boat was becoming worse, with the enormous weight of those traps which now covered the working deck four deep. Looking back, Jonathan could see that the stalactites which Big Boy and Yank had chopped away were gradually being replaced by a new growth of ice. It was his mounting fear of this that kept his weariness at bay. He had been near collapse when they had finished their work but now he was strung tight, and his senses were sharpened by threat. He could feel the tingling of the blood as he worried what to do: at what point in the growth of that ice should he rouse the others?

Would the Skipper say it was his turn, now, to go out along one of those rails and chop the ice away? In spite of the wheelhouse warmth, Jonathan shivered at the thought.

He had been gazing astern at the traps and the ice longer than he knew. When he turned around it was a moment before his eyes adjusted after the arc light glare. Then he saw a white speck over on the starboard bow, before it disappeared in the plunging of the sea. As the Boat itself rose on a swell, the light twinkled again; and this time there were others scattered dead ahead, some of them white, most of them red. Quickly, Jonathan moved his head to the eyepiece of the radar, and sucked in his breath at the telltale signs. There were twenty boats out there, between two and four miles away, lying in a great curve across their path and over to the east; maybe there were more much closer than that, hidden in the disordered light on the screen from the breaking waves. Jonathan knew well enough what they were. It wasn't the first time his watch had coincided with the deployment of a foreign fishing fleet. Usually the watchkeeper cursed his ill luck at having to con the Boat through a pack of other vessels at night. The foreigners habitually lay close together and you had to keep on your toes to find your way through them, vigilant for the goddamn fool who might have his gear down without hoisting the proper international light signal. You could be into his trawl and have cable wrapped right round your screws before you realized you'd hit it, when that happened.

But tonight, as he switched off the automatic pilot and turned the steering to manual, Jonathan was not cursing the foreigners. They were welcome, as far as he was concerned, to catch anything they could get out here in weather like this. That growing multitude of lights represented potential help in the danger of this night. In spite of his sudden need to concentrate on the helm, Jonathan's mind was more than half on that potential help. Maybe another six hours, he thought, before we reach the land. That's only six hours of being out here in a storm. If something happens in the next hour or two, maybe the foreigners will get to us in time. If it happens on the last stretch, the Coast Guard will come and help. The worst bit, when we're between the two, will be in about three hours.

His mind returned from its anxious wandering as the first of the foreign fishing boats came up on the bow. Now that it was this close, so close that Jonathan could make out the individual lights at portholes, he could see that it was merely drifting through the night. At first sight, he hadn't been able to make up his mind whether the fleet was steaming west or not. But it looked as if they were all laid-to. No one was fishing. No one had any arc lights switched on above their working decks. That made things much easier. He pulled the throttle back to half speed and turned the wheel a couple of spokes. The foreigner, wallowing mysteriously in the blackness of the night, seemed to revolve in some orbit of its own as the Boat's head came round and nosed past the alien stern, three or four hundred yards away. A trickle of sweat began to run down Jonathan's back and he gnawed at his lip as the Boat heeled over to starboard in the heavy sea. The foreigner suddenly seemed much closer; too close for safety. He must give the next one a wider berth. She now lay dead ahead though, when Jonathan brought the Boat back onto course, she was somewhere over to his right. He allowed the wheel to turn off course the other way and, praying that his guess about them all being laid-to was right, crossed in front of her bows. It wasn't exactly the rule of the road at sea, but you could never apply that when cutting through these foreign fleets. They were too closely packed and they were spread too far, one after the other in parallel lines. He'd once had to do this through eight lines of the goddamn things, ducking behind one and steaming parallel with the next until he got ahead of her bows, then nipped over and steamed parallel with the next line until the right moment to cross. But that had been on a quiet night in the fall, when you could see everything clearly for miles. Tonight the sea was throwing those foreign navigation lights all over the place, illuminating the blackness like stars one minute, snuffing everything out the next. Big boats they were, much bigger than theirs. Jonathan tried to see if they were iced up, but could not study one for long enough. It struck him that it wouldn't be so bad for their crews in this cold; he reckoned it must always be cold like this, where the Russkies and the Poles came from.

Gradually, the Boat threaded her way through the foreign fleet and, as she came back on course for the last time, as Jonathan switched back to automatic steering, he felt the loneliness of the empty sea again. He'd be very glad when this night was over. He looked back, as soon as they were clear, and tried to judge by how much the ice on the traps had grown in the past hour. He couldn't tell: but it was still there; perhaps a dozen milky spikes slithering down from the traps. He looked at the clock, relieved that he had less than an hour to go. So long as nothing happened while he was on watch, he'd be all right. When he woke up in the bunk room, they'd probably be tied up at the mart. If they could get across the Bay.

He was almost through with his watch when they reached the edge of the blizzard. The Boat ran into it quite suddenly. Jonathan was watching the surges of white water just ahead, where the sea tore itself apart in its violence. He blinked as it vanished, as though a shutter had been dropped; and the world outside the wheelhouse had become a blinding snowfall. Instinctively, his vision obliterated, Jonathan looked at the radar screen, though he knew nothing was within its range. He looked astern, where the greatest danger lay, but could see nothing of the traps now behind the vortex of snow. At the rate this was falling it would soon cover the traps, the way it buried cars ashore. Jonathan wondered whether the flying spray would dissolve the snow as it lay, or whether it would soon turn it into solid ice. If that happened . . .

He looked again at the clock. Another four and a half hours and they'd be in the lee of Nantucket and almost safe. Jonathan could bear this dangerous time no longer. He waited for the wheelhouse to level off from one of the deep rolls and dashed for the ladder to waken Carlo for his watch, though he was selling the Italian short by ten minutes and more. Back in the wheelhouse, he waited impatiently for Carlo to appear, but Carlo was in no hurry this night. Jonathan was about to go below again, in case the man had dozed off after being roused, when he heard steps behind him on the iron rungs. "Took your time," he said shortly, as the Italian came up to him.

Carlo clambered heavily into the chair and started rolling a cigarette. "My apologies," he said, squinting at the roll. "Was just enjoying a last look round. Ya know, you fellas really oughta give this bucket a lick of paint. That bunk room's a disgrace. Next boat I'm on, I'm gonna inspect the accommodation 'fore I sign on. Nothin' but the best for Rosario from now on."

"Whadya mean, next boat you're on?" Jonathan was irritated. This was no time to be hearing Carlo's yarns.

The Italian looked up, eyebrows arched in heavy mock surprise. "You mean you haven't heard? Skipper never told ya? Told me after supper. 'Keep on goin',' he sez, 'when we hit the dock. Don't come back. We can't use you anymore.' Yes'm." He raised the roll to his mouth and licked the gum. "Yes'm. Face don't fit aboard this Yankee boat. They'll be crewin' it soon with Daughters of the fuckin' Revolution." He gave Jonathan a gentle push in the chest. "No offence, Jonathan, now. It's just your old scapegoat talkin'."

Jonathan scratched his head, uncertain what to say. "I'm sorry, Carlo. I really am. I suppose somethin' like this was bound to happen, the way things are with you and Yank." He looked out at the snow, driving almost horizontally past the wheelhouse. It was soothing, the way it flowed. On the starboard side, where the green navigation light glowed, it swept past like bubbles seen from below the surface of the sea, as though some almighty propeller were passing by overhead. Jonathan shook his head, to clear it of a haze. Perhaps they'd gone under without him noticing, with all that ice. Perhaps they'd turned into a goddamn submarine. He had to get his head down, that was for sure. "Hey, look, Carlo," he said. "We'll talk some more in the morning, huh? I'll give ya a hand with your gear. We're steering 345, there's nothin' on the screen and the beam's still floatin' down below. But we've been icin' up back there ever since I came on." He gave Carlo a pat on the shoulder and turned to go. "Take it easy," he said. Carlo waved him off. "*Diamine!*" he replied.

Jonathan's weariness dragged him to its depths the moment his head hit the pillow. When he awoke, it was to the grinding crash of something close to his ear. He came upright and, from force of habit, grabbed at the sideboard of the bunk to steady himself against the next roll. But it was unnecessary. The Boat was motionless, although the engines were still running, making the bunk room door reverberate against its clip. Bemused, Jonathan thrust his head forward, toward the porthole. He screwed up his eyes, uncomprehending, not sure whether he was awake or in a dream. The sky was clear and bright with stars, and the waves had vanished. The sea had been transformed into a white, flat plateau which stretched as far as Jonathan could see. He rubbed his forehead and tried to clear away his sleep; and remembered the Skipper's news at supper. The top of Buzzards Bay was frozen over. So that was where they were. He looked over the side of his bunk and counted three figures fast asleep. He pulled his watch from under his pillow. It was 4:30, six hours since he came below. Anxiously, he levered himself down to the usual mess on the deck between the bunks. The crash that woke him had sounded serious and, as he stumbled toward the door, he thought, Those crazy bastards, sleeping through this.

In the wheelhouse the Skipper was muttering crossly to himself but showed no signs of alarm. His hand was on the gear lever and the Boat was moving again, going slowly astern. "Could you take a look down below?" he said, as Jonathan arrived. "We just hit a big one. And there's a lot more of it to come. Never saw nothin' like this before." On every side of the Boat the ice extended into the darkness, smooth and unbroken except for that serpentine track of black water astern, the way they had come.

Jonathan hurried down to the forepeak and looked quickly at the plates. They gleamed with condensation, as they had done from the start of the trip, but there was no evidence of a leak. Then he went down to the engines and the Caterpillar's roar was deafening as he opened the door. Fantastic, inexhaustible machinery that could take them out there and back without stopping. He ducked his head into all the corners of the cavern, but could see nothing wrong there, either. As he climbed the ladder out of the engine room, the hull suddenly shook again with a fresh impact against the ice. Up top, the Skipper seemed glad of the company. He was tired of talking to himself.

Jonathan gazed at the whiteness around. And saw, in the distance, lights that could only belong to the land. He felt safe now. If the worst happened, he thought, if they sprang a leak and started to go down, they could probably walk ashore across that ice. It was a comforting thought. But it would be a long walk. Buzzards Bay was about six miles across at this point; he could measure that on the radar screen which now showed, not tumultuous sea, but the projecting arms and irregular inlets of the land. Every inch of those six miles seemed to be frozen tight. As the Boat backed off again, Jonathan craned forward to look at the fractured edge of the plateau, where they had last rammed it. From the size of the smashed bits now slopping up and down in the water, he judged the ice must be damn near a foot thick. Strong enough to hold a man. It would be an easy walk. He almost looked forward to it. He felt so secure again that he hadn't bothered to look astern at the load of traps and the ice that almost covered them and oozed sluggishly down the sides. The Skipper had also put them out of his mind. But two hours before, when they were still in the open sea, he had wondered whether they were going to make it. A couple of rolls had very nearly not come back again.

"D'ya reckon we're goin' to get through to the canal?" Jonathan asked, his voice casual, as though the question didn't matter.

The Skipper blew out his cheeks and shook his head. "Hope so," he answered. "If the Lord's willin' and the creek don't rise. But there's been nothing through here since noon and the canal's starting to freeze up, too. Trouble is, we don't have too much choice but try. New Bedford's closed now and it's still Force Nine round the outside of the Cape. Can you see a red buoy anywheres ahead? On-off every two and a half seconds." They peered across the icefield together and it was minutes before the Skipper himself picked up the flashing light. "Well, that's one of 'em still working," he said. "Half of 'em are out since last week's storm. Every buoy in Nantucket Harbor out to Number Five and Number Six has shifted off station. Sooner I get to Florida the better."

Slowly the Boat battered its way through the ice. "Don't know how those guys sleep through it," said the Skipper, after a particularly heavy crash and lurch.

"Yeah," said Jonathan; and decided to risk it. "Hear Carlo's gettin' paid off," he said.

"Yep," said the Skipper crisply.

But Jonathan couldn't leave it alone now. "Why's he goin' when it was him who got jumped? He never saw Yank fall off the rail."

The Skipper drew in his breath. There were times when he wished he were much older in this job; he could sometimes use the insulation of age. He resented being questioned, but he'd sound a damn fool if he said so. "Cos Yank's a good hand," he said.

Jonathan persisted. "But Carlo's a good hand, too."

"Yep," said the Skipper. "But Big Boy's a better one. Could you get me some coffee?"

So that was it; Carlo had it exactly right; he was the scapegoat because Yank and Big Boy were buddies. Two on one and might is right. Carlo had said something like that himself once. Jonathan went below to the galley, wondering how he could stay friendly with all three. He didn't see the sense in not being so.

Yank and Big Boy came up to the wheelhouse, one after the other, as dawn slipped in from the east, just as they smashed through the last of the ice and cruised into slush at the entrance to the canal. Carlo did not follow them. Big Boy blinked in the early light and surveyed the channel ahead, where lumps of ice bobbed and eddied in the current. "Engineers done a great job keeping the canal open," he declared. Yank, leaning on the dashboard ledge, yawned widely. "Ol' Skip, here, he didn't do too bad bringin' us through the ice." He grinned, enigmatically.

"We knew we was in good hands. That's why we slept so well."

The Skipper took the banter easily, now that the worst was past. Crossing the bay home would be rough, but they could get that ice off their backs after unloading at the mart. There was no need to sweat now. " 'S all right," he drawled, "I'll get bedtime in when I hit Miami. You guys can take care of the conversion." They bantered some more, all four of them, as the Boat crept down the canal, between the thick snow newly fallen on either bank. Carlo was never mentioned. It was as though he had already left the Boat. And he never showed up; either then or later, when they docked at the mart and the unloading began. As Jonathan went out onto the freezing deck to take off the hatch cover and go down into the tank, he heard the Italian moving about in the bunk room. By the time Jonathan had sent up the last basket of lobster to Yank and Big Boy by the hatch, Carlo had gone. When Jonathan came up top, he saw the man's figure trudging down the snowbound road, kit bag humped over shoulder, heading for the shed where Carlo knew a lumper who would give him a lift to New Bedford, where his own vehicle was parked. Jonathan decided it was too late to catch up to him now. He would see Carlo later sometime, back in the Town.

Big Boy caught Jonathan's gaze, came over to him, and clapped a hand on the young man's shoulder. "Don't you worry yourself about him," he said. "Carlo can take care of himself. Better he find another site. Too much bad blood, my friend, too much bad blood."

Jonathan nodded absently. "Yeah," he said, "I guess so." They went through the sea-door together, into the galley, where Yank had already sat down. "Hey, Jonathan," he called. "Come in and get your feet warm."

Painlessly, Jonathan switched into the easy vulgarity of

muscular men, the passport to acceptance in the world he had chosen for himself. "It ain't my feet that's freezin'," he replied, with a deadpan face that was grinning inside.

"Never you mind," said Yank. "She'll take care of 'em soon. How's it feel like, bein' a hero, nearly home from the sea?"

Not bad, thought Jonathan. He looked at his wrists, chapped and scratched open into sores, as though they had spent a long time in manacles. He hoped Ellen appreciated what he was going through for her. "It sure was frisky out there," he said.

SPRING

IT TOOK A LONG TIME for that winter to wear off. The snow had fallen too thickly and too often upon the land for the thawing breezes of spring, when they finally came, to disperse it quickly. Even in April ribs of ice still clung to the roads, on shady corners which the sun did not reach, and the wasteland at the top of the harbor was still treacherous with sheet ice made filthy with grit. Where ice had melted by then, deep potholes were revealed, that had been gouged out by months of frost. It was weeks before all were repaired and in the meantime the motorists of the Town became accustomed to swerving past the ones they could spot and cursed when those they didn't see ahead jarred them to the bone. In winter, scarcely anyone had driven anywhere that could be avoided, but now they began to reclaim the rest of the Cape and the country around from its long hibernation and its legendary freeze. These people had new tales for the history of the Town that generations to come would shake their heads over and

find hard to believe. They themselves had sometimes
scoffed at the story of how the harbor had frozen over in
1856, right out to the Point, but now they knew such a
thing was possible. It would have happened again, this
winter past, with ice stretching unbroken from shore to
shore if that butty little boat belonging to the Coast Guard
hadn't kept smashing a narrow passage to the sea.

Even 1856 had not left such a memory as the one they
now had of the frozen fish. It had happened in February,
when the winter was still blasting them bitterly at its
height. Men brooding irritably by their locked-in boats
down at Fisherman's Wharf had noticed clouds of gulls
screaming above the ice farther out and slowly moving
toward them without any visible cause. But presently,
when the fishermen looked down at the water's edge, they
saw fish lying motionless beneath the ice, drifting into the
cove on the incoming tide. There were hundreds of them
in the end, young pollock four or five inches long, and in a
way they had been frozen to death: not literally, but as
good as. They needed oxygen to live, like every other
creature, and the ice had prevented oxygen from circulat-
ing in the water. So the fish had died, to become carrion
for the gulls as soon as they drifted out of the harbor
and from under its ice cap. No winter in anyone's memory had
ever left a tale to tell like that.

But one day, toward the end of that month, the
temperature rose enough to transform the ice in the
middle of the harbor from a white sheet that sparkled in
sunlight into a dirty gray scum, full of bumps and
roughness, with all manner of flotsam strewn upon its
surface. Bits of wood, tin cans, beer bottles and rubber
tires were all visible now that they were themselves
stripped of white crystals, making the harbor look as messy
and derelict as the wasteland at its head. There was more
snow to come, but now the stranglehold of the ice was

broken and it began to recede from the seaward end, and fishing boats began to put out once more as regularly as they had done before it came. It was another storm that finished it for good, blowing straight up the harbor so fiercely, brushing up waves and forcing itself into the land so strongly, that the last of the sheet ice was cracked open. After that, for a week or so, only great slabs floated in the water, becoming smaller as each day passed. Then they were gone. As February turned into March, the cormorants reappeared from the exposed rocks on the outer shore of the Cape, for an icebound harbor had been no use to them. Now they bobbed on the sheltered water once more until they spotted their prey, dived out of sight and surfaced again, half a minute later and maybe a hundred yards away. Each day now, people around the Cape were to hear an agitation in the sky as the Canada geese began to limber up for their long flight to the north. It would be weeks more before they finally went, and there would be one or two false starts on days of unusual warmth, but the birds sensed their season here was coming to an end, were fretful in the change and only biding their time. It was in March that the first sea mist came sagging over East Main, and that was the best indication that the air was beginning to warm up. A wisp of vapor appeared one forenoon, creeping forward through the trees and houses on the ridge above the harbor; then a great weight of fog rolled down the rocky, scrubby hillside toward the road and the dilapidated wooden wharves facing the Town. That same week a dory was to be seen crossing from the Town side toward the Neck, its oarsman well muffled in spite of the warmth generated by the exertion of his steady pulls: on that day the temperature had dropped again, the air was cold and the wind cut through his clothes. But no dory had crossed that water for three months or more.

Jonathan and Ellen moved into their apartment the day

the last floes of ice vanished from the harbor. Neither of
their families had taken kindly to the move and Jonathan
might have weakened under the waves of parental shock if
Big Boy hadn't filled him with Budweiser one lunchtime in
a Main Street bar and convinced him that it was time for
him to live his own life. "Jesus Christ," the older man had
said, "you work too goddamn hard at sea for folks to be
tellin' you what to do when you get ashore — even if they
are your own folks. If you're old enough to risk your ass
out there then you're old enough to lay it where you want
back here." Jonathan had not relieved the anguish at
home much when he repeated this philosophy, almost
word for word, a few hours later. But when, that evening,
Ellen told him she had discovered a place, he mustered
enough sober courage to make the move. Within twenty-
four hours he was wondering why he had found it so hard
to leave, for he had not known such delight as this. He
could have Ellen any time he wanted now and he could
come and go from their place just as he pleased.

They occupied three rooms on the second floor of a
house by the harbor, just above the state fish pier,
sandwiched between another fellow and his girl in the
rooms above, and a young and amiable family in the
apartment below. It was sparsely furnished and he kidded
Ellen that it looked more like a new branch of her plant
shop than anything, when she brought home a large
variety of vegetation in hanging baskets and pots the night
after they moved in. The house was separated from the
water only by a narrow street and a thin strip of wasteland.
It rose high above these on a small hillock, with thirty-nine
wooden steps to be climbed before you reached the
veranda that ran across its wooden front. From their
window over the veranda they could look out across the
pontoons of the Pier 7 yacht basin to some of the
tumbledown jetties long since abandoned in front of East

Main Street, and watch the great refrigerated trucks from
distant parts of the States laboring up the gentle slope of
East Main toward the fish-processing plant by the deep-
water berth. If it hadn't been for the gable of the house
next door they would have been able to see right down the
harbor to the breakwater light, from the windows at the
side. As it was, they had a view from the bedroom of the
Town rising from the other side of the inner harbor to the
ridge landmarked by the three churches and City Hall.
Sometimes at night, they raised the blind above the head
of their bed and looked down at the Coast Guard cutter
moored alongside the fish pier. Its Stars and Stripes,
fluttering across the beam of its masthead light, made
giant shadows leap grotesquely over the planking of the
wharf, as though these were illuminated by some great
candle flame. Then they turned away and shut out the
world and made their own shadows writhe frantically on
the bedroom wall.

With the last of their money they got a five-year-old
Plymouth and, heady with freedom, joined the tentative
weekend exodus of townsfolk who had been too long
confined to their homes and their familiar streets. The
Boat was now high and dry on the railway lines of the
shipyard over at the Neck, while welders and riveters
clamped new machinery to her deck, and Jonathan had
little more than weekday fetching and carrying to do. It
would be the end of March before they were ready to go to
sea again, and he and Ellen made the most of their time in
between.

They drove round the Cape one Saturday to the little
harbor on the other side that would soon be inundated
with even more tourists than the Town itself. There was
nothing much there, these days, apart from pleasure craft
and a handful of small boats belonging to inshore lobstermen who pottered round the headland beyond and

laid their traps off the rocks of the Cape's many coves. Once, this had seemed a fishing port with a big future, but the Town's superior vitality had sapped its strength, and now it was no more than a very pretty place to visit by the sea. There was an old shed perched on the edge of the harbor, where fishermen had once stored their gear, whose boxcar red walls contained nothing now, but made a recurring motif for anyone with an easel and a satchel of paints. The streets around were narrow and wound haphazardly, having been built by seafaring people who preferred to break up the wind when they were ashore, but now these sheltered only commerce of the most self-conscious kind. Rings 'N' Things gave way to the Patio Shop and Serendipity on one side of a street, and exchanged customers with Briny Breeze, Mr. Bag Man and the Sea Fencibles Shop on the other. Over in the Town, only the byways of the Neck harbored anything like this, and in both places the fishing people mostly passed them by. By the time the tourists started to roll in at the end of April all these shops would be crammed with goods, ready for a new season's haul and the continuous tinkling of the bell behind the door. But now most of them were shut tight, with crusts of snow unmelted yet on the street along their fronts. The building in which the summer visitors could pick a lobster from a tank and have it boiled before their eyes was securely boarded up. A few couples sauntered up and down, like Jonathan and Ellen, holding hands, walking close for warmth, and pausing at shop windows to put their faces to the glass and peer inside.

The reawakening of the Town was fully signaled on St. Joseph's Day in the middle of March. Like Fiesta in summer, the feast was a Sicilian one at heart, and sentimental to the core. In many a household round the Fort and the well-to-do terraces beyond, vows had been

taken in the past to render perpetual thanks to the saint on
this day for some blessing in time of need. A son had been
restored to a full life after lingering on the brink of death.
A young wife had become pregnant after doctors had
sworn she was barren. The vows had generally incorporated a shrine in the very best room of the house and all who
entered that home on St. Joseph's Day paid homage to the
saint before receiving food and drink from the family.

Rita Rosario, for one, would have thought something
sadly amiss if thirty people had not shared her piety and
her hospitality in the house on Portuguee Hill that day.
The shrine occupied a large corner of the room, its plaster
saint standing above tiers of angels and flowers, and
candles in colored glass goblets, whose light flickered at
the wrought-iron gondolas on the wall opposite. There
were lilies at that shrine, and these she had promised the
saint if he would bring her husband back from the sea that
morning long ago when a phone call had put her in a
panic until he strolled in heedless from the club: and
although, years later, it was his mangled dead body that
had come home from the sea, the lilies had always been
placed at the shrine because, when she had sought St.
Joseph's help, the saint had done his part. For three weeks
before the feast day, Mrs. Rosario had been preparing the
food for her visitors — the Santo Giuseppe pasta ordained
for the occasion, fifty pounds of it, rolled into balls,
kneaded and thumped, then cut and pressed into the
finest of strips, as thin as paper. It was eaten with a special
sauce, thick with locoli, fava and ceci, and flavored with the
aniseed that Mrs. Rosario still thought of as fenoique. She
pressed this upon her visitors as they dropped by during
the day, together with the fish and the olives that were also
made ready for the feast, urging them to eat their fill when
they were already gorged. "*Mangia, mangia,*" she said,
offering a fresh plate; and giving Carlo a gentle shove in

the back to go and get some more. No one left that house
on St. Joseph's Day without feeling heavy and ready for
sleep. Each person went home with a parting gift of fruit
and some were shown an orange that had been left over
from this feast day some twenty years before. Rita Rosario
kept it in an old cardboard box in a cupboard, where its
skin had hardened and dulled; but the fruit inside had not
rotted with age and it still smelled, faintly now, as sweet as
the day it had been picked. She gestured to the saint at the
shrine when she showed this special thing. It was, she said,
a small miracle that could happen in a house that was well
blessed and kept its faith.

In the evening, still with more energy than many of her
departed guests, Mrs. Rosario was to be found at St.
Peter's Club, where everyone was bidden to the feast. At a
long trestle table down one side of the clubroom, the wives
presided over mountains of food that mostly came from
the sea, while the men congregated around the bar
opposite and handed out the drink. By the time Jonathan
and Ellen arrived, the space between these two focal points
was thick with other people trying to hold conversation
while juggling paper plates and plastic forks and glasses of
wine and beer. The air was so heavy with the smoke of
cigars that Ellen waved her hand in front of her face as
they walked in, and paused to catch her breath. It had
been cold and sharp in the night air outside, but it was
warm and dense in here. Jonathan glanced round cautiously, saw one or two other Yankee faces that he knew,
and took Ellen's coat and his own off to a side room.

When he got back, she was over by the trestles, accepting
guidance from Mrs. Rosario on what to eat. "You try some
of that cioppino, dear, it's delicious and I should know 'cos
I made it myself." She was beaming happily at the girl,
proud that her invitation to the feast had been accepted,
secure in the pride that so much of it revolved around her.

Her warmth did not falter as the young man approached, but her mouth twitched at one corner before she greeted him. "Hallo there, Jonathan. Glad you could make it. Haven't seen much of you lately. How's life treatin' you?"

It was a small rebuke and Jonathan acknowledged it with a blush. "Well, you know, Mrs. Rosario," he mumbled, "it's been a bit heavy lately, convertin' the Boat and all. And she keeps me pretty busy, too, you know."

Rita Rosario nodded briskly. "That's the way it should be, boy. Stop you gettin' lazy. You'll find Carlo over there. He was wonderin' if you'd be comin'."

Jonathan turned and saw Carlo's back, leaning against the white ropework that covered one of the pillars supporting the roof. He was talking rapidly to three other men whom Jonathan faintly recognized as Sicilians from one of the draggers that berthed over at the Neck, his head jerking forward in quick bursts of energy, with one hand bunched and pawing the air. It looked as though he was describing how to butt somebody in the face, and the other three were laughing as this pantomime went on. Carlo's doing his big number, Jonathan thought, as he pushed his way through the crowd. He reached behind him to take Ellen in tow as he covered the last few feet, and the thought crossed her mind, as she let her hand slip into his, that he was probably more nervous than he showed.

Carlo turned abruptly at the tap on his shoulder and for a moment he and Jonathan were motionless, taking each other in. Tall and blond Yankee boy in shirt, sweater, and jeans looked down, with caution in his eyes. Short and dark Sicilian with slicked-back hair looked up and never let his twinkle fade. He had been grinning when they reached him, but now his face creased open with pleasure. "Hey kids," he shouted, "how ya doin? How'd'ya like the garb?" He pulled the sides of his check jacket open to show off the patterned shirt and the slim jim tie secured by a silver clasp. Then he shot his cuffs and rattled the links like two pairs of castanets. Ellen burst out laughing and Carlo took his cue. "At no extra cost to the lady on my left," — wagging a finger under her nose — "the leg show complete with rawhide boots." He bent to draw up a trouser bottom and a calf-length boot was revealed, with a curling design in pokerwork on the side. Ellen laughed some more and Carlo stamped down on two four-inch heels, raised arms like a matador presenting his cape, and broke into a tap-dance that made people within earshot turn around and look. "Real dude stuff, Carlo, real dude stuff," said Jonathan, managing a grin.

Carlo reached over and took him firmly by the arm, but it was to Ellen again that he spoke. "This guy takin' care of you all right? He ain't goin' after the other tootsies on the quiet? 'Cos he's a dark old horse, this Jonathan. D'ya know that?" He laid on a laugh to take away the sting.

"He's doin' fine, just fine, Carlo. You should drop by and see us some time. Come up and I'll cook you a meal."

"Yeah, do that Carlo. We'd like that a lot." Jonathan meant it, and he was glad for Ellen's lead.

"Hey, whaddya know, I'm making big on the popularity stakes. An' I got me a new site, d'ye hear about that, Jonathan?" He looked the other man straight in the eye for the first time and there was mockery in his gaze.

"Yeah, I know an' I was real pleased about that. I'm sorry I didn't get round . . . but, well, you know . . ."

"Sure I know, you don't have nothin' to apologize for. I should have shifted my butt off that boat a long time before. You know we take more cookies and popsicles aboard the *Santa Maria* than even I can eat? And we just get stinkin' every trip on that old Hawaiian Punch." Carlo fluttered his eyebrows, like his idea of Bob Hope ogling Dorothy Lamour.

He chattered on, as though there had been no hurt in

his leaving the Boat, as though he hadn't hoped Jonathan would give him a hand with his gear that morning — or at least come round to see him the next day, when the Boat got home from the canal. But he never mentioned Yank or Big Boy or the Skipper once. Jonathan was too relieved that there seemed to be no hard feelings about his own feeble part to bring the subject up himself. It crossed their horizon only when Carlo kidded him about becoming a real fisherman soon, one who worked with nets instead of traps. "An' just you mind, Jonathan," he said solemnly, "how you all move round that goddamn deck. If anyone goes half over the side, give him a hand to keep goin' and save yourself some hassle." He roared with laughter, and pushed Jonathan on the arm. They parted with humor, as though they had never lost touch, and Jonathan repeated Ellen's invitation that Carlo should drop by soon. As they moved off to say good night to Mrs. Rosario, Carlo raised a hand in farewell. "*Ciao, bambino,*" he said to Jonathan. He winked at Ellen. "You 'n me'll go up to the Common in summer and pick up some more blueberries, eh?"

The Boat came back from its conversion at the Neck the following week, and tied up at the fish pier dock for a couple of days until Jamie's boat followed it from the shipyard, ready to act as consort in pair-trawling for herring. This was a relatively new way of catching fish along the North American coast, although it had been practiced in European waters for many years. Traditionally, the Americans who fished with nets did so by dragging, by seining, or by gill-netting, and most of the craft working out of the Town were either draggers or seiners. The draggers did what their name implies: they cast their great bag of a net over the side and dragged it behind them as they steamed ahead, the fish entering the net's wide open mouth and being trapped in its closed and narrow end. The seiner's art was more subtle than this, for it involved the more careful stalking of prey. Whereas the draggers would blunder through the sea, catching anything that wandered across the mouth of their nets, the seiners could not operate profitably unless they had found a school of fish large enough to warrant the intricate laying of their nets. With the seiner hove-to in the vicinity of a school, a launch was put out to circle the mass of fish and to lay the seine net around them before returning to its parent boat with the end of the net. The fish were thus effectively corralled inside the net, whose two ends were then hauled in by the seine boat until the mass of fish had been drawn close to its hull — so many of them, sometimes, drawn so tightly together, with no escape either below or to the side, that it sometimes seemed possible to walk across their bodies to the perimeter of the net. Then, crudely, an enormous hose was dropped into the mass of fish and they were sucked aboard into the hold. Stealthiest of all were the gill-netters, who laid their long walls of mesh at night and either drifted at the end of them until the dawn or even went away and left them hanging from buoys until the boat's return next day. Whichever method they adopted, they relied for their living on the likelihood of fish swimming into the net, getting their heads through the mesh as far as the gills — and then being held fast, incapable of escape either forward or back.

Pair-trawling was the invention of men with insatiable appetites, the attempt to catch fish on a gargantuan scale. Essentially, it was nothing more than dragging had always been, except that the mouth of the net was so wide, the potential capacity of the bag so great, that one boat could not possibly have hauled it through the sea unaided: so two boats dragged the net astern between them. Pair-trawling was still in its infancy that year along the Atlantic coast, but the rumor was spreading of huge profits that could be made by boats which found the herring shoals and kept track of them for weeks on end. So many fish could be caught in one trawl if the two skippers knew their business — sixty thousand pounds at a time, the gossips said — that small fortunes were being made out of every trip to sea. A couple of boats had come down from Maine the previous summer and based themselves on the Town, which meant shorter steaming time to the grounds than from their home port farther north. In seven months, it was said, every man on those boats had collected thirty-eight thousand dollars for his work. This was in spite of the fact that the fish was sold ashore for a mere sixty-five dollars a ton to an entrepreneur whose trucks were waiting at the wharf when the pair-trawlers came in. The trucks took the herring north to his factory in Maine and there they were gutted, cleaned and pickled in a variety of ways unacceptable to the American taste and dispatched to the supermarkets of continental Europe, where such things were much prized. There were some who, mindful of the European boats fishing the American sea and the European freighters bringing fish to American homes, snorted at this commerce as yet another example of a world gone mad. But the pair-trawlermen themselves counted their dollars and hoped their luck still held. With money like this they were becoming the envy of those who held to traditional ways. As their luck continued, the word began to spread. Pair-trawling was the thing to get into if you could. A few years before, they had said the same of deep-sea lobstering.

Converting a lobsterman to this new trade had entailed a rearrangement of the working deck. When the Boat was returned to its owners by the riveters and welders over at the Neck, it had lost the metal table by the starboard rail, on which the lobster traps had been landed from the sea and their contents taken out. The deep coaming of the hatch above the water tank had also disappeared and the cover had been refashioned to lie flush with the deck. In exchange for these removals, the Boat had acquired many pieces of fresh equipment, which so cluttered the deck that it was scarcely possible to move three paces in any direction without running into something. A large winch had appeared on the port side, close by the sea-door, and steel cable ran knee-high from its drum straight across the deck to the starboard rail. There it turned through pulleys inside the rail to a gantry close by the stern, whence it would disappear into the sea when a trawl was being dragged. In the middle of the deck, a few feet from the stern, stood the tall white hoist with a drum on the end, over which the net would be pulled aboard when the fish were caught. It was articulated for flexibility in dealing with the tremendous strain and, bent at its joints in repose, rearing high above men standing on deck, it resembled nothing so much as a giant dentist's drill. Step back from it incautiously and you came hard up against the coaming of the fish pound, which occupied the center of the deck, erected to accommodate a surplus of herring when the tank below was full. The pound itself when empty provided the only clear space on deck. Big Boy, observing the transformation of his acknowledged home, declared that it looked more like a fuckin' obstacle course than a fishing boat.

The two crews sailed with the breezy high hopes of men bound for a gold rush, though no one aboard the Boat or its consort had ever been pair-trawling before. They had gleaned what they could about this new craft from the Maine men at odd encounters in the bars of the Town, though information from that quarter had been sparse, fishing being the competitive business that it was. The crews were relying most of all on their own common sense

to see them through, on their ability to tackle anything that
might come their way at sea. A few of them had worked in
draggers before turning to lobster fishing and therefore
had some acquaintance with the use of nets. Big Boy was
one of these and so was Gus, who had taken Carlo's place
aboard the Boat. He was a tall, raw-boned man in his
midthirties who looked ten years older than that, restless
with nervous energy, perpetually muttering to himself as
he loped around looking for things to do. His face was all
bone and hollows and, underneath the tam-o'-shanter that
he perpetually wore, it might have belonged to an early
American pioneer of the backwoods, displaced perhaps
from the Scottish Highlands by famine or religious zeal.
When he spoke to others it sometimes seemed to be no
more than a continuation of talking to himself. He and
Jonathan were stowing away the ropes after the Boat cast
off from the fish pier and, without once addressing his
companion directly, Gus was explaining how lately he had
given up the booze. "Mind you," he said, stooping low over
a coil of rope, "I've had a lot more women since I went on
the wagon." He paused, thoughtfully, staring at the hemp
in his hands. "Well, a better class of woman, anyway."

They went out on a morning tide into a sea that rolled
low and gray under heavy clouds, away from land that was
piebald with patches of lingering snow. They turned past
the buoys beyond the breakwater that always marked the
way in and out of the harbor, and moved out beyond the
new buoy put down by the Coast Guard to mark the place
where the sunken coaster's bows had been dragged by the
current. As the Boat made its turn and steamed along the
outside of the breakwater, Jonathan wondered whether
Ellen was watching from the apartment: if you looked out
of the front window, straight across the low land on the
inside of the Neck, it was possible to see vessels for a
moment or two at this point. But then he remembered that

she was at work, too, on the other side of the Town, where the only view was of houses on the road that led to Boston. She slipped out of his mind then and he turned his attention to Jamie's vessel, half a mile or so ahead. Was that what the Boat looked like when it went out to sea; head dipping like a horse's to the motion of the waves, surge of white water on either side when the wide stern came down with a smack? Jonathan leaned against the wheelhouse dashboard, only half hearing the chatter of the others who were also loitering there. Their spirits were up after the long time ashore, fueled with the prospect of making big money at last. Jonathan himself was ready for this but for the first time in months another feeling was there. He was bound on a new adventure, as he had been the first time he sailed in the Boat. But this one spoke to something primitive in his soul more strongly than the first voyage he had made to catch lobster. The lobsters were there for the taking once the Boat had reached the grounds, trapped by a crude technique that took advantage of their stupid greed; all you had to do was pick the poor bastards off the sea floor. This fishing offered the prospect of the hunt, for they had to find the herring before they made a catch. These fish weren't going to swim into anybody's trap. His eyes glistened with pleasure as he dreamily watched the land slide away, the shoreline of the Point and the forbidding houses just beyond. Some of the buildings still had shutters across their windows at the seaward end, just in case winter had not yet gone.

The two vessels curved around the Cape and made way to the northeast, up the Gulf of Maine. The herring had been shoaling on Jeffreys Ledge within the past week and the boats from Maine had returned the day before with holds full of fish. Their crews had been deliberately vague about where in that great patch of sea the fish were running, but the Skipper and his opposite number had reckoned Jeffreys Ledge was worth a try for a start. Mysterious the movements of fish might be, but there were some areas they frequented more regularly than others and Jeffreys was one of them, just over the horizon from the New Hampshire coast. Since the days of the schooner-men, herring had been taken abundantly there and the mackerel seiners had usually found it a profitable place to plunder, too. But you never could tell, when you set sail, whether this would be the trip that might yield nothing at all. Fish that had been almost stationary in their millions for a week could suddenly vanish overnight, and fisher-men became hunters again, tracking the sea for days before recovering the scent. The miracle was that they generally did. The Skipper, unsure of his skill in this new game, fervently hoped that they wouldn't draw blank first time out. He was relaxed after his weeks in the Florida sun, anxious to try the new technique that he had studied at college but not yet practiced on his own command. At the same time, he knew how quickly the spirits of the crew would droop if they got off to a bad start in pair-trawling. He didn't want a repetition of the miseries they'd all endured last fall.

The other pair-trawler steamed off at an angle once they were around the Cape, and within the hour it was out of sight over the rim of the sea. The Boat sailed more directly toward the ledge, aiming for its landward side while its consort approached Jeffreys from farther offshore, the two vessels spreading themselves apart to increase their chances of picking up the trail. Both were equipped with sounding devices now, that traced the seabed and any-thing else under the keel on a roll of paper in the wheelhouse. Jamie's vessel had also been provided with the most expensive new toy of all, a scanner that operated like radar to reveal what was under the surface within 1,500 feet all round the hull. These were the devices in which the Skipper placed most of his trust. But he also knew that it was wise to keep a weather eye lifted for signs on which the old schoonermen relied long before science had come to the fishermen's aid. If you were out looking for herring, pay attention to whales because the two often went together, though no one had ever explained to the Skipper why. He was watching the empty sea around as much as he kept his eye on the tracing of his sounder and before long he was trying to decide which of the two was more monotonous.

As the morning wore on and became afternoon, as the Boat drew nearer to Jeffreys Ledge, the two captains consulted each other about their progress, by radiotelephone. But when all the crackling in the wheelhouse had stopped, neither had anything to report. It was three o'clock before they were cruising around the ledge, and in spite of his desire for a kill, the Skipper could feel the boredom of his watch seeping through the marrow of his bones. Only Jonathan had come up to the wheelhouse after lunch. The others had stayed below playing crib and the sounds of their laughter and challenge drifted up to the two men above. It was a dull gray day, without a patch of blue in the sky, and the occasional white-capped wave only served to emphasize the general glumness of the sea. The Skipper yawned as he contemplated it all without enthusiasm. "If you were a herring," he said, "would you want to get caught on a day like this?" Then he turned his back to the bows, propped himself against the dashboard, and resumed his glassy-eyed stare at the sounder.

So it was Jonathan who saw the sea suddenly part just ahead of the Boat and the great back rise out of the water, sending waves crashing on every side. "Christ, it's a whale," he shouted, jumping with the shock of it. Before the words were out of his mouth the dorsal fin on top of the back had disappeared again, though it had seemed to sink very gently into the sea, not a hundred yards from their bows. Almost simultaneously the Skipper straightened up in front of the sounder, at the sudden thickening of the trace.

"Well, I'll be darned," he said, "there's a spike showing up." He turned to look where Jonathan was pointing, but nothing was visible except a telltale circle of froth on the gray water. "Which way was he going?" he asked.

Jonathan nodded to port. "Bloody great thing he was. Never seen one that big before." He was elated, sap rising with the prospect of the chase.

The Skipper checked the trace again, its lines now coming thick and deep. He reached for the radio microphone with one hand, switched off the automatic pilot with the other, and called up Jamie as he began to turn the Boat onto the track of the whale. "Better get over here," he said. "Look's like we're into some fish." He asked for the other boat's position and swore under his breath when the crackling voice on the other end of the line estimated a dozen miles to the east. "Okay. Well get over as fast as you can. We don't want to lose 'em."

But they did lose them. It was an hour before the other boat appeared out of the eastern horizon, another twenty minutes before it drew close. The whale reappeared half a dozen times in the first half hour, though it never came as near to the Boat again as when it had risen almost beneath the bows. The Skipper throttled back the engine until they were barely making way at all and he steered with one hand and his back to the bows, so that he could watch the trace and try to judge his course from it. For a while he kept track and the Boat moved in circles and haphazard curves in response to the pen marks on the paper roll. The cardplayers came up from their game when the Boat slowed down, and by the time Jamie showed up they were cursing him for their loss. Long before his boat came into view, the lines of the trace had thinned out and gone, leaving nothing on the paper but an outline of the sea floor, thirty-three fathoms down. The two captains spoke to each other again and agreed to stay close from now on. As darkness fell, the pair-trawlers steamed north and resumed their hunt, like a pair of hounds quartering the ground. When they reached the top of Jeffreys Ledge they turned and padded back again over a fresh sector of the sea, carefully keeping themselves just four miles apart. When they reached the southern extremity of the ledge they wheeled once more and returned to the north.

They were steaming south down the outer side of the ledge, and it was two in the morning, when Jamie's boat picked up the trail again. If it hadn't been for the expensive scanner they might never have caught herring that trip, for the fish showed up on the starboard beam at the outer limit of the scanner's range. As the Boat turned away from its course and headed toward its consort, the Skipper rang the alarm bell to waken his sleeping crew, for they had long since taken to their bunks and left him to his lonely watch. By the time Big Boy and the rest had tumbled out, the other vessel had hove-to, no longer a distant twinkle of navigation lights in a deep black night. The arc lamps above her deck had been switched on and her outlines were clearly defined in the glowing white light that made the sea sparkle in response. The Boat's own arcs were turned on as she closed up the distance between them, and the sea was no longer an empty and a lonely place. Before the Boat drew close to her consort, maybe fifty yards away, the other crew was already out on deck preparing to put the net, its buoys and its weights over the stern. When Big Boy and the other three deckhands got into the open air they could see the net being slowly paid out over the tall articulated winch, with men stretching and tugging to prevent it from jamming on the drum.

They themselves readied their own deck for action. Yank and Big Boy bent over the winch by the sea-door, which would take the strain when the trawl was paired, and gave its wheels a few experimental turns. Gus was down by the gantry, examining the shackles on the end of their own steel wires by which they would link themselves to the trawl. It was vital to match the shackles correctly when the trawl line was passed across from the other boat, if the net was not to be twisted at the mouth so that no fish could possibly get in. "Top shackle to this one, lower shackle to this one," said Gus to himself, pointing with his finger to be sure he was getting it right. Jonathan grinned as he cleared some loose gear out of the fish pound and opened the hatch in the middle, where the herring would be poured into the hold. He had heard nothing like Gus's monologues before; was already committing them to memory so that he could repeat them to audiences ashore.

A shout from the other boat caused them all to move to the port rail. The net was now gone into the sea, the pink Day-Glo buoys above the mouth bobbing dimly on the surface astern. It was time to pass over their wire and Jamie was maneuvering his vessel alongside so that a line could be cast over first. He came in too close and the sea's slop brought the vessels together with a heavy thump and the tortured squeak of compressed rubber fenders. Men shouted their alarm, were bounced off balance, and the line was not cast in the confusion. It took the best part of ten minutes and three attempts before the turk's head at the end of the codline landed square on the Boat's deck. A frantic grabbing by three pairs of hands lest it should be lost again, then a rush round the stern by Jonathan and Big Boy, pulling the heavier line in toward the gantry hand over hand, and the wire hawsers after that, with the trawl shackles on the end. They were apprentices all at this game and they fumbled anxiously as they tried to move fast; as they needed to if they were to secure the net before it twisted in the water and had to be reset from the start.

They fumbled most of all in trying to match the shackles up. For all his concentration, Gus got them the wrong way round in the end, so that the Skipper had to back the Boat off to reduce the strain while Big Boy and Gus together struggled to reassemble the massive links and chains. Their bodies contorted with effort and their hands drew back from each movement in exaggerated jerks, to miss the split second when metal ground against metal, in which they might be horribly crushed. Jonathan had never been so much aware of tension in watching two men at work. Nor had he ever been so conscious of strain in anything as when their winch had finally paid out its hawser and the two vessels began dragging the trawl between them for fish. The creaking of the nylon rope when they had been hauling in lobster traps was ominous enough, but it contained nothing like the threat implicit in this evil sound of straining steel cable, which was not a creak but a thrumming that suggested something unbearable to the steel itself. Every inch of the cable was alive with that sound, from the point where it left the winch by the sea-door, in its passage across the deck to the starboard rail, in its taut length of the Boat's side and in its crossing of the stern. Only when it vanished into the sea did the steel cable cease to threaten every man on that deck. It had them cornered and Jonathan shivered under his sweater and his oilskins when the thrumming began. There would be no escape for one of them if that hawser snapped under the strain of the trawl, and a severed limb would be the least he could expect. In spite of himself, Jonathan was hurrying when he left the deck and made for protection inside the sea-door.

The two boats steamed ahead for half an hour, each lugging hawser that cut viciously into its wake. The success of the trawl was entirely in the hands of the two captains now, jockeying their vessels fifty yards apart, glancing across at each other's bows to be sure they kept their distance and their speeds absolutely constant. Vary the distance, and the mouth of the trawl might begin to twist. Go too fast or too slow, and the net would either rise too near the surface or sink too near the seabed. They wanted it in the middle water of the sea, where the shoal of herring cruised. In the galley, the deckhands were boisterous with relief that they had accomplished the first maneuver of the night. Gus was apologizing for his failure to make the link. "Y'see, I got it into my head that their top cable would have red bunting tied on. That's how I got confused. It was all my fault, so I'm sorry and that's that." He pushed the tam to the back of his head and went on muttering crossly to himself as he took off his oilskin. "It was the top shackle that went wrong. If I'd got that right we'd have been okay."

Big Boy beamed magnanimously over his beaker of milk. "Never you mind, old son," he said, "we'll get you a pair of fuckin' glasses next trip, then there'll be no problem."

Jonathan nodded toward the porthole, where the lights of the other fishing boat glowed. "Better make it two pairs. Jamie could use 'em, too. What was the matter with that guy, banging us up like that?"

"Did you see Hoboe's face? Thought he was goin' to shit hisself." Big Boy's gut wobbled with mirth beneath his heavy sweater.

Yank, bending to get a loaf from the refrigerator, was expressionless as usual. "Guess poor old Jamie just got tired of waiting," he murmured. "Decided to come and stir you bastards up a bit." He was an amiable man beneath all the resentments of his origins and the toughness of the ex-Marine.

Hauling the trawl in began with the same process as before. The two vessels hove-to and then maneuvered close so that a line could be cast across to the Boat, which this time was taking the net. As soon as Jamie's boat had passed over its hawser, it backed off and lay there wallowing in the low sea, its part done until the setting of a new trawl. Its crew made tracks for the galley and left the others to work without spectators. Yank pushed his winch into gear, and slowly the hawsers crept out of the sea. Once again the thrumming of their strain was heard along the deck, the deadly sound that penetrated even the heavy clanking of the winch. As the buoys holding up the mouth of the net came close to the stern, Yank stopped the winch so that Gus and Jonathan could grapple for the buoys. A new sound as the winch stopped. A loud creak, then another, after it a third. A great tree might make that sound, just before it topples to the woodsman's ax; but this was the sound of bunched steel wires tightening even more toward the breaking point. Jonathan, busy on the very edge of the stern, heard that sound above the slap of the waves below his feet and pursed his lips involuntarily. He dragged up one of the buoys, Gus retrieved the other, and they cast them aside and waited for the net to follow.

Its mouth came up from the darkness of the sea like a serpent, the mesh all bunched together. There was another pause, while Big Boy started up the stern hoist and caused its articulated arm to dip under the net so that this would come over the big drum. The drum began to revolve and the arm rose until the net could be guided down off the drum and stowed in layers across the middle of the stern. Gus and Jonathan stood on either side of the net when it came down, their oilskins glistening as water cascaded over them. It was a new net and there was no slime on it yet, no pieces of rotted fish that had clung from previous trips, no skeletons picked clean by gulls at the dock but still entangled in the mesh. It merely brought seawater with it, which sloshed down their oilskin cuffs when they raised their arms, saturated their sweaters and wet them to the skin almost as much as if they had stood there naked in the cold night. Slowly the net was drawn aboard, while the Boat lolloped sideways in the gentle swell and dipped a little at the stern under the weight coming out of the sea. They were, in effect, hauling a long cylinder of mesh aboard and the first sign of the prey it contained was a disturbance on the surface of the water fifty yards or more astern. This sounded like many pigeons flying out of trees some distance away, but it was the noise of herring struggling to be free from the net that was closing more tightly about them. As the net came out of the water now it was wider than before, its sides held apart by the mass of fish further back. Then the bag was under the stern and there was another pause, while Big Boy fiddled with the controls of the hoist so that it would swing the catch aboard.

As the bag was drawn closer to the Boat, the surface around it for many yards started to gleam with the millions of scales scraped from the fish struggling inside the net. At first sight the shiny spectrum light of the scales made it look as if there were soapsuds deep in the water. Then some shift of glare from the Boat made the sea round the net milky. Now, as Big Boy prepared his machine for the last act in catching the fish, another trick of light presented the scales on the surface of the sea, so many millions of them so closely packed together that the water appeared to have been inlaid with a mosaic in mother of pearl. Jonathan, looking down at this, caught sight of a movement that was not made by the swarming fish inside the net. A large tail swung casually around and a long and thick body appeared from under the net, glided through the bottle-green water illuminated by the arc lights above, and vanished into the darkness beyond. It was not a very big shark, maybe five feet at most, but it was a hungry one, nosing round the bag, waiting for any herring that might manage to struggle out.

With a jerk, Big Boy's hoist made the lift and the bag came thickly out of the sea, spouting water in jets on all sides. It swayed and swung as the hoist's arm carried it over the side and poised it above the fish pound in the middle of the deck. It hung still there for a moment, but it was heaving with the life inside. Then Gus reached over, took hold of the rope dangling from the cod end, gave it a mighty tug, and jumped back as the bag shot open and the herring poured into the pound. They hit the deck with a rushing thud, the first ones smothered at once by the torrent behind. Wriggling, somersaulting, inert, the herring came, showering Gus and Jonathan with their scales as they poured down, and with flecks of blood from the ones that had been flayed alive in the struggle of bodies against the fine cords of the net. When the rush had finished, when the herring caught in the top of the bag had slithered over the mound made by those at the bottom, and lay flipping and gaping around the sides of the pound, some fish were still caught up above in the net, hanging by the gills from its meshes. Jonathan shook the limp net to drop them free, and some of them fell out onto the mass of bodies below. But others stayed there, where they would presently rot and lose parts of their bodies bit by bit to the sea or the gulls.

Imperceptibly at first, then more visibly, the mound of fish in the middle of the pound subsided, as they descended through the hatch into the hold below. All four men were gathered around the pound and the Skipper was looking down from the fo'c'sle rail, calculating the amount of herring they had caught. "What do you reckon," Big Boy shouted up to his captain, " 'bout twenty thousand pounds maybe?"

The Skipper shook his head doubtfully. "Nearer fifteen, I should say." He turned and went into the wheelhouse, to call Jamie with the news.

Yank picked up a shovel and began to heave live herring from the edges of the pound into the hold. "Better than a kick in the arse, though, isn't it?"

His blade uncovered a larger shape in the middle of the pile and Gus strode over the coaming of the pound and bent down to recover the codfish before it slithered through the hatch. "Sometimes you get lucky, you know. Sometimes you don't do too badly at all. Will you just look at that now?" He grunted with the effort of pulling the cod free, hooking his fingers into its gills, embracing the long body as it came out of the heap. As Gus was about to step over the coaming the fish suddenly leaped from his arms and went flopping across the deck. "Bastard!" shouted Gus, sitting down abruptly on the herring. He picked himself up, fetched another shovel, and gave the cod a hard crack on the head, then threw the shovel down. "You'll make a fine chowder, you will, old fella," said Gus. "We'll put you in the freezer right now till we're nice and ready for you." He headed for the galley with the cod in his arms, murmuring inaudible things to the corpse as he went.

By the time the fish pound had been cleared, the end of the net had been tied up again and laid ready for the next trawl, the two vessels were under way. They steamed back toward the spot where the net had first been shot and the captains decided to try again a little way to the west, where herring were still showing up well on the trace. This time it was Jamie's boat that bore the brunt of the work after the net had been put into the sea and after Yank, standing on top of the starboard rail and swinging the turk's head round and round like a bolas, had cast the codline over to the other deck. He landed it square amidships first time and, as two oilskinned figures scrambled for it, he gave them a V-sign which, in Yank's case, was a token of comradeship as much as of derision. The hawser was taken across without a hitch and, when the trawl was over, the Boat relinquished the second hawser without trouble and hove-to while Jamie's men began to haul in the net. Big Boy and the others were down in the galley, taking their ease and eating some food while this was going on.

"They must be making good time," said Big Boy, cocking his head as the radio crackled into life up in the wheelhouse. "Sounds like Jamie's telling what they've hauled." He paused and grinned mischievously. "Or else he's telling how they've fucked it up."

Jonathan got up from the table and went over to the porthole. He peered out at the glow of light a few yards away and saw four figures struggling with the net under the hoist. "Nope," he said. "Looks like they're still hauling in."

The wheelhouse had gone quiet again, but they heard the Skipper coming down the ladder. He was red in the face as he entered the galley, strode over to the stove and reached for coffee. "Show's over for tonight," he said curtly. "Net's got a hole in it you could drive a truck through."

The grin disappeared from Big Boy's face. "The stupid bastards," he cried. "What they gone and done? Run their fuckin' screws right over it."

The Skipper sipped his coffee and rubbed a hand over eyes that felt they were about to burst. He'd been in the wheelhouse for eighteen hours and that was too much of a first day at sea in weeks. "No, sir," he replied. "Looks like we screwed it up between us. Tide's turned and I guess we weren't making enough speed against it. Anyways, she ripped up on something at the bottom that didn't show up on the trace. If she was that low to start with, she probably wouldn't have caught much fish anyway." He tossed the remains of the coffee into the sink impatiently and turned to go back up above. "Sooner we get going," he said, "sooner we get back and start mending that net."

Gus watched his retreating back with a long face and rolled his eyes toward his tam-o'-shanter with disgust. "If there's one thing I fuckin' hate," he said, "it's standin' about all day on a dock in March, catching me goddamn death of cold mendin' fishin' nets." His bony nose wagged emphatically across the table at Jonathan. "I'm tellin' you. I'd sooner stand on deck all day in December haulin' the bleedin' things in."

It was still cold when they crept up the harbor in the morning, though the sun was out and the Town was etched bright and sharp in clear light. The three churches poked into a blue sky and the stone tower of the indeterminately European City Hall looked deceptively warm facing the sun. A couple of inshore lobstermen were hauling traps just inside the breakwater and the Boat passed three draggers outward bound as it rounded the island just before the Neck. The only pleasure craft around were the small handful of deep-water yachts that had ridden out the winter at moorings in midchannel, where men had walked across the ice to inspect them from time to time to make sure that all was well aboard the forsaken craft. But spring was in the air at last. A faint scent of damp earth came off the land and that had been missing last time the Boat had returned from the sea.

They did not head directly for the dock, but turned into another berth a little way down the fish pier, where two trucks were waiting on the road beyond a shed which extended almost to the end of the jetty. A conveyor belt sloped high above the first of the trucks and from the other end of the shed an enormous hose pipe dangled, ready to ingest the catch. As the Boat tied up alongside, seagulls lining the roof of the shed began to flex their wings and rise from the crouch, anticipating the opportunity to come. The hatch cover in the fish pound was removed, the end of the hose was dropped in and the herring were sucked out of the hold and up the pipe to the conveyor belt. As the fish cascaded from the belt into the truck, the gulls rose in spirals from the shed and clouded the air above the belt, shrieking with rage at the daring ones that darted lower than the rest and plucked at the silvery rush of food. Gus cocked an eye in their direction and shook his head disapprovingly. "Do you think," he asked no one in particular, "those poor bastards in Europe know their herrin's been pickled in American gull shit?"

Inside the hour the hold was emptied and the Boat was tied up at her own dock. Jamie's vessel came into sight as the last rope was cleated fast, and the two crews exchanged sardonic thrusts about the tearing of the net as they came within each other's range, pretending that one or other of them had been to blame for the mishap on the seabed. There was no spite in this, but these were competitive men by nature as well as by reason of the trade they pursued. It was as tradesmen with a common cause, however, that they hauled the net off Jamie's stern and manhandled it along the dock.

The net was bunched tight as it came off the boat and it was sodden with water, heavy and cold, as the ten men locked their arms around it and staggered in a leaning line to lay it out full length. The hole was three-quarters of the way from the mouth toward the bag, several yards long, and when the net had been spread out to reveal its full extent, the two crews gathered round and gazed at it gloomily for a while before doing anything else. Only five of the ten had ever mended a fishing net before. The Skipper, Big Boy, and Gus went into a long discussion with Jamie and a deckhand from the other crew, full of pointing fingers, optimistic exclamations, skeptical shakes of the head and ultimately rough agreement on how the matter should proceed. The rest of the men meanwhile stood round and looked vaguely at the mess of slashed panels, frayed cords, and dangling threads. They bent down and squatted on their heels, lifted edges of the hole and wondered how the hell anyone could possibly put it all together again; and how long this would take.

It took the best part of two days, because half the men in those two crews had everything to learn. The ones who had done this sort of thing before had to teach as they tried to remember what they themselves had been shown years ago. "Nothin's easy," said Big Boy, when he realized, in the nick of time, that the panel he had just told Yank to cut out was an undamaged piece of net on which the success of the repair job largely depended.

The trouble with a torn fishing net out of water was the difficulty in seeing it as it really was. Its mesh did not naturally hang square in the open air but became merely a bundle of threads, a series of flattened diamond shapes, almost anything but what it was designed to be unless you held it at arm's length with fingers wide apart, as though you were helping to wind wool for somebody's knitting. Unless you could visualize it as it would be in the water, you could not know which damaged sections were best cut away altogether and which could profitably be incorporated into newly made mesh. But slowly the teachers and the novices groped their way through the reconstruction of the thing. One by one, each man took up an appointed task. The dangling threads were carefully cut away, the ragged edges of the hole meticulously trimmed. Wide flat plastic needles were loaded with fresh cord. Some men

simply stood holding sections of the net up so that
experienced hands could braid new mesh into it. Clumsily
at first, but gradually acquiring a deftness of sorts, fingers
long out of practice began to fashion the new mesh, with
its rhythm of side knots, round turns and sheet bends;
sheet bends upside down, mind, where you had to take up
a mesh into the one above. There was little conversation
on that dock those two days. Natural babblers became
tongue-tied in the concentration of this work. Get the
thing wrong now, and it might produce an even bigger
mess next time the boats were at sea. A fishing net is an
artful thing, with finely balanced tension throughout its
complicated shape, from its gaping maw down the belly to
the narrowness of the bag. Disturb the balance, and the
first shoal of fish that swims inside it is liable to burst the
net where it hangs slack. Understanding this well, rough
men whose lives had been built on their manual strength,
who exulted above all things in the domination of anything weak, now submitted themselves painstakingly to
delicate craft. Stubborn Yank, most macho of them all,
stood for hours holding net for Big Boy to braid, watching
carefully the manipulations of the cord. As his buddy
paused to study a fresh row of mesh before going on,
Yank lit cigarettes for them both and handed one across.
"They said pair-trawling's as easy as shooting fish in a
barrel," he murmured. "I'm fucked if it ain't."

The two crews discovered, in the next few weeks, how
misleading such gossip had been. On their next trip they
took twenty thousand pounds of herring in their first trawl
but were in trouble again on their second. The captains,
still unaccustomed to working as a pair, were driving
neck-and-neck through a roughish sea when one of the
boats yawed away from the parallel course. It was not
much of a deviation, but it was enough to place intolerable
strain on one of the hawsers. It parted below the water but,

even so, it whiplashed back at the Boat. The deckhands
were in the galley, waiting for the trawl to end, and heard
the loud clang as the severed steel smacked against the
sea-door with enough force to flake off a foot of its dirty
white paint. "Just above your head, that would have been,"
Big Boy informed Jonathan cryptically, when he spotted
the mark in the daylight on their way home. They lost a
whole day, collecting a fresh cable and attaching it to the
net. After that, for three trips in a row, they came home
with holes in the net and with few fish in their hold.

Each time this happened they spent more than a day
repairing the damage at the dock. But as they became
more practiced they fumbled less, and presently everyone
was taking a hand in all the work that had to be done,
though the novices still moved slowly in the braiding of
mesh. Realizing that this might be a recurring feature of
their lives from now on, they got some timber and made
benches with a beam sticking upright at one end, which
took the weight off their feet and made it easier to follow
the pattern of the net. You sat astride the bench (which
was why fishermen called it a horse) and snagged the net
on a nail driven into the top of the beam, so that no one
need stand and hold it out for you while you braided.

The sight of these men sitting at their horses, in line
ahead along the whole length of the wharf, became so
familiar to people passing by the state fish pier that a
schoolteacher turned up one day, leading a large platoon
of children on extramural exercise. "I thought you'd be
here," she said brightly to Big Boy who, for once in his life,
merely grunted balefully at a woman. There was little
response from any of the others, either, apart from a few
distant nods as the kids stood and watched, and a warning
growl from Gus when a small boy got his foot tangled in
one of the nets and, giggling, nearly went full length. The
fisherman looked up at the young woman in charge, as she

stood smiling uncertainly at the work. "If I was you," he said, "I'd watch your step out here." He took a pull at his cigarette and replaced it carefully in a notch he had cut for the purpose on his beam. "You just might get your panties wet." The teacher blushed, almost replied, thought better of it, and began to marshal the children away.

Each time they put to sea, after the mending of nets, they spent fruitless hours hunting for fish again before getting a trace that looked worthwhile. The herring were on the move down the Gulf, in that mysterious passage along the Atlantic coast which was a source of speculation to fishermen and scientists alike. The shoals had departed from the region of Jeffrey's Ledge shortly after that first attempt at pair-trawling and were rediscovered over Stellwagen Bank, about fifty miles off the coast opposite Boston. They lingered there for a week or more and then they moved closer inshore, between Cohasset and Scituate. The lights of the two towns were clearly visible to the hunters at sea and the beam of the Minots Light swept the horizon as the boats fished the Tar Pouch away to the south. Four days later the herring had moved off again and the next time they were found, they were deep inside Cape Cod Bay, massed on Billingsgate Shoal. They seemed inexhaustible, those fish. The men spoke admiringly of their capacity to keep going over such distances as these and carelessly assumed that the herring had supernatural powers of regeneration as well as phenomenal endurance. They believed only the evidence contained in their nets and, even though the novice pair-trawlers experienced uneven luck, it was known that the older hands at this game, like the trawlers which had descended from Maine, were taking big catches wherever the fish could be found.

The two boats from the Town had their best night off

Billingsgate, where Cape Cod begins to curve toward the bottom of its hook. The water runs shallow on the shoal, eighteen fathoms at best, but it is adequately protected by the land from the Atlantic seas and storms, even though the land is very narrow there. This is where the Cape consists of little but high sand dunes on both of its sides, between the cranberry bogs and the clapboard villages to the south, and the regimental rows of vacation cottages which announce Provincetown to the north.

It was the warmest day since the fall when the Boat led Jamie's vessel out past the breakwater at the Town, the first time that every man had not hurried to shelter inside, the moment the ropes had been cast off. Fishing was not so bad after all, Jonathan thought, as they plodded through the April sun toward Cape Cod. The weather seemed to have settled and it was a month since they'd had a real storm. The sea was rolling sluggishly, as though composed of oil, but it was not only the tranquillity of the day that contented Jonathan so much. He had quickly picked up the knack of mending nets and he was pleased with his new skill; he wondered vaguely whether one day he might aim for the exams that would qualify him for a command. The rest of the men were in good heart, too, after three consecutive trips without mishap.

Gus, retrieving his forgotten codfish from the freezer, had informed them that he would make a chowder with it, "just like my mother showed me."

Big Boy sniffed the trophy in Gus's arms, frozen stiff with a half-open mouth and a slightly turned tail, looking much like the museum piece it had almost become. "Getting a bit old, isn't it?" he asked dubiously.

Gus agreed that it might be best if the creature was put outside to thaw and strode out on deck to place the cod carefully on top of the winch. He stooped to tidy a couple of shovels someone had left lying around, straightened up and shaded his eyes to inspect a red sun sinking down to the land. But there was a dark purple haze in the sky above it. "We'll be fishin' in the fog tonight, boys," he told the others when he went back in.

It had rolled up densely by the time they reached Billingsgate Shoal. For a couple of hours the two vessels cast about for a scent, invisible to each other except on their radar screens. Then Jamie called across the obscure night that he'd found them, and that it was the thickest trace he'd ever seen. They were to get over as fast as they could. The Boat turned on its heel and tramped over three miles of water that had become even more viscous under the fog bank, in the lee of the land, than in the crossing of the bay in the afternoon. The fog was so dense there that the Skipper, measuring his distance from Jamie's boat by radar, had throttled back to a gentle five knots to avoid collision before the arc lights of the other vessel were seen glowing faintly through swirling clouds of mist. They were only three hundred yards apart then. As the men went out on deck, the figures across the water were heaving the net out over their stern, their oilskins already gleaming with moisture that had settled upon them from the air. Jonathan spotted something else as he marched to his own position by the rail. The cod had vanished from the top of the winch, though neither Gus nor Big Boy appeared to have noticed its departure.

Nothing else was lost that night. In spite of the fog, the two captains kept perfectly abreast, managing to hold exactly the right distance between the boats; this must always be half the distance between the boats and the trawl astern, and it had been the hardest trick of all for the captains to learn. The turk's head found its mark faultlessly every time it was slung from one deck to the other and the shackles were matched properly whenever the trawls began. They could see nothing of the buoys once these had gone over the stern, could see nothing of the net when hauling in until it appeared spectrally almost beneath their feet. But this densely foggy night was also a very quiet night, containing no natural sound other than the gentle slopping of the sea against the hull. And so, when the men waiting under the arc lights in the curling wraithes of mist heard a loud fluttering as of a multitude of birds, they knew the net was near, though they could not see it yet.

It was so full of fish, the first time it was hauled, that the articulated hoist flexed visibly as it took the weight of the bag and the Boat dipped into an appreciable slope from bow to stern. When Gus tugged the cod end open there followed such a rush of herring into the pound that he was up to his knees in them before he could move back, and Yank and Jonathan had to help him clear. The first haul alone brought twenty-five thousand pounds of fish. A second run over the same ground put nearly thirty thousand pounds in the hold of Jamie's boat. At their third trawl, the two vessels netted another twenty-eight thousand pounds. Then the herring turned toward the shore, where the water ran to only half a dozen fathoms at high tide over Smalley Bar. By then it was four in the morning and the tide was ebbing fast. So the hunters called off the chase and left the herring for another day. For the first time since they had gone pair-trawling, the men aboard the Boat felt they were at last within sight of the great plunder they had sought.

They were halfway home, eating an exuberant breakfast, when the Skipper came down with the news. He looked disturbed as well as tired when he walked into the galley and sat down at his place on the bench. "Just picked up a Mayday to the Coast Guard," he said. The others looked up from their plates, paused in the chewing of food, a mixture of curiosity and caution on every face. The Skipper looked across the table at nothing in particular;

his eyes just happened to rest blankly in the region of Big Boy's plate. "They've had an explosion on the *Santa Maria*," he said. "One dead, three hurt."

"Who is it?" Jonathan didn't recognize the sound of his own voice; it sounded strangely distant, as though it had come from somewhere to his right.

"Not absolutely sure. They're all Italians on that boat and there was a lot of static." The Skipper paused and picked up his fork. "Sounded like Carlo, though."

His eyes flicked up at Yank, then quickly down. He began to prod at a piece of sweet sausage. Yank took a deep breath and started eating again, stopped, reached for a beaker of milk, poured it into his mouthful of food.

"Poor bastard. That's real tough. Gets hisself a new site and turns out to be the wrong one." Big Boy, philosophical as ever. Also Big Boy, the always interested one. "Where'd it happen? Did she go down?"

The Skipper had recovered a bit now. He began to look boyishly tired again; no worse than that. "Just round the Cape. They were dragging inshore. Something exploded in the engine room. Blew the wheelhouse half over the side. Coast Guard's gone to tow her in." He was eating properly now, letting hunger take over. So was Yank. But he never said a word.

Jonathan was silent, too, scarcely aware of what was being said. Gus had started into a rambling tale about accidents at sea. They were all beginning to relax round the table, except where Jonathan sat. He felt slightly sick and his head was buzzing with some words that came dimly out of his past. Something about "those things we ought to have done and those things we ought not to have done." He thought it must be something to do with church; or maybe it was something his father had said to him once. He couldn't remember. He didn't really want to know. He felt pursued. Later, as they approached the breakwater, he felt this even more. He wasn't looking forward to telling Ellen about Carlo. He hoped she'd already heard.

There was no public mourning for Carlo Rosario, though many people went around to the Neck by car to see the wreckage in which he had been killed. The Coast Guard cutter had towed the *Santa Maria* to a berth where Italian boats usually tied up, until it was decided what should be done with her next. For two or three days the smashed-up wheelhouse, with its shattered windows, was a local sight, and fishing people were not the only ones to go and take a look. Commuters into Boston found time to appreciate the scorch marks on the wheelhouse side. Some of the artists with studios on the Neck strolled around to the wharf and shook their heads, impressed, at the crazy angle of the wheelhouse across the starboard rail, and the splintered metal and wood marking the place where it had originally stood. It must, the sightseers all agreed, have been some explosion to do a thing like that. They spoke quietly to each other; a man, after all, had died. But mostly they discussed the strange effects of blast, the unexpected directions it could take.

No flags were hauled to half-mast the day they buried him and no bell tolled across the Town. It was a bright and warm day, and shops on the sunny side of Main Street had their awnings drawn over the sidewalk for the first time in months. A couple of blocks up the hill behind Main, the windows of the Yellow Sub Shop (Sandwiches and Cokes) were a little steamed up as people sipped coffee and tea in their midmorning break, gossiped through mouthfuls of pastrami, or simply idled behind the smudgy newsprint of the *Globe*. Occasionally they took in the Italian church across the way, and the solitary figures who climbed its steps and went inside. A couple of nuns arrived, but there was nothing unusual in that, either. Those people were always praying. Then cars began to lurch into the parking lot round the corner and people began to cross to the church in twos and threes, looking up and down the street as they crossed, as though they were a bit unfamiliar with this place or as if they were keeping their eyes open for who else was in sight. It became apparent to the watchers in the shop that the Catholics were having a funeral today. People talked to each other when they were going to weddings. These people just looked uneasy.

Jonathan was the uneasiest of them all, when he and Ellen arrived. He just might have dodged it if it hadn't been for her. He was still stricken with his guilt about Carlo and he had never been to a Catholic church before. Most of all, he was uneasy because Big Boy and the Skipper had decided to go and he felt that between them, the men and the woman, they had him over a barrel. Ellen had been deeply upset by Carlo's death in a way that Jonathan could not understand. She seemed to be hurting at Carlo's loss; he only felt the oppressive ache of guilt and he wished all this was a long way behind. Beyond this, he was not at all sure what feelings he had. He hoped that nothing at all would show, in front of his buddies from the Boat.

The church was almost full when they arrived and they had to squeeze into the end of a pew at the back. Jonathan had only been to a couple of funerals in his life and at neither of them had there been anything like the number of people who had turned up for this. By the time the service began, only the side aisles had space in them; the rest of the building was packed. He picked out the Skipper and Big Boy at once, a few rows ahead. Only one of them was six feet tall, but both stood higher than almost everyone else in sight. Jonathan himself had a clear view to the altar across the hundreds of heads in front. They were stocky, dark people in that church, but Jonathan was most surprised by the way they had dressed. He had put on the darkest clothes he possessed, but some of these Italian men wouldn't have dressed any differently for Fiesta. Many of them wore bright flowery shirts, wide open at the neck so that you could see the hair curling up from their chests. There were a lot of imitation leather jackets, shiny and new, which creaked when the guys in them moved. A number of women were dressed in dark things, but not many had anything on their heads. He sat very still while Ellen was kneeling down and looked round at the strangeness of it all. Palm Sunday had just passed and some of its decorations were still upon the pumpkin-colored walls. A poster hung from a pillar and in big lettering said "Long have I waited for your coming home to me." Jonathan wondered why these people had to rub it in.

He jumped when the coffin arrived at the door, draped in white with something embroidered on the top. Loud anguish came with it and he had never heard that shocking sound before. Six men bore the coffin up the church (four of them were Rosarios, come down from Detroit) and behind was a stream of people, every one in black, showing grief so openly that Jonathan was seized with a desire to get out of that place and run for it. At the head of these mourners a short and heavily-built woman was bent almost double, close to hysteria, virtually carried along by a man. A shawl covered her head, there were gloves on her hands, not an inch of her flesh was visible from where Jonathan stood. Her face was buried against the body of the man, who held it tenderly there, as though it belonged to a child. It was Rita Rosario and Jonathan did not recognize her in this state, for Mrs. Rosario was a rock to which many other people had always clung. He wondered for some time where on earth she could be. Other women followed, their bodies shaking with sobs, supported by men who were trying to control their own faces. But men in the congregation were weeping openly now, and women were wiping their eyes with white linen. Ellen blew her nose, while Jonathan stood tight and held fast to the pew in front. Uncertain of everything in this church, he followed her movements except when she knelt. He had not done that since childhood and he could only bring himself to lean forward awkwardly in his seat now. Some people, he noticed, sat from start to finish; others stood. Some had their arms folded throughout; others crossed themselves and bobbed down at words from the priest. Big Boy and the Skipper seemed to move as awkwardly as he.

He did not understand a word of that service, for all of it was in Italian. The prayers, the Bible reading, the communion, the address — all were foreign to him. The name of Carlo Rosario was uttered several times by the priest in his address and, each time, a wail of women, a strictured gasp of pain, broke out from the people sitting at the front. Jonathan wished he knew what was being said of the dead man. A cantor stood and sang "Panis Angelicus" at the communion, his thin tenor dipping and climbing lonely above the shuffle of feet, the murmurs of the priest, the terrible sadness of it all. Jonathan faintly recognized the tune. But he was glad when it was all over. The body of Carlo Rosario and his mourners came back down the church and the congregation began to follow them through the door. More women than ever were sobbing now; there were many young women, sobbing most loudly of all. Across the road, in the Yellow Sub Shop, people paused, pastramis in hand, to watch this exodus of grief, and to shake their heads, reprovingly, at the traffic jam building up in the street. City Hall should have sent a cop along, to sort that tangle out. Some of the watchers wondered who this big turnout had been for and the knowing ones told them it was for that Italian boy, killed on the fishing boat the other day. The explosion had made the front page of the evening papers when the Coast Guard towed the *Santa Maria* in.

Jonathan nodded to the other two men from the Boat, across a score of heads, as the three of them turned out of their pews and joined the slow procession of people moving down the center aisle of the church. Big Boy's face was set at blank, his eyes wide and shiny in the stained glass-windowed light. The Skipper's mouth was pursed, as though he was concentrating hard. Jonathan followed Ellen into the lobby beyond the door, where the walls had been frescoed crudely with depictions of local fishing boats, steaming across ultramarine sea. She paused above the steps leading down to the street and he was ready for what she had to say.

"Jonathan, we've got to go on to the Calvary. Mrs. Rosario asked us specially, you know. And she wants us to go back to the house after."

He looked past her reddened eyes, shuffled, half shrugged his head. Big Boy and the Skipper were coming closer through the crowd. He moved impatiently as they advanced. "Look," he said, "I've got to live with these guys. You know how it is. You go on. I'll see you later. Tell Mrs. Rosario I'm sorry."

Ellen's eyes glittered for a moment with something fiercer than tears. Her mouth and her chin went hard, and he wanted to run away from that, too. "Very well," she hissed. "I'll go. But you can say you're sorry in your own good time." She turned quickly away from him and darted toward the steps, made her way down them, and disappeared into the street.

Jonathan waited for the other two men to catch up. The Skipper nodded to him again, offered an embarrassed smile. "Hi, old buddy," said Big Boy. "This is a very sad day and I think we all need a drink. You comin'?"

Jonathan began to relax. "Sure," he said. "I really could use one after all of this."

They made for the crew's usual bar at the top end of Main Street, where the street wound between junk shops below Portuguee Hill and a high wire fence that separated it from the emptiest stretch of waterfront opposite the fish pier, the untidy reminder of urban non-renewal that became the wasteland parking lot for refrigerator trucks a few hundred yards beyond. The Skipper left the other two there, saying he had some work to do aboard the Boat, whose wheelhouse top and mast were visible across the water and the pier. Big Boy and Jonathan settled behind beer in the corner by the door, where they could watch the hostesses pushing drinks and sandwiches to other customers over the bartop.

"Life goes on, my friend," said Big Boy. "Life goes on." He was in one of his instructive moods, the parable-teller home from the sea. "You never know what's going to hit you out there, so you gotta make the most of all this while it's here." He eyed one of the hostesses speculatively. "Carlo could be a pain in the ass and he was a lazy bastard at the best of times. But he understood all of that. He lived his life ashore to the full. Did you see all those women cryin' in the church? If it's like that when it's time for you and me to go, Jonathan, we won't have done so bad." He stroked his mustache gently, then held his hand up to acknowledge a man who had detached himself from one of the pinball machines and was on his way out. "Funny thing about Carlo," he said, "comin' back from the Midwest just to keep an eye on his old lady. Had a great little business goin' for him out there, y'know. He'd have had it made by now."

Jonathan shrugged and gulped at his beer. "Maybe he just couldn't keep away from the sea," he said. He hoped that was it. He didn't care, just then, for any other explanation. Big Boy looked sharply at the younger man's face. The kid was still green in all sorts of ways.

When they parted, Jonathan intended to go home, but what Big Boy had said about Carlo's return to the Town made him sit still in the car for a moment before moving off. He looked at his watch. An hour and a half had passed since they came out of the church. It would be all over by now and all the people would be gone. On impulse he took a left at the green liquor store, and headed for the highway that eventually fetched up at the opposite end of the Cape. He knew the Calvary lay somewhere up there. It was one of several burial grounds on the outskirts of the Town, and the only one Jonathan had visited before was in the other direction, where a corner had for more than a century been set apart for the fishermen of the Town. Low white headstones cut from the granite of the Cape lay in row after row up there, with small Stars and Stripes fluttering in the grass beside some. Beyond these memorials a rough wall ran under a belt of trees, with white-washed anchors and Stoddart wheels leaning against it. Most of the headstones were very simply inscribed, with the names of the men, the years they had lived and died. Some had died ashore, others had been lost at sea; and 1938 had been a bad year for both. It had taken Henry Ingalls and five other old-timers, Stephen S. Fudge and four other men in their prime. A handful of graves was more elaborate than most, with large stones bearing verses, graven codfish, and anchors sculpted from the rock, but all the memorials on that plot of ground spoke of hardness, righteousness, and pride. It was a quiet, inland place, hidden from all but the strongest of the Atlantic winds. The people of the Town knew the place as Fishermen's Rest.

Calvary was where Catholics were laid and on a stormy day the winds rushed fiercely over this ground, for it curved in bare slopes that were open to the sea. When Jonathan drove in through the gates, he saw at once where that day's burial had been, for fresh flowers were heaped in the one place where the ground was newly disturbed. A man about his own age, whom he didn't recognize, was kneeling not far away by a large gravestone surmounted by a cross, with angels wing-spread on either side. Otherwise the Calvary seemed deserted. But it was a while before Jonathan got out of his car; he felt an intruder in here, and he wondered whether anyone could see him from the road. He walked very slowly up the gravel path, pretending to scrutinize the headstones he passed. He tried to look casual when he stood where the earth of New England was still sweetly damp on the Italian grave. They had heaped gladioli and chrysanthemums all around, with labels mass-produced, not written by hand. One said "Son," others said "Brother" and "Brother-in-law," all of them in English. At the head of the grave a model fishing boat had been placed, fashioned from carnations in pink, white and light blue, all sprayed with glitter like a Christmas wreath. The boat had a wooden mast, though, with a paper Stars and Stripes attached to its tip, and with the Italian flag stuck just below. Between the fo'c'sle and the wheelhouse, a glass tube arose, containing a little water and a solitary deep, red rose. Jonathan was staring at all of this when the young man came up to him. "That's the Italian boy who got blown up the other day," he said. "Did you know him?"

Jonathan's shoulders shifted grudgingly and he made a small gesture with his hand. "Saw him down at the waterfront now and then," he said. "Never knew him real well."

The young man rubbed the back of his neck, untroubled by the paraphernalia with which the living come to terms with their dead. "Never knew him myself," he said.

"That must have been some explosion. They said he was messed up so bad, they didn't think they'd be able to let people view him at the funeral home." Jonathan took a deep breath and gulped. "But they did let people go in the end. I guess Mr. Rushton did a real nice job on him."

Jonathan swung away quickly. "Yeah, I guess so," he said. "Well, I've got to get back to Town." He strode back to the car, feeling sick. When the nausea had gone, on the drive home, he was wondering who had put the rose on Carlo's grave, and why he had never known about a brother or a sister.

The Boat went to sea again the next day. Jonathan and Ellen struggled through long silences in their apartment the night before; she wishing to make up with him before he went away, but angry at his refusal to see Carlo's funeral through to the end; he sullen and resenting the guilt she made him feel. They lay apart in bed, did not touch at all until just before he left. Then she came forward and hugged him hard, and told him to take care. He went easier, at that, squeezed her in return and said they'd make it up properly when he got back. Then he grabbed his bag and hurried out of the apartment, down the steps to the street.

She watched him walk along towards the pier, where the Boat lay in wait, three figures already moving about the machinery on her deck. The sun was slanting down from the ridge above East Main, where the trees were still bare, but almost ready to burst into leaf. One of the houses up there had the Stars and Stripes on a pole outside its porch, which had flown night and day since the owner came home from Iwo Jima, a generation before. This morning it drooped limply in the warm, quiescent air. New England was at that brief moment when its seasons leaped from winter into summer. Already, the bicycle wheels were beginning to flash in kaleidoscope along the gentle slope of East Main and soon their riders would abandon light woolens and ride sunburned with bare limbs. A kid sauntered along the street crumbled by the ice just below the apartment, socking a fist into the baseball mitt on his other hand, dreaming of Opening Day at Fenway and Little League dramas to come. The children on the first floor would soon be hunting grass snakes on the slope above the street and the weekend sailors would bring their boats in and out on the water beyond. Ellen pressed her face against the window until she saw Jonathan climb aboard the Boat. Then she turned away.

This morning she was troubled by the tale that you must never watch them go. She moved about the front room for a moment or two, picking things up and putting them down, nagged by her contempt for Jonathan's behavior the day before, hurt by his indifference to Carlo since the fight aboard the Boat. She went into the kitchen to wash the breakfast things. As she approached the sink she saw, through the open doorway beyond, that he had left his carton of cigarettes upon the bed. They lay where he had lain, upon the rumpled sheet, with the smoothly pressed strip just beyond, which neither of them had crossed in that exhausted, distant night. She smiled and shook her head; he'd be real sore at forgetting his smokes; it meant he would have to beg until he got back. Then she remembered that the Boat was stopping at the ice store down the harbor before going out to sea. Now that the weather had come warm they needed it to keep the herring fresh. If she hurried, she could catch up with Jonathan there. She grabbed the carton and went, excited, down the stairs.

As she drove along Main, she sensed the relaxation of the Town at this turning of the year. Outside the fish-food factory the women were taking a break, white-stockinged legs swinging lazily as they sat along the wall. People were driving cars with their elbows out again, steering with one hand and enjoying the breeze. Three old men had returned to the bench at the top of the hill, exchanging the news of how they'd survived all that ice. Down at Fisherman's Wharf, people were strolling again, looking at the boats, not anxious to keep on the move. Ellen could see the Boat itself, tied up by the store, the men lounging idly on its deck. She parked the car along the road and started walking down the wharf, content to do this errand for her man. This was their chosen world, right here they belonged amid the mewing of the gulls and the keen, tinny smell of fish; and, yes, the dangers of the sea. Jonathan and the others were roaring with laughter at something as she came alongside the Boat and looked down at them from the wharf. His face was happy and wide when he swung round and he concealed his impatience at the interruption well. She affected a mocking smirk as she held the carton in the air. "You know, you'd forget your head if it weren't screwed on," she said. She slung the carton through the air to him and the others bellowed their applause. "That was a great throw, Ellen," shouted Big Boy. "You got a great future at second base." She grinned back across the mooring ropes. "I know it," she said. "You all set now?" Jonathan nodded, as though approving of some careful plan. "Yeah, we just about ready to go now." He looked her up and down. "Well," she said, hesitating, "I guess I'd better go and get cleaned up for work. Take care. I'll see you tomorrow night." He grinned, knowingly. "Yeah. I'll see you then."

The four men watched her retreating back, one of them absentmindedly, the other three with twinkles of lust. "Look at that ass," said Yank with a sigh. "Wouldn't mind having that on my hands. Wouldn't mind at all." Big Boy gurgled and agreed.

Jonathan opened his palm. "Be my guest," he said, and

was pleased when Big Boy rumbled with mirth. It had taken him a long time to learn cool, but he reckoned he'd made it in the end.

Ellen did not hear this exchange, but the laughter followed her along the wharf. She frowned a little at the sound, but dismissed the thought from her mind. The day was bright, on the edge of new growth, and she dearly wished to hold on to that. She stood for a moment before driving away and looked across the Town, at its patchwork of wooden homes glowing gently in the sun, at the way it rose and fell around the harbor in its arms. It was a fruitful place and it had toughness in its soul, and Ellen knew both these things were echoed in her own. But she also knew of the dark things here. She tried not to think of the sea just beyond, and the awful treachery it might reveal this day.